GOOD KARMA

Good Karma

HOW TO CREATE THE CAUSES OF
HAPPINESS AND AVOID
THE CAUSES OF SUFFERING

Thubten Chodron

SHAMBHALA
BOULDER
2016

Shambhala Publications, Inc.
4720 Walnut Street
Boulder, Colorado 80301
www.shambhala.com

9 8 7 6 5 4 3 2 1

First Edition
Printed in the United States of America
(∞) This edition is printed on acid-free paper that meets the Amer-
ican National Standards Institute z39.48 Standard.
♻ This book is printed on 30% postconsumer recycled paper. For
more information please visit www.shambhala.com.

Distributed in the United States by Penguin Random House LLC
and in Canada by Random House of Canada Ltd

Designed by Gopa & Ted2, Inc.

Library of Congress Cataloging-in-Publication Data

Names: Thubten Chodron, 1950– author.
Title: Good karma: how to create the causes of happiness and
    avoid the causes of suffering / Thubten Chodron.
Description: First Edition. | Boulder: Shambhala, 2016.
Identifiers: LCCN 2015038921 | ISBN 9781611803396 (pbk.:
    alk. paper)
Subjects: LCSH: Religious life—Buddhism. | Happiness—
    Religious aspects—Buddhism. | Suffering—Religious
    aspects—Buddhism.
Classification: LCC BQ4302 .T47 2016 | DDC 294.3/422—dc23
    LC record available at http://lccn.loc.gov/2015038921

For as long as space endures
And as long as sentient beings remain
Until then may I too abide
To dispel the miseries of the world

—Shantideva, *Engaging in the Bodhisattva's Deeds*

May I be beloved of beings,
And may they be more beloved to me than myself.
May their bad deeds ripen upon me
And may all my virtue, without exception, ripen upon them.

—Nagarjuna, *Precious Garland*

Contents

Preface

EVERY BOOK HAS a story behind it—how and why it was written. I'll share part of that story with you now, and another part in the first chapter. From my own experience as a young Westerner encountering the Dharma—the Buddha's teachings—and my experience now many years later as someone introducing people to these teachings, it's clear that the functioning of the law of karma (our actions) and its effects is both difficult and important to understand. In fact, it's said that only a buddha completely knows the intricate details of how it works. People new to the Dharma, as well as people who have been practicing for decades (if not lifetimes), have questions about how karma works and how it applies to our lives. Fortunately, the Buddha and the great Buddhist masters that came after him have given us a wealth of material explaining karma and its effects that will give us the fundamental knowledge we need to create the causes of happiness and avoid the causes of suffering.

One of these kind masters is Dharmarakshita, the author of the poem *The Wheel of Weapons Striking at the Vital Points of the Enemy,* also called *The Wheel of Sharp Weapons* (Tib. *blo-sbyong mtshon-cha 'khor-lo*). This poem belongs to a genre of teachings in the Tibetan Buddhist tradition called "thought training" (*lojong*). These teachings help us train our mind to apply compassion and wisdom in our daily lives, especially to transform adversity into the path. They are immediately applicable to our lives, and when we practice them correctly, they reduce our anxiety, fear, and depression and replace them with wise acceptance, compassion for ourselves and others, determination to be free from cyclic existence (samsara) with its constantly recurring difficulties, and liberating wisdom.

This poem is attributed to the late-tenth-century Indian Buddhist sage Dharmarakshita, a teacher of the great Indian sage Atisha (986–1054), who revitalized Buddhism in Tibet. Unfortunately, very little is known about Dharmarakshita's life. Some say he was a Vaibhāṣika master; others say he was a great bodhisattva abbot.[1] It is said that Atisha studied with him at the great Buddhist monastic university of Odantapuri in India.

The thought-training teachings in Tibet are traced to Atisha. From him they passed to the Kadampa geshes in Tibet and then down to the masters of the present day. I received this teaching from Geshe Ngawang Dhargye and Geshe Jampa Lodro, two of my most kind spiritual mentors.

OVERVIEW

Before actually embarking on Dharmarakshita's poem, it's helpful to understand the Buddhist worldview: that we currently exist in a cycle of constantly recurring unsatisfactory experiences that is caused not by external people and objects, but by the ignorance, anger, and clinging attachment in our own minds. This is explained in chapter 2.

The third chapter, "Brave Peacocks and Cowardly Crows," introduces us to Yamantaka (the fierce form of Mañjushrī, the buddha of wisdom) and to bodhisattvas, those beings who aspire for full awakening for the benefit of all sentient beings. It contrasts these altruistic bodhisattvas with us ordinary beings, who focus primarily on our own well-being. The heart of the text begins with the fourth chapter, where Dharmarakshita presents us again and again with unpleasant situations we frequently encounter in life and tells us that these are not random occurrences or the fault of other living beings, but are in fact the result

---

1. See the introduction by Michael Sweet and Leonard Zwilling in Geshe Lhundub Sopa's *Peacock in the Poison Grove* for more about the authorship of *The Wheel of Sharp Weapons* and Dharmarakshita.

of our own self-centered actions. In doing so, he sparks us to realize that by changing our mental states and our actions, we have the power to learn from suffering and to change our experiences. In this way, we gain the power to transform difficulties into the path to full awakening. This continues in chapter 5, which contains ways to deal with sickness, laziness, and distractions, and in chapter 6, where we look at our spiritual obstacles and how to remedy them.

Chapter 7, "Seize the Enemy: Identifying Self-Grasping Ignorance and the Self-Centered Attitude," identifies the real culprits, our self-centered thought and self-grasping ignorance. We learn how Yamantaka, the symbolic representation of clear wisdom and strong altruism, can help us dance and trample on these inner enemies. Chapters 8, 9, and 10 go into this in more depth, pointing out our mistaken behavior and ways of thinking and increasing our determination to abolish these through cultivating love, compassion, *bodhicitta*, and the wisdom realizing the ultimate nature.

Chapter 11, "Safe at Last," speaks of the benefits of taking refuge in the Three Jewels and of building up our internal strength, as a prelude to chapter 12, which shows us the way to compassionate action and to becoming the person we want to be, a person unencumbered by self-centeredness and ignorance. This leads directly into chapter 13, which deals with the way to cultivate the wisdom realizing the emptiness of inheren existence and to understand that emptiness and dependent arising are complementary, not contradictory. Chapter 14 is the colophon and conclusion, with an inspiring poem by Atisha and the dedication. A section on recommended reading follows.

APPRECIATION

While working on this book, I received a request from a Dharma friend to write a book explaining the ins and outs of karma in detail. While the present volume does not go into the details found in the Abhidharma and stages-of-the-path literature about the various types of karma, their strengths, their results, and so forth, it does speak about karma in a most practical way. Dharmarakshita, in his directness, guides us to understand that our actions are not simply items in categories and numbered lists—which are definitely helpful to understand—but that we are creating karma and experiencing their results all day long. Karma is intertwined in the fabric of our life, and training ourselves to be aware of this can transform how we live. We become more mindful and thoughtful, making choices with care, understanding that our past actions, present experiences, and future circumstances originate in our minds.

I bow to the Buddha as the source of this marvelous teaching, and to Dharmarakshita, Atisha, and the sages of Tibet for developing the genre of thought transformation teachings. I also am eternally grateful to Geshe Ngawang Dhargye for teaching this text and waking me up, and all my other teachers, including His Holiness the Dalai Lama, Tsenzhap Serkong Rinpoche, and Zopa Rinpoche, among others, for continuing to guide and teach me. It's amazing that they never gave up on this thick-skulled person. And I'm also grateful to the kitchen staff who didn't wash the vegetables, so that I got hepatitis A, for without this event, my Dharma practice might have stalled long ago. Much appreciation to Geshe Thupten Jinpa for translating *The Wheel of Sharp Weapons*. All mistakes in this book are my own.

Bhikshuni Thubten Chodron
Sravasti Abbey
June 2, 2015

GOOD KARMA

1

Sick as a Dog

GENERATING OUR MOTIVATION

I HAVE A SPECIAL connection with this poem. It impacted my life in a strong but unexpected way. In 1976 I was living at Kopan Monastery outside of Kathmandu, Nepal, where, as someone new to the Dharma, I was studying and practicing the Dharma. I became sick and weak, my skin turned yellow, and anger percolated inside me. I had contracted hepatitis A, a disease that Western medicine had no cure for. The illness totally knocked me out physically and mentally, and my bad mood was accentuated because hepatitis A affects the liver, which, according to Tibetan medicine, is related to the element of bile and the defilement of anger. Some friends kindly took me to Kathmandu to see a homeopathic doctor, who prescribed some medicine. On the return to Kopan, I was so weak that a friend had to carry me on his back up the hill to the monastery. Taxis were few and far between in those days, and in any case, I couldn't afford to take one.

At the time, I stayed in a dormitory where the floor was made of irregularly spaced wooden planks. When someone from the upper floor swept their room, the dirt fell through the planks and onto the people in the room below. Instead of toilets, there were outhouses—pits in the ground with two boards across. Grass mats formed the sides of the outhouses. At night, you had to navigate carefully to avoid falling into the pit. I was so sick that walking from my room to the outhouse was like climbing Mount Everest. Exhausted, I just lay in my room all day.

While in my sickbed, somebody brought me a little booklet called *The Wheel of Sharp Weapons,* published by the Library of Tibetan Works and Archives in Dharamsala, India. I had enough strength to turn the pages. Verse 9 stopped me in my tracks. It read:

> When my body falls prey to unbearable illnesses,
> It is the weapon of destructive karma returning on me
> For injuring the bodies of others;
> From now on I will take all sickness upon myself.

Until that moment, I had blamed my illness and its attendant discomfort on the cook, who had not cleaned the vegetables thoroughly, and on the kitchen helpers, who had not washed the dishes well. Now Dharmarakshita was telling me that my experience was the result of my own actions! Looking at it from a karmic viewpoint, I saw that the sickness was rooted in my own actions—probably created in previous lives—of physically harming others. Or perhaps the karma was created when, as a young child, I piled up all the snails in the garden and stomped on them with glee, mistakenly thinking I was doing something good by ridding the garden of these pests. Or perhaps it was due to swatting flies in the summer, another activity I took great delight in as a child.

That my misery was due to my own actions doesn't mean I deserved to suffer; karma is not a ticket to punishment. Rather, it meant I could no longer blame my misery on others. Whatever I had done to others was now coming back to me, and I had to take responsibility for my previous actions, even if I couldn't remember them or didn't know specifically which destructive actions were now ripening as my suffering. Actually it didn't matter because I knew I certainly had not been an angel. *The Wheel of Sharp Weapons* made it clear to me that karma is like a boomerang. Whatever actions we do return and have a similar effect upon us.

That moment was a turning point in my Dharma practice. Previously I had thought, "Dharma is nice. I *should* practice it." But I was lazy in doing so. Seeing that my miserable experiences were the results of my own actions, which could be traced back to the ignorance, anger, and clinging attachment in my own mind, I now *wanted* to practice

Dharma. The difference between *should* and *want* is enormous. The latter is supported by wisdom; the other is limp obligation. Looking back on having hepatitis, I am grateful for the experience of being sick because it dramatically changed my approach to life and to Dharma practice. It got me going on the right path, a path that is still benefiting me—and others—four decades later.

In the middle of my recovery from hepatitis, while I was still very weak, the Nepali government decided that it was time for all the foreigners at Kopan to leave and stopped extending our visas. This was in May or June, 1976, the time just before the monsoon rains, the hottest and muggiest months of the year. It was not the time anyone in their right mind wanted to travel overland from Kathmandu to Dharamsala, India—a several-day journey in buses on winding roads and trains packed with people. I was a monastic wannabe, not a nun, then, but nevertheless the monastic community of Westerners took me under their wing as we schlepped up and down mountains and across plains and again up mountains to arrive in Dharamsala, where we could continue our study and practice of the Dharma with compassionate and wise Tibetan spiritual mentors.

The kindness that others gave me then was yet another real-life Dharma teaching. It made me wonder what I possibly could have done in previous lives that created the cause for this. "Why previous lives?" you may wonder. Because now alert to the machinations of my self-centered thought due to having read *The Wheel of Sharp Weapons,* I was aware that in this life I had not created such causes. Experiencing the kindness of others in this way fortified my confidence in the wisdom of Dharmarakshita's message to *dance and trample on the head of the betrayer* of self-centeredness and self-grasping ignorance and to cherish others and take delight in benefiting them in whatever way possible.

MOTIVATION

To fully benefit from reading a Dharma book or listening to teachings, having an open mind is essential. We need to be willing to reflect on the teachings to make sure we understand them correctly and then take them to heart and use them as a mirror to show us the condition of our minds.

In addition to describing the results of our actions, the teachings in this book center on the generation of bodhicitta, the wish to attain full awakening for the benefit of all sentient beings. They also explain how to transform adverse circumstances into the path, so that everything we experience will become part of the path to full awakening.

Our motivation is the chief factor that determines the karmic result of our actions. If we act seeking worldly happiness for ourselves in this life, sometimes our aim is fulfilled, but frequently it isn't. However, when our aim goes beyond the limited scope of this particular life and expands to seeking a fortunate rebirth in the future, liberation from cyclic existence, or full awakening, then the actions done with those motivations will bring those corresponding results. This is the meaning of "karma is infallible": happiness comes from constructive actions, never from destructive ones, and misery arises due to destructive actions, never constructive one. Constructive and destructive actions are principally differentiated based on the motivation with which they were done.

In terms of the functioning of the law of karma (actions) and their effects, being hypocritical spells our own doom. While in ordinary activities we may adopt pretenses to make ourselves look good and we may sometimes be successful in deceiving people to get what we want, this strategy doesn't work when our goal is to purify our mind. The results of our actions are determined principally by our motivation, not by what others think or say about us. Being a spiritual practitioner requires complete sincerity and self-honesty.

To cultivate the courage such self-honesty necessitates, we reflect on the shortcomings of our self-centered attitude, the kindness we have received from sentient beings, and the advantages that accrue to ourselves and others from cherishing others. Seeing the misery of sentient beings, we train our hearts and minds to respond with love, wanting them to have happiness and its causes, and with compassion, wanting them to be free from suffering and its causes. With that heartfelt intention, we then cultivate the great resolve to work for their benefit, and in order to do that most effectively, we generate the aspiration to attain the full awakening of a buddha. This motivation of bodhicitta is the source of all happiness and success for all sentient beings throughout all times.

2   The World We Swim In

THE BUDDHIST WORLDVIEW

B EFORE DELVING INTO *The Wheel of Sharp Weapons*, it is first helpful to have a brief explanation of our current situation of life in
cyclic existence, the self-grasping ignorance and self-centered thoughts
that fuel our difficulties, liberation and full awakening as desirable
states of peace, and the Buddhist path that transforms our mind into
those states. These form the context for the teachings in *The Wheel of
Sharp Weapons.*

From our usual perspective, we see ourselves as real individuals with
our own unique essence, Self, or soul. Everyone and everything around
us appear to be objectively "real," existing from its own side, independent of everything else. This is the view of self-grasping ignorance.
While people and things are fluid, changing, and dependent on other
factors, ignorance confines them to being "solid," independent, objective things "out there."

Meanwhile, self-centered thought thinks, "I'm the most important
one in the world. Everything should be the way I want it to be." From
this perspective, our task becomes to navigate our way through the
external world so that we will encounter what gives us pleasure and
avoid all that causes us pain. Security, comfort, and success are of great-
est importance.

This view is limited in many ways. One is that it takes only ourselves
into account. We primarily think about what *I* want, what makes *me*
happy. While there are over seven billion human beings on the planet,
we care principally about only one. Since everyone sees the world this
way, we are left to quarrel about who really is the most important.

Disputes, from family arguments to international wars, result from this limited view.

Another drawback is that it assumes only this life exists in the way that everything appears now. But a little reflection will show us that who we are is in fact fluid. Try this simple exercise. Ask yourself: "Am I the same person I was when I was one month old?" Our present body and mind are completely different; we are not exactly the same person as the infant in our baby pictures. Nevertheless, there is a continuum that connects the baby to the adult we are now. Similarly, there is a continuum that goes on after we die.

What we call "I" or "me" exists by being merely designated in dependence on a body and mind. While our body is physical and its continuity can be traced back to the sperm and egg of our parents, we also have a mind—the cognitive, perceptive, emotional part of ourselves that is not material form. If we trace back the continuity of our mind—each moment of mind being preceded by a previous moment of mind—we reach the moment of conception. Our mind at this time, too, had a cause, its preceding moment before taking place in the combination of sperm and egg. In this way, the continuity of mind can be traced back to before this life—the mind in previous lives. Although our body, mind, and self were different in our previous life, there is the continuity of the mind.

Going back from one moment of consciousness to the previous moment, from one lifetime to another, we see that we have been born into many different bodies in what we call cyclic existence, or samsara. Cyclic existence refers to taking a body and mind under the control of ignorance, mental afflictions, and karma. Cyclic existence is not our environment; it's the state of our body and mind.

There is a saying, "Be careful what you want because you might get it." In our case, at the time of death of one life, we wanted another body, and we got it! Why does our mind seek to be born in a body at the time of death? Having a body makes us feel real. On the basis of our body, we create many identities that we cling to, without which we would feel lost.

What makes our mind take one rebirth after the next? The fundamental cause is ignorance, a mental factor that misapprehends how phenomena exist. Once we grasp at a "real me" and think that our body and mind exist objectively and independent of everything else, mental afflictions arise: attachment to what gives us pleasure, anger at what interferes with our happiness or brings us pain. We become jealous of those who have what we don't, arrogant regarding those who we think aren't as good as we are, and competitive with equals.

Due to grasping a "real me," we create identities based on our body: "I am this race, this ethnic group, this nationality, this gender, this sexual orientation, this age, this degree of sexiness, this degree of physical strength and athletic ability." We also create identities based on our mind: "I am talented." "I am stupid." "I am creative, articulate, emotional, uneducated," and so forth. Clinging to these identities, we react with attachment or anger toward what confirms or threatens them.

Motivated by these afflictive mental states, we then act—this is the meaning of "to create karma." Sometimes we connive how to get what we want; other times we speak in inconsiderate ways; in other situations we may steal others' possessions or use our sexuality in ways that harm ourselves or others. These actions leave on our mindstream—the continuity of consciousness—a residue, which may be called "karmic seeds." Many different karmic seeds are planted on our mindstream in just one day, depending on the various intentions we have and actions we do. Depending upon which karmic seeds ripen at the time we die, our mindstream will be attracted to one or another type of body, and we are reborn. Sometimes we have kind intentions and act according to them, but because the fundamental ignorance is still present, these actions bring rebirth in cyclic existence nonetheless. These actions will influence the type of rebirth we take, where we are born, our experiences, and our habitual thought patterns and actions.

At the time of death, craving for our present life arises, and some of the karmic seeds on our mindstream ripen, making a particular rebirth appear attractive to us. We assume that new body and mind, and then cling to that new existence. When our sense powers contact various objects, feelings of pleasure, pain, or neither pleasure nor pain arise. Attachment arises for pleasant feelings, and hostility, for unpleasant feelings. Wanting happiness and not suffering, we again act to get what we find desirable and destroy or distance ourselves from what we find unpleasant. We respond to neutral feelings with apathy or boredom and distract ourselves. Actions motivated by kindness, compassion, wisdom, and the like lead to happiness in the future, while actions rooted in greed, hostility, and closed-mindedness bring us suffering.

This cycle goes on and on. We are born into one body after another, experiencing sickness, aging, and death repeatedly. Between birth and death, we try so hard to get what we want and avoid what we do not want, but are never completely successful. Meanwhile, suffering that we don't wish for comes our way.

This is cyclic existence, and we have been experiencing it beginninglessly. From a Buddhist perspective, there was no initial moment in which this cycle began. Cyclic existence is not the creation of an external Creator. Rather, everything arises due to its own causes, and everything that functions must have causes and conditions that produced it. Therefore, there can be no beginning; everything is preceded by its own causes and conditions.

Spending our time and energy searching for a first beginning is unproductive. The Buddha encouraged us to be practical by giving the example of a man shot by an arrow. If, before getting medical treatment, he insisted on knowing who made the arrow, how fast it was traveling, and where it came from, that person would surely die. It's best to deal with the present circumstance and get immediate treatment for the wound. Similarly, if we become immersed in theories of a beginning, our life will go by without confronting our suffering and its causes. Instead, it is more useful to deal directly with how afflictions create our misery.

MIND CREATES OUR EXPERIENCES

Our mind creates our experience in two ways. First, our mental afflictions motivate the actions that leave karmic seeds on our mindstream and eventually ripen in our experiences, as described above. Second, our thoughts influence our experience in each moment. Dwelling on perceived injustice to ourselves, we become unhappy and angry. Contemplating the kindness we have received from others, we perceive others as friendly and generous, and our mood lightens. A simple exercise is to observe the thoughts behind each of our moods, seeing how those thoughts—and not the external situation—affect our emotions and feelings of happiness and misery.

The moment afflictions arise, our mind is in a state of suffering. Attachment breeds dissatisfaction or fear of losing what we cling to. Jealousy creates a burning sensation inside of us. Arrogance stirs up restlessness. Anger may give us a lot of energy, but inside we're not peaceful or happy.

In this way, the afflictions disturb our inner peace when they are manifest in our mind. In addition, they motivate actions that will ripen later in unsatisfactory situations. These situations, in turn, are the field in which more afflictions arise, creating more karma, bringing more uncontrolled rebirths. This is the meaning of cyclic existence. Seeing this clearly, the strong intention to oppose the three poisonous attitudes of ignorance, attachment, and anger arises within us, and we are motivated to attain liberation from this unrelenting cycle of unsatisfactory experiences.

The first step in doing this is to reverse the eight worldly concerns—four pairs of emotional responses that wreak havoc in this life and plant the seeds for misery in future lives. The first pair is delight at receiving and possessing money and material possessions, and dejection at not getting them or losing them. The second pair is delight at receiving praise and approval, and dejection when confronted with blame and disapproval. The third pair is delight at having a good reputation and displeasure when having a bad one. The fourth pair is delight at pleasurable sights, sounds, smells, tastes, and tactile sensations, and unhappiness when encountering unpleasant sensory experiences.

Spend a few moments contemplating how these four pairs affect your life. From morning until night, and even in our dreams, most of our time and energy are spent trying to get money and possessions, approval and praise, good reputation, and pleasurable sensory experiences, and avoiding their opposites. The attachment to the pleasant four worldly concerns and aversion to the four unpleasant ones are so powerful that we will act unethically to procure these or protect ourselves from them. Even when we are successful in getting the pleasant four, our attachment to them creates problems as we cling to them and fear losing them. When we don't get them, our dejection leads to depression, anger, and even rage. As a result we act in ways that harm others and create suffering for ourselves.

The eight worldly concerns also distract us from spiritual practice, consuming our time and energy with plans, anxiety, and worry. They get us involved in destructive actions: fighting with others, taking their possessions, using sexuality unwisely and unkindly, lying, creating disharmony, speaking harshly, gossiping, coveting, thinking malicious thoughts, and pursuing wrong views. There is no space in our minds for virtuous mental states, such as genuine love and compassion, generosity, ethical conduct, fortitude, joyous effort, meditative stability, or wisdom.

In addition, the eight worldly concerns corrupt our Dharma practice by stimulating us to do the right thing for the wrong reason. For example, instead of meditating in order to attain liberation, we sit in a meditation position with a distracted mind, trying to appear like a spiritual practitioner to others. Rather than give a donation to a charity with the motivation to benefit the recipients, we do so with the wish to appear rich or generous in others' eyes.

WORLDLY LIFE AND DHARMA ACTIONS

The difference between worldly actions and Dharma actions is the presence or absence of the eight worldly concerns. Subduing the gross forms of these eight is the first step in living a spiritual or Dharma life. Doing this requires time and persistent effort and leads to a peaceful mind. We will begin to consider that we will be reborn, and we will become concerned with creating the causes for a good rebirth that will enable us to continue our Dharma practice. On that basis, we can then cultivate even more noble motivations, such as seeking liberation from cyclic existence and progressing on the path to full awakening, so we can be of the most effective and long-lasting benefit to each and every living being.

Genuine Dharma practice is not the superficial appearance of reciting prayers, making prostrations, reading scriptures, or looking holy. It is about monitoring and improving what is going on in our mind, especially our emotional state. By taming the mind, our speech and physical actions will naturally improve as well. Is our mind seeking only the happiness of this life, or is there mental space to think about future lives, liberation, and full awakening? Is our attention focused on our own self-centered concerns, or is it directed toward the welfare of others? Are we thinking about long-term benefit or short-term pleasure?

In short, actions done with *only* a concern for this life and for the sake of the eight worldly concerns are worldly actions. Actions done seeking a good rebirth, liberation from cyclic existence, or full awakening are Dharma actions. Bearing this in mind is worthwhile since there is a huge difference between worldly and Dharma actions, and it is very easy for us to fall into old habits, seeking wealth, praise, good reputation, and sensory pleasure.

Sometimes people mistakenly think that practicing Dharma means having to give up everything that brings us happiness. In fact, chocolate cake, money, or a boyfriend is not the problem. The attachment, resentment, arrogance, and jealousy that arise in us in reaction to those things or people are the sources of problems. In other words, the deeper cause for our suffering is not the inability to get what we want. It is the craving that is obsessed with getting it. The moment we give up the self-centered craving that seeks "my happiness now!" our mind is peaceful and relaxed.

We begin practicing the Dharma by observing our mind and investigating our thoughts and emotions. What am I thinking? What am I feeling? What is the story behind this emotion? Is this mental state realistic? Is it beneficial? Am I exaggerating the good qualities of someone or something? Am I focusing on a particular goal because it will bring me happiness in the short term, even though it may interfere with others' well-being or even cause me problems in the long term?

Am I overestimating someone's faults? Are my expectations of others unrealistic?

When we begin in earnest to observe our mind and investigate our thoughts and emotions—especially the habitual ones that arise so easily—we have begun real Dharma practice. Then, by studying the Buddha's teachings, we learn the antidotes to the afflictions, practice them, and learn to cultivate constructive, realistic mental states. This will lead us to experience happiness now and in the future. In addition, we will become able to benefit others temporally and ultimately. This is what gives meaning and satisfaction to our lives. Such fulfillment coming from a life well lived is more worthwhile than possessions and money, praise and approval, good reputation, and sensual pleasure.

KARMA AND ITS EFFECTS

Causality functions in so many areas of our lives—physics, chemistry, biology, politics, psychology, economics, sociology, to name a few. In these areas, understanding causality enables us to shape our environment and experiences. In addition to these systems of causality, the law of karma and its effects influences us. The law of karma—actions of our body, speech, and mind—and its effects involve the ethical dimension of our lives. It answers the questions, Why was I born me? Why do things happen the way they do? What are the long-term results of my thoughts and deeds? The law of karma and its effects explain the link between our actions and our experiences and demonstrate why ethical conduct is so vital to having happy lives.

Karma means "action" and refers to volitional actions done by our body, speech, or mind. Karma has to do with our intentions; our mental plans, verbal communications, and physical deeds are all preceded by an intention. From the viewpoint of their causes, actions done with wholesome or virtuous intentions—such as kindness, love, compassion, wisdom, care, friendliness, and so forth—bring happy results, and thus are called "constructive (positive) actions." Actions motivated by unwholesome intentions—such as anger, resentment, and greed—are considered and called "destructive (negative)." Here we see that hypocrisy and manipulation in spiritual practice don't work to our benefit. While we can look good to others, if our intentions are rotten, so are the actions motivated by them.

We can also differentiate actions based on the long-term results they bring. Through supernormal powers, the Buddha was able to see the karmic causes of sentient beings' present experiences. He labeled as *constructive* those actions bringing long-term happiness to the person who does them, and designated as *destructive* those actions that lead to that person's suffering. Actions that lead to neither particularly pleasant nor unpleasant results are termed *neutral.* Thus our actions are neither inherently virtuous nor nonvirtuous; they become so in relation to their long-term results. The Buddha did not invent the law of karma and its effects, nor does he give out rewards and punishments. He merely described how this natural law operates.

What are the physical, verbal, and mental actions that cause long-term unhappiness to the person who does them? The Buddha observed ten unwholesome paths of action. Three are done with our body (killing, stealing, and unwise or unkind sexual behavior), four with our speech (lying, creating disharmony, harsh words, idle talk), and three by way of our thoughts (coveting, malice, and wrong views). The simple act of restraining ourselves from these ten creates constructive karma. In other words, when we are tempted to speak harshly, for example, restraining ourselves from harshly criticizing the other person is a wholesome action that will bring happiness. So is taking outside an insect in our house, instead of swatting or stomping on it.

Furthermore, doing the opposite of the ten nonvirtuous paths of actions creates constructive karma: saving life, protecting others' possessions, using sexuality wisely and kindly, speaking truthfully, creating harmony with our speech, speaking kindly and encouraging others in constructive actions, speaking at appropriate times and in an appropriate way, thoughts of giving, love, and forgiveness, and correct views.

The law of karma and its effects has four basic principles. First, karma is definite. That is, happiness comes only from constructive actions, never from destructive ones, and suffering arises only from destructive actions, never from constructive ones. While the specific way in which a particular action will ripen is not fixed or predetermined, destructive actions will always bring misery and constructive ones will always bring happiness. Thus trying to justify our harmful actions by saying they will bring good results doesn't work.

Second, a small action can bring a strong or long-lasting result in much the same way that a small seed can grow into a huge tree. For this reason, it is important not to rationalize our negative behavior by saying, for example, "It was just a little lie." Similarly, being lazy, thinking, "It's just a small act of kindness and isn't of much significance, so why bother?" is a lost opportunity to create good karma.

Third, if we don't create the cause, we don't experience the effect. We ourselves are the creator of our experience, not another person or an external god. When we refrain from stealing, for example, we will not experience poverty or having our own possessions stolen. If we don't practice the Dharma and create the causes for happiness, happiness will not come our way. The great masters say that simply praying for worldly happiness or for spiritual awakening is not sufficient. We have to create the causes for it through our actions.

Fourth, karmic seeds—the "residual energy" left on our mindstreams after we have done an action—don't get lost. We will definitely experience their results, unless intervening forces arise. In the case of destructive actions, doing purification practices makes the results of those actions weaker, shorter, or occur later. The strongest purification practice is meditating on the nature of ultimate reality—the emptiness of inherent existence. Direct perception of this has the power to uproot seeds of destructive karma from our mindstreams so that they can never ripen in suffering.

Anger and wrong views have the power to interfere with the ripening of our virtuous actions, delaying the result or lessening the duration or strength of the happy situation. Therefore, we want to take special care not to destroy our own future happiness by allowing anger or distorted conceptions to govern our mind.

Once complete with three branches, our actions mature or ripen into three types of results. These three branches of a complete karma are the preparation, the action itself, and the completion of the action. (1) The preparation involves our motivation: we have a wholesome or unwholesome intention to do something, there is a certain thing or person that is the object of our intention, and we identify that person or thing correctly. (2) Then the action is done: either we do it ourselves or ask another person to do it. (3) Finally, the act is completed, fulfilling the aim that motivated it. In addition, we rejoice in doing the action.

Three types of results may come from actions done with all branches complete. These results usually come in future lives, but especially strong actions may bring their results in this life. The three types of results are (1) the ripening result, which is the body and mind we will take in a future life; (2) the causally concordant result, which is of two types, experiential (that is, we will experience a situation similar to the one our actions caused others to experience) or behavioral (that is, we will tend to do that action again in the future); and (3) the environmental result, which is our experience of the environment and climate where we live.

In the case of lying, for example, the ripening result is an unfortunate rebirth, the causally concordant experiential result is others lying to us, the causally concordant behavioral result is our tendency to lie repeatedly, and the environmental result is living in a filthy place where people are corrupt and dishonest.

Verses 9 to 47 of *The Wheel of Sharp Weapons* speak of the unpleasant causally concordant experiential results we are currently experiencing and what kinds of actions we did in the past to bring them about. This discussion enables us to identify our self-grasping ignorance and self-centered thought as the chief culprits that activated the afflictions that, in turn, motivated the destructive actions we did in the past that led to our present difficulties. Understanding this enables us to stop blaming others for our misery by realizing that the principal causes of it lie within our own minds. It also will make us more careful about the actions we choose to do in the future because we will be more aware that we're creating our own futures through our present choices and actions.

Verses 54 to 89 focus on the causally concordant behavioral result— the habitual actions and attitudes underlain by self-grasping ignorance and the self-centered thought that we repeatedly do, which create the causes for future suffering. Learning these will make us more mindful of the values and ethical precepts we want to implement to guide our lives. It will also strengthen our introspective awareness so that we will be more aware of what we are thinking, saying, and doing, thus giving us more choice to either continue these actions or disengage from them. Instead of operating "on automatic" with little self-awareness of our choices and actions, we will be able to guide our lives with wisdom.

In short, our minds are the creator of our experiences. As the Buddha says in the *Dhammapada* (v. 1–2):

> We are what we think.
> All that we are arises with our thoughts.
> With our thoughts we make the world.
> Speak or act with an impure mind
> And trouble will follow you
> As the wheel follows the ox that draws the cart.

> We are what we think.
> All that we are arises with our thoughts.
> With our thoughts we make the world.
> Speak or act with a pure mind
> And happiness will follow you
> As your shadow, unshakable.

BUDDHA-NATURE: OUR POTENTIAL TO CHANGE

Because our minds create our experiences, it is possible to free ourselves from cyclic existence by abandoning the ignorance, anger, and clinging attachment and the polluted karma that are its principal causes. These afflictions obscure the pure nature of our mind and can be removed. We have buddha-nature, the potential to become fully awakened buddhas, within us. As the very nature of our mind, buddha-nature can never disappear; we can never be separated from it.

What is this buddha-nature? There is a lot of discussion about this in the various Buddhist philosophical tenet systems. The view explained here is according to the Madhyamaka, or Middle Way, system, which most Tibetans consider to be the most accurate description of the nature of reality.

Buddha-nature is of two types: naturally abiding buddha-nature and transforming buddha-nature. Naturally abiding buddha-nature is the natural purity of the mind: its emptiness of inherent existence. That is, the mind lacks an independent essence of its own. If it had such an essence, mental afflictions would inherently abide in the nature of the mind; they would be inseparable from the mind and thus could never be eliminated. However, since the mind lacks inherent existence, it can change and the afflictions can be eradicated such that they can never arise again.

How is this possible? As described above, ignorance is the root of the problem. Because we misapprehend how we and other phenomena exist, anger, attachment, jealousy, conceit, afflictive doubt, wrong views, and a host of other disturbing mental states arise. These mental afflictions motivate actions or karma, and these karmic seeds then continue along with our mind. When suitable conditions arise, they ripen as our experiences in cyclic existence.

Ignorance is an erroneous consciousness—whereas people and phenomena exist dependently, it apprehends them as existing independently. By cultivating the wisdom that sees how things actually exist, ignorance can be eliminated. This wisdom correctly sees that people and phenomena are empty of inherent or independent existence because they exist dependent on other factors. All of us know that our bodies depend on the bodies of our parents, that our mental acuity is influenced by our education, that social problems and their solutions arise due to causes and conditions. Nothing exists alone, independent, isolated from everything. All phenomena are interdependent.

The wisdom that realizes that everything is empty of inherent existence because it arises dependent on other factors perceives the opposite of ignorance. While ignorance apprehends things as having an inherent nature, wisdom apprehends things as being empty of such a nature. Because wisdom apprehends phenomena as they actually are, ignorance cannot stand up to it. Ignorance cannot be manifest in the mind at the same time as the wisdom directly perceiving the emptiness of independent existence is manifest. When the wisdom directly realizing the absence of independent existence grows increasingly more powerful through familiarization and repeated meditation, it is able to overpower ignorance, uprooting it completely from our mindstream, eliminating it so that it can never arise again. In this way, it is possible to attain nirvana and full awakening. In the state of full awakening, naturally abiding buddha-nature becomes the Buddha's nature body—the emptiness of inherent existence of a buddha's mind and the true cessation of defilements.

The second type, transforming buddha-nature, is the seed for the unpolluted mind. It consists of virtuous and neutral phenomena that can transform into a buddha's omniscient mind. These include the mental factors of concentration, love, compassion, wisdom, faith, and other virtuous mental states that we have now, but are currently undeveloped. The conventional nature of the mind, its clarity (luminosity) and aware (knowing) nature, is also part of the transforming buddha-nature. It is neutral—afflictions and defilements have not entered its nature—and can be transformed into a virtuous or wholesome state.

Every sentient being has two types of buddha-nature that are always present within them. No matter how disgusting someone's actions may be at any particular moment, that person is not inherently evil or depraved. The actions are not the person. The person has buddha-nature, and thus change is possible; there is always hope, and that is a sound reason to respect each and every living being.

Afflictions are like clouds in the pure blue sky. The clouds are not in the nature of the sky. Although they may temporarily obscure the sky, they are momentary, adventitious. The pure nature of the sky remains untainted. The clouds can be removed. While we don't have much control over the weather and the presence or absence of clouds, we do have the power to remove the clouds of defilements obscuring our minds. We can purify our negativities and create the causes for happiness and liberation. This is what this book is about.

The fact that we have buddha-nature also means that there is a valid basis for self-confidence. Instead of basing our self-esteem on tran-sient factors—such as physical appearance, wealth, athletic or artistic ability, social status, others' approval, reputation, and so forth—that will surely disintegrate with the passage of time, we can now base our self-confidence on a stable factor, our buddha-nature. No matter whether we are healthy or sick, rich or poor, appreciated or neglected, our buddha-nature is still present and gives us the possibility of attain-ing buddhahood.

3 Brave Peacocks and Cowardly Crows

NOW WE WILL begin the actual text. Please read the verses and explanation slowly. Stop and think about each verse: see if it makes sense logically and make examples of how it pertains to your life. Reflect on each verse from the perspective of cyclic existence and the law of karma and its effects as described above.

HOMAGE

Homage to the Three Jewels!

This is the wheel of sharp weapons striking at the vital points of the enemy.
Homage to the wrathful Yamantaka!

Dharmarakshita begins by paying *homage to the Three Jewels:* the Buddha, Dharma, and Sangha. The Dharma Jewel—the true cessation of *duhkha* (suffering or unsatisfactory circumstances) and its causes and the true path leading to that—is the real refuge because actualizing the true cessation and true path in our mindstreams is what actually protects us from misery. The Buddha taught the path to achieve those cessations, and for this reason he is the supreme teacher or guide for us sentient beings. The Sangha Jewel consists of all those who have direct realization of the nature of reality and in that way become reliable friends on the path.

Our relationship with the Three Jewels is similar to that of a sick person with a doctor, medicine, and nurse. We are the sick person suffering from the pain of cyclic existence: birth, aging, sickness, death, not getting what we like, being separated from what we find desirable, and experiencing problems that we don't want. We want to be well but are ignorant about the cause of our illness and the treatment that will cure it. The Buddha is the doctor who diagnoses the causes of the illness of cyclic existence—ignorance, afflictions, and polluted karma. He then prescribes the medicine of the Dharma—ethical conduct, concentration, wisdom, love, compassion, and altruism. The sangha are the nurses who encourage us and help us take the medicine. This is the way the Three Jewels guide us to spiritual health.

When faced with an attack, warriors seek to strike at the *vital points of the enemy* to kill him or her and stop the harm that person is causing. For bodhisattvas seeking full awakening, the vital points to eradicate are the self-grasping ignorance that grasps persons and phenomena as existing with their own inherent essence, and its accomplice, the self-centered attitude that considers our own happiness and suffering to be more important than those of everyone else. The teachings in this poem form the wheel of sharp weapons that will strike at and kill these sources of misery.

Dharmarakshita then pays homage to Yamantaka, the wrathful form of Manjushri, the buddha of wisdom. While Manjushri's appearance is peaceful and compassionate, Yamantaka's is extremely fierce. His body is dark blue, and he has nine heads and thirty-four arms that hold weapons and bodily parts of his foes. His sixteen legs trample various animals and worldly gods. He stands amid a raging fire and roars like terrifying thunder.

Yamantaka, whose name means "Vajra Terrifier of the Lord of Death," counteracts the enemy of death in cyclic existence. To stop death, the last of the twelve links of dependent arising, we must eradicate the first link, ignorance, from which arises the karma causing rebirth in cyclic existence. While phenomena exist dependent on other things, such as their causes and their parts, ignorance apprehends them as existing with an independent nature. Realizing that phenomena have a dependent nature, wisdom negates their having an independent or inherent nature. Because wisdom sees things as they really are, it is capable of overcoming and eventually completely eradicating ignorance so that it can never arise again.

I

When peacocks roam through the jungle of virulent poison,
Though the gardens of medicinal plants are attractive,
The flocks of peacocks will not take delight in them;
For peacocks thrive on the essence of virulent poison.

2

Likewise when heroes (bodhisattvas) enter the jungle of cyclic
  existence,
Though the gardens of happiness and prosperity may seem beautiful,
The heroes will not become attached to them,
For heroes thrive in the jungle of suffering.

In this poetic metaphor, peacocks symbolize the great bodhisattvas, the jungle represents cyclic existence, and the virulent poisons are the afflictions, especially the three poisons of ignorance, anger, and attachment. Although the peacocks have the opportunity to enjoy medicinal gardens, they are not captivated by the beauty and shun them in favor of poisonous plants. While they live in treacherous jungles and eat poisonous plants, peacocks are not harmed by these. Instead they thrive, and their feathers take on the beautiful colors that draw us to them.

In the same way, *arya* bodhisattvas—those who have the wisdom directly perceiving reality—could choose to enter nirvana and be forever free from cyclic existence. However, due to their strong compassion and bodhicitta, they choose not to stay in the state of personal peace and voluntarily take birth in cyclic existence. Although they appear in cyclic existence, these bodhisattvas are not overwhelmed by the afflictions that cause repetitive rebirth. Instead, they thrive on the afflictions that have not yet been totally cleansed from their mind and transform these mental poisons into the path to full awakening. For this reason they are called *heroes*. Arya bodhisattvas are not seduced by the joys and pleasures of cyclic existence, but steadily continue on the path, happily enduring whatever hardships they encounter for the noble aim of attaining buddhahood and thus being able to benefit all sentient beings most effectively. They practice until all their afflictive obscurations and cognitive obscurations are eradicated due to the force of the wisdom realizing the ultimate truth supported by bodhicitta.

The Mahayana path leading to full awakening has five paths: the paths of accumulation, preparation, seeing, meditation, and no-more-learning. Lower bodhisattvas, who are on the paths of accumulation and preparation, have not yet realized emptiness directly or begun to eradicate defilements. The great bodhisattvas who are spoken of in verses 1 and 2 are on the third and fourth paths: the paths of seeing and meditation. On the path of seeing, they have their first direct, nonconceptual realization of the ultimate nature of phenomena—the emptiness of inherent existence. They strengthen this realization on the path of meditation. On these two paths, they use this wisdom to eradicate the two obscurations, the afflictive obscurations and the cognitive obscurations, from their mindstream.

Afflictive obscurations consist of ignorance, afflictions (such as attachment, anger, arrogance, jealousy, and so forth), and their seeds, as well as the polluted karma causing rebirth in cyclic existence. The afflictive obscurations prevent liberation from cyclic existence. Cognitive obscurations are more subtle and difficult to eliminate. Consisting of the latencies of ignorance and the dualistic appearance they cause, cognitive obscurations impede attaining the full awakening of a buddha.

Due to having directly and nonconceptually realized emptiness and thus begun the process of uprooting ignorance, arya bodhisattvas no longer create polluted karma. They create unpolluted karma, which is motivated by bodhicitta and acts as a cause for them to attain full awakening. After arya bodhisattvas become buddhas, they no longer create karma at all. Buddhas' actions are called "awakening activities"—their spontaneous and effortless actions that continuously benefit sentient beings by leading them on the path to awakening.

We ordinary beings differ from great bodhisattvas because we are seduced by the pleasures of cyclic existence. Our first thoughts in the morning usually center on "How can I experience pleasure today?" The images of a cup of coffee, a hot shower, and breakfast get us out of bed. Most of the things we do during the day are similarly fueled by self-centered thought, seeking our own pleasure and happiness. Although we may not verbalize it, our motivation is "If there is happiness and advantage, I'll take it; if there are problems, others can have them." Although this may sound crass, if we look closely, we will see that these are the kinds of thoughts our ignorant and self-preoccupied minds latch onto.

Completely caught up with the eight worldly concerns, we see cyclic existence as a garden of happiness and and delight in playing in it. In the process, we act in harmful ways, creating the karmic seeds that bind us to cyclic existence. Again and again we take a body that gets old, sick, and dies, and a mind that is constantly dissatisfied.

Arya bodhisattvas see through the glittering appearance of cyclic existence as a garden of happiness. Seeing its deceptive quality, they know it is actually a hellhole. Instead of running after the glitter of sense pleasure, prestige, or romance, they seek a higher type of happiness and a deeper purpose in life. Having realized the three principal aspects of the path—(1) renunciation of duhkha and the causes of duhkha, (2) the altruistic intention of bodhicitta that seeks full awakening for the benefit of all beings, and (3) the correct view of reality—they are able to manifest in cyclic existence but not be beguiled by it. They have the ability to transform afflictions into the path to awakening.

In the Sutrayana—the path described in the discourses (sutras) spoken by the Buddha—bodhisattvas do not actually take the afflictions as the path, but use them to do things that benefit others. For example, they may have children who grow up to be bodhisattvas and spread the Dharma. On the Tantrayana—the path taught by the Buddha in the tantras—bodhisattvas actually take the energy of attachment and transform it into the path. This is a much deeper level of practice.

3

Those who avidly pursue happiness and prosperity
Are brought to suffering due to their cowardice.

The bodhisattvas, who willingly embrace suffering,
Always remain happy due to their heroism.

Motivated by clinging attachment and greed, we ordinary beings *avidly pursue happiness and prosperity.* Trying to find security, we want others to meet our needs. By aggressively trying to control others or surreptitiously manipulating them, we try to arrange the world and everyone in it to be the way we want them to be. However, we are never successful in doing this and remain perpetually dissatisfied.

In cyclic existence we experience three types of unsatisfactory circumstances, or duhkha. The duhkha of pain—physical and mental pain that no one likes—is easy to renounce. Even animals do not like it. However, the duhkha of change—what we ordinary beings usually call "happiness"—is difficult for us to give up because we think it is real joy. When we get what we want—a promotion, a new home, a romantic relationship, an award—we believe that to be genuine happiness. However, it if were real happiness, it wouldn't disappear, and the object or person that brings us joy one day would not be problematic the next. The duhkha of pervasive conditioning—having a body and mind under the control of ignorance, afflictions, and polluted karma—is even more difficult to relinquish because we do not think of it as undesirable. Quite the opposite, we cling to our body as the basis of our identity and the source of much of our pleasure.

The *cowardice* that brings us suffering refers to our clinging attachment, a mental factor that seeks happiness through obtaining external possessions, relationships, praise, status, and so on. This craving prevents us from facing the unsatisfactory nature of our existence and the disadvantages of greed and attachment. Instead, we are attracted to the pleasures of cyclic existence, create more karma by pursuing them, and as a result are repeatedly reborn. We are cowardly in the sense that we are afraid to see attachment for what it is. We fear that if we don't follow our attachment, we won't have any happiness at all. Due to our cowardice in facing the reality of the situation, we are *brought to suffering.*

Great bodhisattvas are the opposite. They are heroic in that they stand up to their craving and refrain from chasing after samsaric happiness. In addition, they do not fear the duhkha of cyclic existence in the same way we ordinary beings do. We fear the first kind of duhkha but happily embrace the second and third, while bodhisattvas want to be free of all three. But if they are faced with experiencing pain in order to benefit others, they will happily do that, whereas we run away. Bodhisattvas' "fear" of cyclic existence is not the panicky, anxious fear that plagues ordinary beings who seek to avoid discomfort. Theirs is a wise awareness of danger that propels them to practice the path and liberate themselves from cyclic existence. Such a fear of cyclic existence is useful on the path as it instigates us to study and practice the Dharma.

Unlike common beings, bodhisattvas willingly undergo suffering for a higher purpose. With fortitude and compassion for all sentient beings, they learn the Dharma and practice the path whatever physical or mental difficulties they may encounter. Not fearing unpleasant tasks, they willingly go through hardship for the benefit of others, and as a result, their minds are always joyful.

We can gradually train our mind to look at the world the way bodhisattvas do. We do not have fixed personalities, and our habitual emotions and responses are not cast in stone. Let's say somebody makes a reasonable request that we do a task that we dislike doing, and our mind silently screams, "I don't want to do this!" Mentally step back from the situation and reflect, "How would a bodhisattva look at this situation? What would this situation look like if I had compassion for everyone concerned? What options would I have if I weren't confined by my complaining mind?" Here we imagine looking at the situation with a kinder attitude and from a broader perspective. Doing this, we see that it's possible to view it in an entirely different way because there's nothing unpleasant inherent in the situation. What is so painful about washing the dishes, helping our friends clean their yard, or talking with our ex about how to help the children we both love?

Then we reflect, "Wouldn't it be nice to do the chores, so my aging parents can relax?" Imagine how they would feel, and reflect how good you would feel knowing that you contributed to their well-being. We discover that by doing a small action with genuine compassion, our minds become joyful. Indeed, researchers have found that people experience a greater sense of well-being from helping others than they do from just seeking their own benefit.

4
Here now, desire is like the jungle of virulent poison;
The peacock-like heroes {alone} can digest this.
But for the crow-like cowards it spells death,
For how can the self-centered digest such poison?
When you extend this {analogy} to other afflictions,
Each similarly assails liberation's life force, like {poison to} a crow.

Here refers to bodhisattvas who have developed confidence and compassion on the initial levels of the path. *Now* indicates they have progressed so that their compassion aiming to benefit others is strong and stable and they have the correct view of reality. This gives them the special ability to use clinging desire to accomplish the path without being polluted by it. Just as the peacocks can digest poisonous plants and it makes their feathers bright and beautiful, arya bodhisattvas can work with afflictions, thereby increasing the power of their realizations.

However, if crows tried to eat poisonous plants, they couldn't stomach them and would surely die. Similarly, ordinary self-centered beings cannot do the actions of great bodhisattvas. If we tried to take desire on the path, it would overwhelm us, causing us to get involved in many destructive actions. This would spell the death of the opportunity to attain liberation. Just as crows need to avoid poisonous plants, we need to stay away from our afflictions.

When we hear that tantra practice can transform afflictions into the path, our minds may invent a variety of excuses about how we could use desire on the path. We rationalize going against the five lay precepts of abandoning killing, stealing, unwise or unkind sexual behavior, lying, and intoxicants. Holding skewed views and an inflated opinion of our present abilities, we imagine being further along the path than we actually are. This is a recipe for spiritual disaster that unfortunately many people fall prey to.

Dharmarakshita's disciple Atisha described the path to full awakening as having three tiers. A clear understanding of this schema enables us to accurately access our present capabilities and what we at present need to emphasize in our practice. People of initial capacity cultivate the aspiration for a fortunate rebirth and practice abandoning the ten destructive paths of action in order to do so. They may also choose to live according to the five precepts for lay practitioners or the various sets of monastic precepts. People of intermediate capacity cultivate renunciation of cyclic existence and the aspiration to attain liberation. They continue to practice ethical conduct as above and in addition cultivate concentration and wisdom. People of advanced capacity are motivated by bodhicitta, the aspiration for full awakening in order to benefit all sentient beings most effectively. To accomplish this they assume the bodhisattva precepts, and when they are well trained in those, they may receive tantric empowerment and take on the tantric commitments and ethical code. We don't start out as beings of advanced capacity. Even though we may admire bodhicitta and be attracted to the bodhisattva path, we still have to build up to them by practicing the paths in common with the initial- and intermediate-capacity beings.

Until we are well trained in all three aspirations and their corresponding practices, it's important to be vigilant regarding our interactions with objects of attachment. This is not because those objects or people are bad, but because we are not yet skilled in restraining our attachment and maintaining a balanced state of mind when we're around them. Bodhisattva practitioners on the higher levels of the path can enjoy objects of attachment because they know the pleasure is deceptive: it is impermanent and lacks inherent existence. Due to their wisdom, they do not become entangled in attachment. Instead, well-trained tantric practitioners are able to generate the blissful wisdom that realizes emptiness by enjoying those pleasures. However, if those of us whose minds are overwhelmed with attachment surround ourselves with objects of attachment, we get sucked in by them and create more causes of suffering trying to procure them and then to protect them.

Those of us who take monastic precepts live simply. We accept what we need to stay alive and train our minds not to chase after more. For example, at Sravasti Abbey, the monastery where I live, we eat only food that is offered to us, although we will prepare and cook what others give us. This helps us deal with attachment to food. If our minds crave cookies and no one offers them, we confront our attachment, asking ourselves, "Will I be forever happy if I have cookies? Will cookies stop my mental restlessness?" Clearly the answer is no, so we let go of the attachment and cultivate contentment. Living in this way also helps us to develop a sense of gratitude for the kindness of the people who support us.

Meditating on impermanence is important to help us understand what is actually important in life and to set our priorities accordingly. In light of our mortality and the possibility of having an unfortunate rebirth, having cookies—or whatever we are craving—is not important. Those things won't bring us the lasting joy and fulfillment we seek, whereas taming our mind and relinquishing craving and attachment will. Meditating on the defects of cyclic existence enables us to see its unsatisfactory nature, and this reduces our interest in its transient pleasures, thus making our minds more peaceful and satisfied. Eventually, by realizing emptiness, we will cut the root of our craving and attachment completely. In short, genuine joy and fulfillment come from transforming our hearts and minds. This is something that each of us can do.

5
Therefore the peacock-like heroes must convert
Afflictions that resemble a jungle of poisons into an elixir
And enter the jungle of cyclic existence.
Embracing the afflictions, heroes must destroy their poison.

Arya bodhisattvas enter the jungle of cyclic existence and transform poisonous attachment so that it becomes an aid to accessing the subtlest level of consciousness. With that very refined mind, they then meditate on the nature of reality and use that realization to uproot all afflictions and their seeds so that they are forever gone.

Penicillin is actually a poison that when taken in appropriate ways becomes a medicine that cures diseases. In the same way, arya bodhisattvas use afflictions skillfully so that they become the means to generate the liberating wisdom of bliss and emptiness that cuts all afflictive and cognitive obscurations. Through the example of peacocks and crows, the first five verses clarify the difference between arya bodhisattvas and ordinary beings and the ways they are able or unable to transform afflictions.

The homage introduces Yamantaka, the destroyer of death, who conquers death by generating the blissful wisdom realizing reality. Yamantaka's appearance is of terrifying wrath, while his nature is compassion and wisdom, love and tolerance. His anger is not like ours, which is based on self-centeredness and self-grasping ignorance. We get angry with sentient beings because we think they are the cause of our problems. Bodhisattvas and deities such as Yamantaka are wrathful toward the afflictions, polluted karma, self-centered thought, and cognitive obscurations, because those are the real enemies that cut off our life and make us suffer.

When we invoke Yamantaka to slay all the afflictive mental states that keep us bound in cyclic existence, it is important to remember that he symbolizes wisdom and compassion. Wrathful deities do not punish or inflict harm on sentient beings. They know that we have the potential to become fully awakened buddhas, and with compassion they want to help us. Their ferocious energy is directed toward the causes of our duhkha, not toward us. In other words, we are not our afflictions; we are not our faults or our bad habits. We are not the destructive actions we have done. None of these things exist inherently in us, and they can be separated from us. Understanding this opens our minds to the possibility of change and the confidence to make these changes. In addition, it allows us to view others in a more open way. No one is inherently evil or beyond hope. No matter what horrible actions people may have engaged in, they are not those actions. Those actions can be purified, and the people who did them still have buddha-nature.

The next verses spur us to awaken our courage to confront the enemies of self-grasping ignorance and self-centered thought.

6

From now on I will distance myself from this demon—
Self-grasping that {makes me} wander helplessly,
And its emissary—self-centeredness that seeks {only} selfish happiness
  and prosperity;
I will joyfully embrace hardship for the sake of others.

We *wander helplessly*, taking birth in one body after another in cyclic existence, with no end in sight. The *demon* behind this sad story is the self-grasping ignorance that grasps at the inherent existence of ourselves and all other phenomena. It is the root of samsara that gives rise to all the afflictions, and its eradication is the key to attaining liberation.

Self-grasping is in cahoots with self-centeredness; they are companions in evil. Self-grasping ignorance resembles a dictator who decrees that "I and everything else inherently exist as objective entities." Self-centeredness is the *emissary* that executes this vicious dictator's decrees by unrelentingly insisting that our own happiness and suffering are more important than anyone else's.

Following the self-centered thought narrows our perspective on life. Instead of seeing others as living beings with feelings, we focus on how they can benefit us. Rather than approach situations with openness, curiosity, and sharing, we think, "What can I get out of this?" Ignoring the other seven billion human beings on the planet as well as the zillions of animals, insects, and fish, self-centeredness demands that its own concerns and needs be fulfilled before anyone else's and even at the cost of others' happiness.

Examining our experience, we see that the more self-centered we are, the more miserable we become. Because self-centeredness interprets everything as revolving around us, we become extremely sensitive to small actions others do, believing that they indicate what others think about us. We are easily hurt and offended. We become preoccupied with our appearance, our status, wealth, reputation, and there is little space to consider others' feelings and needs. We treat others inconsiderately and then are angry when they avoid us. We try to control others in an attempt to make them do what we want. In the process, we make enemies and create a lot of destructive karma.

Giving up self-preoccupation does not entail making ourselves suffer. We must take care of ourselves, but in a proper way, not a self-indulgent way. This human body is the basis of our precious human life that gives us the possibility to learn and practice the Dharma. We need to keep our body clean and make sure we exercise and sleep enough and eat nutritious food to stay healthy. We do this with the motivation to practice the Dharma and gain realizations, so we can benefit others. This way of taking care of our physical needs is not self-centered.

In opposing self-grasping and self-centeredness, we may encounter difficulties. Problems arise naturally in cyclic existence, and when we start to practice Dharma, we shouldn't expect this to change instantly. Sometimes our previously created destructive karma will ripen as health problems, relationship difficulties, financial problems, and so on. But now we respond to problems differently because we want to benefit others. So rather than get angry or feel sorry for ourselves when we face problems, Dharmarakshita advises us to *joyfully embrace hardship for the sake of others*. In this way we transform the situation so it becomes an aid to help us cultivate love, compassion, and inner strength.

In other words, while we don't go looking for hardship, if it comes our way in the process of helping others and practicing the Dharma, we accept it. Experiencing hardship can teach us a lot. We discover internal resources we didn't know we had, and we develop good qualities we may not have developed otherwise. Our empathy and understanding of others' situations increases, stifling our arrogance and helping us to connect with others better.

In our beginningless samsaric existences, we have experienced many hardships. We have been born in unfortunate realms countless times and been separated from our loved ones and possessions countless times. We have been under the control of repressive regimes, imprisoned for exercising our human rights, and humiliated although we have done nothing wrong. While experiencing these hardships in the past, our mind remained self-centered: "I don't like this. It isn't fair. The world should be different. Get rid of these horrible people who abuse me."

This way of thinking increases our present suffering and plants more seeds for suffering in future lives.

However, undergoing hardship with the motivation to attain spiritual realizations is worthwhile, and despite external difficulties, our mind will remain content. Having a noble, long-term goal to gain the wisdom, compassion, and skill needed to best benefit others enables us to put the present difficulties in perspective and to adopt a Dharma approach to them. For example, if we have to make a long and uncomfortable journey to learn the Dharma or endure pain while sitting in meditation, we bear this for the purpose of attaining full awakening for the benefit of all beings. In this way, we learn to transform adversity into the path and counteract the self-grasping ignorance and self-centered thought that are the chief causes of our own suffering. Some Tibetans who were imprisoned and tortured after the communist takeover of Tibet used their hardship to cultivate compassion and the determination to be free of cyclic existence. In this way, they maintained a peaceful mind and transformed their suffering into the path to awakening.

7
Propelled by karma and habituated to afflictions—
The sufferings of all beings who share this same nature—
I will heap them upon the self that yearns for happiness.

Attachment and anger are our "dear companions"; ignorance is the "friend" that never leaves us. We are so *habituated to afflictions* that we often do not realize when they take over our minds. We hear a critical remark, feel offended, and get angry. It all seems so natural. We take it for granted that the right response is to utter a snide remark in return or spread bad tales about our offender. In this way, we plant the seeds of destructive karma in our mindstreams. This karma will ripen as the type of rebirth we will take in the future. It will influence whether we will be healthy or sick, whether we live in a war-torn or peaceful place, and whether people like us or not. Before we engage in actions, we have a choice to create the causes for suffering or for happiness, but after we create destructive karma, unless we purify it, it will definitely ripen in unpleasant ways.

We need to contemplate this and recognize that this is our situation. This will prompt us to generate a strong aspiration to free ourselves from cyclic existence. Then, realizing that this is the situation of all other sentient beings—*the sufferings of all beings who share this same nature*—we generate the wish for them to be free from cyclic existence. Recognizing that our self-centeredness is the real enemy responsible for all of our suffering, we imagine taking the misery of others away from them and heaping it upon our self-centered thought, *the self that yearns for* only my own *happiness.*

Mentally taking on others' suffering does not mean that we blame ourselves for being selfish and thus think we deserve to suffer. Rather, differentiating between the inherently existent self that the self-grasping ignorance and self-centered thought grasp and the conventional self, we want to free ourselves from the tyranny of self-centeredness and ignorance.

The conventional self is the I that exists by being merely designated in dependence on the body and mind. That is, on the basis of seeing the body and mind, we say "I" or "a person." This is the mere I, the conventionally existent I that revolves in cyclic existence, practices the path, and attains awakening. That merely designated self, which cannot be found when we search for exactly what it is, exists now and continues into the awakened state. The problem starts when ignorance grasps that I in an erroneous manner, projecting a mode of existence onto it that it doesn't have. Ignorance believes that the conventional self exists in its own right as an objectively existent person with its own inherent essence. In fact, such an inherently existent self does not exist at all. In short, ignorance makes a big deal about something that doesn't exist. It's like a child believing in the boogey man and becoming paralyzed with fear. The child is afraid of something that doesn't exist.

That doesn't mean that the person doesn't exist at all. The person exists conventionally, by being merely designated. What doesn't exist is the inherently existent person we mistakenly believe is there. The conventional person wants to be happy and free of suffering. Every person has this thought, and there's nothing wrong with it. However, ignorance isn't satisfied with that and believes the I to be quite "solid." Buoyed by ignorance, self-centeredness says, "*I* want to be happy. *I* am most important. *I* should get everything *I* want." Ignorance misapprehends the self, and self-preoccupation makes our self and everything that happens to us more important than they are.

Just as ignorance is not an intrinsic part of us and can be eliminated, so too self-centered thought is not who we are and it can be abandoned. We are not inherently selfish. The above verse instructs us to pinpoint self-centered thought and self-grasping ignorance and give them all of our problems. Since they are the source of our misery, it is suitable to do this. This is very different from masochistically wishing ourselves to suffer. Rather, wishing other living beings to be happy and wanting ourselves to be free from the reign of terror our self-grasping and self-centeredness inflict on us, we take on others' pain and give it to these two culprits.

8

When selfish craving enters my heart,
I will expel it and offer my happiness to all beings.
If those around me rise in mutiny against me,
I will relish it, thinking, "This is due to my own negligence."

Seeing the defects of self-preoccupation, *when selfish craving enters our heart,* we train our mind to recognize the harm it causes us and to *expel it* by imagining taking on the suffering of others. To further harm our self-centeredness, we do something it does not like at all: we *offer our happiness to all beings.* Instead of indulging our self-preoccupation, which only digs us into a hole, we focus on others' needs and concerns and give them our happiness.

Even if others harm us and *rise in mutiny against* us, instead of retaliating and inflicting harm on them, we recognize that the harm we receive is due to our previous negligence in observing the law of karma and its effects. Not realizing or caring that our actions have an ethical dimension, in the past we acted in self-centered ways that inflicted harm on others and created destructive karma for ourselves. Now we are experiencing the result of these actions—the boomerang returns to us. So we assume responsibility for our own actions and bear the result without blaming others or feeling sorry for ourselves. Relishing the opportunity to purify our destructive karma, we do the taking-and-giving meditation.

As preparation for this meditation, we contemplate that all sentient beings—ourselves and others, friends, strangers, enemies—all equally want happiness and not suffering. We then consider others' misery in cyclic existence—the poverty, sickness, emotional betrayal, injustice, and disappointments they experience in life after life. Here we can bring the news into our meditation by reflecting on all the diverse sufferings humans and animals experience. Rather than go to the extreme of despair over the state of the world, we generate compassion for all sentient beings, thinking, "How wonderful if they were free from all unsatisfactory circumstances and their causes."

We then reflect on the kindness living beings have shown us in this and previous lives and will continue to show us in future lives. They grow the food we eat, make the clothes we wear. All our knowledge comes because others taught us; all our talents depend on those who encourage and coach us. Feeling their kindness, we cultivate love, thinking, "How wonderful if they had happiness and all the causes of happiness."

We then reflect on the defects of self-centeredness, becoming convinced of its deleterious effects; we contemplate the benefits of cherishing others until we have an overwhelming wish to act on our positive feelings. This propels us to "exchange self and others." This means that instead of thinking that we are the most important one who deserves everything good, we think that others are more important and sincerely want to work for their benefit. We can even exchange the referents of the words "self" and "others," so that when we say, "I want to be happy," we actually mean "others want to be happy," and when we say, "others aren't important," we mean "I'm not so important."

The taking-and-giving meditation is a win-win situation where we imagine compassionately taking what others don't want—their duh-kha and its causes, self-grasping and self-centeredness—and use it to destroy what we don't want, our ignorance and self-centeredness. Then, with love, we imagine giving them our happiness, good circumstances, and their causes, wholesome mental states and wholesome karma.

To do the taking-and-giving meditation itself, we visualize in front of us others who are afflicted with the three kinds of duhkha. With some people we may focus more on their obvious suffering, the duhkha of pain; with others we may be more aware of their duhkha of change, which leaves them constantly dissatisfied or disillusioned. With still others, their duhkha of pervasive conditioning is more prominent in our minds. We imagine all these unsatisfactory circumstances leaving them in the form of pollution. Inhaling the pollution, we meditate that we are taking on their duhkha and its causes—and feel joyful that these kind sentient beings are now free from them.

We do not simply take their duhkha and its causes into ourselves and sit there and suffer. Instead, we imagine our self-grasping ignorance and self-centeredness as a lump at our heart. The duhkha of others that we have inhaled becomes a lightning bolt that obliterates the lump at our heart (i.e., the heart center in the middle of our chest). We pause and experience the spaciousness and relief of being free from ignorance and self-centeredness. We rest our minds in this space while meditating on the emptiness of inherent existence.

When our concentration begins to fade, we imagine radiant light filling the space in our heart. It is our happiness, and we now give to others without any fear or reluctance. We imagine transforming our body into a wish-fulfilling jewel that becomes whatever or whoever others need, and we give this to others. We imagine doing the same with our possessions, imagining others receiving whatever they need and feeling satisfied. Finally, we imagine giving our merit or good karma to others, thinking it transforms and expands into whatever others need to practice the Dharma—temples, centers, monasteries, teachers, Dharma friends, books, meditation cushions, and so forth. We also imagine our merit becomes realizations of the path and give these to all others. They receive these and become fully enlightened buddhas. We witness them being radiant and peaceful, experiencing true freedom and fearlessness as well as overwhelming delight in working for the benefit of others. The happiness of being able to benefit others overrides any kind of discomfort we may have felt about giving our body, possessions, and merit to them.

People sometimes have objections regarding the taking-and-giving meditation. One objection is that it does not work; the other is that it might work. Regarding the first, we think, "I'm only imagining relieving sentient beings of their misery and giving them happiness. That doesn't change their situation at all, so what use is it?" Regarding the second, we worry, "What happens if by visualizing taking on others' suffering, I succeed? I might get sick by imagining taking on others' illness. I might lose my body, wealth, and merit because I'm imagining giving them away."

Our minds are so contradictory, and self-centered thought is the root of the conundrum. Self-preoccupation doesn't want to waste our time doing something it considers useless (such as imagining others becoming buddhas), but it also doesn't want to take a risk (and possibly get sick if what we imagined actually happened). This recurs in so many aspects of our life. "Will I do this, or will I do that?" We get totally tangled up and cannot make up our mind. We are stuck between two self-centered thoughts, and we cannot make a suitable decision or find a satisfactory solution. We want to think of ourselves as magnanimous individuals who bravely relieve others of their pain and sacrifice our body, possessions, and virtue for them, and yet we don't want to experience any discomfort. In fact, being aware of our discomfort when doing the taking-and-giving meditation lets us see the current limitations of our love and compassion. With this knowledge, sincere practitioners will contemplate more precisely the drawbacks of self-preoccupation and the benefits of cherishing others to the point where they become courageous bodhisattvas.

This meditation is good to do when we experience fear and aversion toward our own suffering. It is also an excellent antidote to self-pity. When we feel hurt, we generally feel weak and helpless. To mask the discomfort of these feelings, our self-centeredness inflames our anger.

Sometimes we may explode in anger, spewing our negativity on everyone around us. Other times we implode, retreating to sulk, pout, and feel sorry for ourselves. We have a "pity party" relishing the thought of "poor me." Our egos get a lot of mileage out of thinking we are victims whom nobody appreciates. However, this thought only makes us more miserable, and our sulking and pouting only push people away from us at the very time when we most want to connect with them.

Instead of drowning in this jumble of confused thoughts, we can do the taking-and-giving meditation. This pulls us out of this unhealthy focus on ourselves and broadens our perspective to see that others are just like us, wanting happiness and not suffering. It elicits our love and compassion, bringing peace into our hearts and lives.

4   The Wheel of Destructive Karma

UNDERSTANDING AND TRANSFORMING DIFFICULTIES

9

When my body falls prey to unbearable illnesses
It is the weapon of destructive karma returning on me
For injuring the bodies of others;
From now on I will take all sickness upon myself.

THIS AND THE subsequent verses follow a similar structure. The
first line describes an unfortunate circumstance we experience: we
fall ill, our friends abandon us, and so forth. Sometimes we may feel
that we're the only person who has had a particular misfortune. The
first line reminds us that it is common to many people.

The second line tells us that this unfortunate circumstance is not a
random event but one caused by the destructive actions we have done
in the past: *It is the weapon of destructive karma returning on me.* Contemplating this increases our confidence in the functioning of karma and
its effects. By taking responsibility for our actions—even those done in
previous lives that we cannot consciously remember doing—we stop
blaming others for our problems. This reduces our anger and self-pity,
and stimulates us to reflect more deeply on our actions and their effects
both on others and on ourselves. So often our self-preoccupation prevents us from seeing that our actions affect others and ourselves. A big
part of our maturation as adults and as Dharma practitioners involves
stretching our perspective and looking at the big picture. We must pay
attention to the fact that our actions have an ethical dimension. Thinking deeply about the law of karma and its effects will enable us to make

some important changes in our behavior and personalities. We'll begin to break old, dysfunctional habits and build new ones.

The third line of each verse describes more specifically what the action was. So often when we experience obstacles in our life, we say, "Why me?" This line answers that question. While it may not be pleasant to recall specific destructive actions we have done, it is useful for it motivates us to purify the seeds of this destructive karma. If filth is hidden under a rug or behind a cabinet, we will smell it but won't be able to do anything about it. Only when we see the dirt in a room can we clean it. Similarly, this line sparks us to look more closely at our life (perhaps to even do a life review), acknowledge our harmful actions, and purify them.

The fourth line expresses a resolution to act in the opposite way in the future. The stronger our conviction in karma and its results, the more we will be motivated to apply antidotes to our disturbing emotions, refrain from destructive actions, and engage in constructive emotions, thoughts, and actions. We then make the determination to act differently in the future, and to solidify this determination, we do the taking-and-giving meditation, taking on the misery of others and giving them our body, possessions, and merit. Doing this increases our love and compassion and weakens our self-centered thought, thus enabling us to act according to our virtuous intention.

Verse 9 is the verse that affected me so strongly when I was sick with hepatitis A. Our illnesses are the result of our destructive actions, in particular injuring the bodies of others. We may think, "But I'm a nice person. I've never killed anyone." We may not have killed another human being, but most of us have killed insects and perhaps animals as well. We may have gone hunting or fishing, or asked someone to cook live shellfish for our dinner. Thinking we were putting a pet out of its misery, we may have euthanized it, or we may have sprayed pesticide in our house or garden. We may recall doing such actions in this life. Sometimes these are actions done in previous lives that we only infer we have done since we are experiencing this type of result.

For example, perhaps we were the powerful leader of a country who led the people into an aggressive war. Even though we may not have killed anyone ourselves, we commanded our troops to take the lives of the enemy. By doing so, we accumulated the karma of taking the lives of many people. Or perhaps for the sake of solely scientific curiosity, we injected many animals with viruses just to see what would happen. We have had infinite, beginningless lifetimes in which we have done every type of action. While we do not remember these actions, their imprints are on our mindstream, and when the cooperative conditions are present, that karma ripens. In the case of my hepatitis, the cooperative conditions were the unclean vegetables, but the principal causes were my own actions in this or previous lives.

In situations such as illness, we can either get angry and depressed, or we can transform the situation into the path to awakening by thinking, "This is *the weapon of destructive karma returning on me,* so I'm not going to blame anybody else. I'm going to learn from this mistake. Since I don't like illness, I must stop creating the cause." We make the firm intention not to injure anybody else's body ever again.

At this point, it is helpful to think about what we will do if we encounter situations in which we may be tempted to injure others' bodies in the future. Do we put ourselves in environments where this could happen? Even if I deliberately stay away from such situations, something could arise unexpectedly whereby I may be tempted to kill someone. How would I want to act in such a situation? How could I subdue the anger or fear that could cause me to take another's life? We may want to spend some time meditating on fortitude in order to strengthen our determination not to succumb to anger or contemplate impermanence to overcome the attachment that breeds fear. Meditating in this way prepares us to deal skillfully with such situations in the future.

To purify destructive karma we may have created through injuring others' bodies and to prevent harming them in the future, we do the taking-and-giving meditation. Since this verse has to do with experiencing illness, with compassion we imagine taking on the sickness of others and using it to destroy the ignorance and self-centeredness that lie behind having harmed others' bodies in the past. Breathing in the pollution that represents their suffering, we think it transforms into a lightning bolt that strikes and demolishes the lump of ignorance and self-preoccupation at our heart. We tranquilly dwell in the empty space at our hearts, relishing that others are free from their illness and we are free from our ignorance and self-centeredness. Then we imagine transforming our body and possessions into medicine, hospitals, health-care professionals, loving companions, and whatever else those suffering from illness may need or find comforting. Giving these to them, we imagine them healing and living happily. Giving them our merit, we think they have all the necessary causes to meet and practice the Dharma. Through this they progress on the path and attain full awakening. Imagining this, we feel satisfied and peaceful..

This is the basic way of meditating for verses 9 to 44. If the verse deals with an experience you have not had in this life, think of what others have experienced. Also, examine if you have created the cause to experience this in the future. We may have created the cause in this life, but not experienced the result yet. Before the result comes, we should engage in purification practice by doing the taking-and-giving meditation, as well as by other practices such as bowing to the Buddha and reciting the Vajrasattva mantra.

Even if you have not done the destructive action described in the verse in this lifetime, make a strong determination to avoid it in the future. Since we never know what kind of situations we will encounter in this or future lives where we may be tempted to do it, making a firm decision now not to behave in such a manner is helpful to restrain ourselves in the future. Then do the taking-and-giving meditation. With each verse, the key is to think about the specific suffering and its corresponding causal action in relation to our own lives. Then our meditation becomes very rich and meaningful.

Some of these circumstances mentioned in the coming verses and their karmic causes may be difficult to think about. They may challenge our image of ourselves or bring up regret that has long been buried. If this happens, go slowly, have compassion for yourself and anyone else involved. Be glad that you are now able to clean up the past, learn from mistaken actions, and go into the future with a kind heart.

10

When my mind falls prey to suffering,
It is the weapon of destructive karma turning upon me
For definitely causing turbulence in the hearts of others;
From now on I will take all suffering upon myself.

Many people in developed countries have much greater mental suffering than physical suffering. They are plagued by depression, anxiety, fear, worry—feelings that arise when we fail to achieve our aims or believe we are being rejected, abandoned, or treated unfairly. Many people in undeveloped nations are usually too busy trying to meet their basic survival needs to have this kind of mental suffering.

When we experience mental anguish, we can use this as an opportunity to learn how our mind works. First, rather than focus on the story behind your feeling, just pay attention to the mental feeling of unhappiness. Be aware of how it differs from physical suffering. Then, be aware of your reactions to mental suffering: we dislike it, get angry, blame others. We crave to experience pleasant mental feelings. We do everything we can to get rid of the unpleasant mental feelings: we may drink or take drugs, speak harshly to others, gamble, sleep around, overeat, overspend, and do many other actions that only create more suffering for us now and in the future.

Instead of repeatedly playing out our responses to unpleasant mental feelings, we can adopt the perspective of this verse and view our mental suffering as the result of our own harmful actions, specifically *causing turbulence in the hearts of others.* For example, in the past we have inflicted mental pain on others by criticizing, ridiculing, humiliating, or shaming them. Being rebellious, inconsiderate, or uncooperative, we have done things that have brought them worry, grief, or embarrassment.

An effective way to transform mental anguish into the path to awakening is to *take all {mental} suffering upon ourselves,* and give others our mental joy. We do this through the taking-and-giving meditation.

While doing this meditation, one part of your mind may protest, "I don't want anybody else's mental pain; I can't even handle my own.

I want someone to take away *my* mental suffering." That state of mind itself is suffering. Build up your courage by thinking, "I'm experiencing mental pain as a result of my own destructive karma. Since I'm experiencing this mental anguish anyway, may I take on the mental pain of everyone else." Take on the pain of people who are grieving the loss of dear ones and people who are fearful because they live in an unstable, war-torn country. Take on the misery of those with mental illness. Take on the pain of those whose trust has been betrayed. Do all of this happily. Use this pain to destroy the selfishness that motivated you to create the karma that brought about your own mental unhappiness. Feel light and relaxed as you use others' mental pain to destroy the self-preoccupation that keeps you stuck in your own mental pain and self-pity.

11

When I am tormented by extreme hunger and thirst,
It is the weapon of destructive karma turning upon me
For engaging in deception, theft, and miserly acts;
From now on I will take all hunger and thirst upon myself.

When *tormented by extreme hunger and thirst* or from a mental state that is dissatisfied and hungry for some pleasure—perhaps we long for companionship, intimacy, or love, or we hunger for praise, acknowledgment, and approval—it is the *weapon of destructive karma returning* on us. What did we do in the past that brought this misfortune upon ourselves? We deceived people and prevented them from getting what was rightfully theirs. We stole others' possessions—not necessarily by breaking into their homes, but through doing white-collar crimes such as embezzlement, altering accounts, and fraud. We did not return borrowed items or pay fees and taxes that we owed.

In addition, we did not share what we had, but stingily kept it for ourselves even when others needed it more. Miserly acts include not sharing our possessions and keeping jointly owned items for ourselves, without giving others their fair share. Fear and stinginess are cohorts that weave the story: "If I give, then I won't have this and may suffer later." They prevent us from being generous even when we have enough.

Dharma practitioners sometimes take the eight Mahayana precepts for twenty-four hours and eat only one meal that day. To counter any hunger and thirst we may feel, we think, "I'm purifying my destructive karma of being miserly, deceiving others, and stealing their possessions. Instead of my experiencing extreme hunger and thirst that have no end in sight, my harmful behavior is ripening in this relatively small suffering of feeling hungry today. I accept this suffering happily, and in the future I will stop creating those harmful actions." In this way, we can be happy when experiencing the hardship of hunger because we are doing it for the sake of the Dharma. We are also stimulated to train ourselves in generosity, which is the karmic cause of wealth and prosperity.

As a new nun, I was very poor. I lived in India, and nobody sent me money. At one time, I had fifty dollars to my name and no return ticket! Even after I left India for Europe, I stayed in a monastery where we nuns lived in converted horse stables. It was cold in the winter, and I didn't have enough money to pay for a heater in my room. Sitting in the meditation hall one day, I realized, "I don't have enough money because I'm miserly." This tight, stingy, fearful attitude was so vivid in my mind that I knew I had to change or things would only get worse.

That was a turning point for me, and I started making more effort to be generous. My miserliness and fear of not having enough were so strong that I had to keep nudging myself to give. Interestingly, as my tight fist gradually became an open hand, I received more support from others. Through my own experience, it is clear that giving is the cause of receiving.

12

When I am powerless and suffer in servitude to others,
This is the weapon of destructive karma turning upon me
For being hostile to the weak and subjecting them;
From now on I will employ my body and life in the service of others.

Being *powerless and suffering in servitude to others* could include a variety of circumstances, such as slavery, sexual exploitation, lack of human rights or civil rights, economic exploitation, human trafficking, and political oppression. This verse could also refer to more general situations in which we feel powerless and disrespected, for example when our boss ignores our ideas for a project or family members dismiss our advice.

In such situations, the karmic cause is taking advantage of the young or powerless, *being hostile to the weak and subjecting them* to servitude. In previous times, or in this lifetime, we might have been bosses who deprecated our employees or manipulated others into doing something against their will. We may have exploited others to our advantage with no concern for their well-being. For example, in 2013 a building containing garment factories crumbled in Bangladesh, killing over five hundred people. Even though an engineer warned that the building was unsafe, factory owners insisted on keeping the factories open. Another example is those who prey upon young runaway girls, inducing them into emotional dependence on a pimp and turning them into prostitutes, often with a drug addiction that makes them further dependent on the pimp. Some people charge exorbitant prices for refugees, such as those from the Rohingya area of Myanmar, to board their ships and then abandon them or sell them into slavery.

Our present powerlessness and servitude is the result of having selfishly used and disrespected others, denying them opportunities and rights. To repair this, we make a strong determination to *employ our body and life in the service of others.* Regardless of whether somebody has high or low social status, we should respect and benefit them. Especially as people who aspire for full awakening, we cultivate the mind that cherishes others more than self and we should try to live that attitude by serving others in whatever way possible. I clearly remember Lama Yeshe addressing us monastics. Holding his prayer beads at his heart, he said, "This should be your mantra." As he turned each bead, he said, "I am the servant of others. I am the servant of others."

We can start modestly. Provided that our job isn't one that involves harming others, such as manufacturing weapons or pesticides, we can transform it into an act of service by cultivating a good motivation. For example, we think, "I am going to work not just to make money, but to help the clients or customers. May they benefit by my work." Or "I wish to benefit my colleagues, boss, and others and try to create a good work environment, so people will feel fulfilled by their work."

If even a few people at a workplace have a generous attitude, everybody else will easily catch on. Conversely, if a few people like to pick faults—"*You* left the coffee table a mess. *I'm* not going to clean it up"—that attitude will permeate the workplace. Rather than waiting for others to do it first, it is up to us to be friendly and helpful at work.

Similarly, at home we can be loving and cooperative. Instead of plopping on the sofa after work and ordering family members around, we can greet them with kindness, remembering that these are the people we cherish the most. If parents want their children to grow up to be kind and considerate, they need to model that behavior themselves. Small actions speak loudly, set a good example, and promote affection in a family.

Take on the suffering of others, especially that of the powerless and those suffering in servitude. Use it to destroy your self-centered thought and self-grasping ignorance. Then transform your body, possessions, and merit into all they need and, with love, give it to them. Imagine them being satisfied in terms of their temporal needs, having all conducive circumstances to practice the Dharma, and becoming bodhisattvas and then buddhas.

13
When unpleasant words reach my ears,
It is the weapon of destructive karma turning upon me
For my verbal offenses, such as divisive speech;
From now on I will condemn flawed speech.

When people criticize or insult us, make comments we find offensive, or talk about us behind our back, our usual reaction is to get defensive and/or aggressive. We may lobby others to be on our side of the conflict or talk badly about others behind their back. This just creates more disharmony and plants the seeds of more destructive karma on our mindstreams. Instead of blaming others for our hurt feelings, we need to see that the cause of hearing unpleasant words is our own *verbal offenses, such as divisive speech.*

Examining our speech, we may discover that we have harshly blamed others, made false accusations, hurt their feelings, and ruined their reputation. We have picked faults and gossiped about them. We have deliberately made derogatory comments about others and widely discussed what was told to us in confidence. Considering what we have said about others, why are we surprised when others speak badly about us? Instead of continuing to misuse our speech, we need to make a determination to counteract the temptation to lie, create disharmony, speak harshly, and gossip. In this way, we will have better relationships now and will not create the karma to have contentious relationships in the future.

As in all the verses of this section, do the taking-and-giving meditation: taking on the pain others experience due to harsh speech and giving them the happiness we have from hearing kind, truthful, appropriate speech.

14
When I am born in a place of impurity
It is the weapon of destructive karma turning upon me
For always cultivating impure perceptions.
From now on I will cultivate only pure perceptions.

A place of impurity is polluted, filthy, and unhealthy. It could be a slum in a large city, a site where toxic waste was dumped, or an area with thick air pollution. Living in such a place is due to *cultivating impure perceptions.* That is, due to grasping true existence, we generate all sorts of afflicted mental states: hostility, attachment, laziness, jealousy, arrogance, and so on. Our mind judges others, seeing everyone as falling short of our view of what they should be. Instead of cultivating these impure perceptions that cause us to be born in an impure place, we make a determination to solely cultivate pure perceptions. We make it a practice to see the good in each person and situation.

Saying that karma from previous lives is the cause for us having to live in such unhealthy places does not mean we ignore the present causes that pollute the air, water, and land. We must hold factories accountable for proper disposal of their waste and use vehicles that reduce and eventually eliminate carbon emissions. As a global community, we need to carefully consider whether we want to continue to use nuclear energy and, if so, how to protect the planet from disasters such as Chernobyl in 1986 and Fukushima Daiichi in 2011.

There are different ways to generate pure perceptions. One is to recognize that we do not know whether someone is a buddha or a bodhisattva. Holy beings manifest as ordinary beings in order to skillfully teach and guide us, but they do not wear name tags identifying themselves, "Hi, my name is Avalokiteshvara. I am a buddha." Since disparaging holy beings is very destructive karma and we do not know whether someone is awakened or not, Buddhist teachings recommend we avoid criticizing anybody.

This doesn't mean, however, that we don't confront difficulties or that we hide the truth. For example, if a potential employer contacts us as a reference for Joe, it's not suitable to either speak of Joe's faults with the motivation to harm him or to praise him for qualities he doesn't have because we think he may be a buddha. If we believe that a person is not a good fit for the job, then with a compassionate motivation that doesn't want either party to be stuck with a poor job fit, we share our honest assessment.

Along the same lines, we can say an action is inappropriate and harmful without disparaging the person who did it. Separating the action from the person is a powerful tool for being able to see that each sentient being has buddha-nature and at the same time acknowledge mistakes and help people grow by holding them accountable for harmful actions.

When we do tantric practice, we try to see the environment as a pure land and the other beings we encounter as deities and enlightened beings. The purpose of doing this is to protect our mind from anger, attachment, dissatisfaction, jealousy, and other afflictions. It does not mean we whitewash negativities or project fanciful ideas of truly existent perfection onto others, as that can lead to problems. For example, if we see others fighting, we do not just say, "These are the wrathful deities Yamantaka and Mahakala doing this as a show." Seeing everyone as a deity does not mean we sit back and let people hurt each other. We must intercede to stop the harm if we are capable of doing so, but we do this without anger.

15

When I am separated from helpful and loving friends,
It is the weapon of destructive karma turning upon me
For luring away others' companions;
From now on I will never estrange others from their companions.

All of us cherish helpful and loving friends, and wise, compassionate spiritual mentors are especially important to us to progress on the path. Being separated from the people we value or having an important relationship not work out the way we had hoped is painful, yet it is a common occurrence in cyclic existence. Because we ourselves, others, and all the conditioned things around us are impermanent by nature, whatever comes together must also separate.

Hindrances interfering with our relationships with loving friends, spiritual mentors, or helpful companions arise due to our *luring away others' companions*. In the past, we may have broken up marriages or separated teachers and disciples by criticizing one to the other or by making it difficult for them to meet. Abusing power, we may have been a leader who implemented policies that separated people from those dear to them. Motivated by jealousy, we may have talked about people behind their backs to provoke disharmony in their relationships. Or people may already have separated, and out of jealousy we prevent them from reconciling.

In all these verses, it is helpful to examine whether we have done the inappropriate action in this life and, if we have, to apply the four opponent powers to purify those karmic seeds: regret, taking refuge and generating bodhicitta, making a determination not to do the action again, and engaging in a remedial action. Doing the taking and giving meditation is a form of remedial action.

Furthermore, we may have acted in harmful or obnoxious ways in previous lives. Although we cannot remember specific instances from previous lives, purifying these karmic seeds is still important. To learn from our mistakes, we then make a determination to do the opposite of the specific harmful action. In the above verse, we resolve not to *estrange others from their companions* with whom they have healthy and mutually beneficial relationships. To go a step further, we also help others have harmonious relations.

There are some cases, however, when separating people may be necessary. For example, a woman is separated from her husband who beats her, but strong attachment for him arises in her mind and she wants to go back to him. Out of compassion, for the sake of her safety and to prevent him from creating destructive karma by beating her, we may warn her, "Remember what he did. Be strong and don't give in to momentary attachment."

Another example is a friend who is attending the classes of a "spiritual mentor" who, while claiming to be a Buddhist, does not teach according to the Buddhadharma. If our friend doesn't yet consider this person to be his teacher, we may want to encourage him to be cautious. We may say, "The scriptures encourage us to learn the qualities of a qualified spiritual mentor and then to check if someone has at least some of these qualities before taking him or her as our teacher. Since this 'teacher' is controversial, please consider doing this."

16

When sublime ones become displeased with me,
It is the weapon of destructive karma turning upon me
For renouncing the sublime ones and seeking bad companions;
From now on I will give up negative friendships.

Sublime ones refers particularly to our spiritual teachers, those whose spiritual guidance is essential to our practice of learning, reflecting, and meditating on the Dharma. If we are training in *vinaya*—monastic discipline—sublime ones include senior monastics whom we trust and are who are committed to guiding us. When these people become displeased with us, our tendency is to blame them: "They're insensitive, closed-minded, and too demanding. They play favorites." Since we have this tendency, some monastic precepts prohibit making such accusations because it is our mind, not theirs, that is under the control of afflictions.

Perhaps the teacher who instructs us in the bodhisattva practice seems displeased with us. He or she is too busy to see us, ignores our questions in Dharma class, and no longer beams an encouraging smile in our direction. Being self-preoccupied, we take everything personally and become riddled with doubts and anxiety that we "did something wrong." In this case, we may need to pause and reflect on whether our teacher is actually displeased with us or whether there are other people or important projects our teacher needs to attend to. If her displeasure is due to our fabricating a story that isn't real, we need to drop our story.

On the other hand, if our teacher in fact is unhappy with us, we need to recall that this is due to our *renouncing the sublime ones and seeking bad companions.* Instead of seeking the advice of those who are skilled and knowledgeable in the Dharma, we have befriended bad companions— people who, by pleasing our ego, distract us from spiritual practice. In addition, in this or previous lives, we have not respected our spiritual mentors, acted contrary to their advice, and even competed with them. We usually do not recognize the disadvantages of these thoughts and actions because we think they are justified. Part of Dharma practice is learning how to correctly identify our intentions and to accurately evaluate our actions.

We have also sought out "bad friends." These people don't have horns on their head. They aren't evil-looking, sinister, or out to get us. In fact, they care about us, but in a superficial, worldly way. When we plan to attend a meditation retreat, they say, "Why don't you get a life? Go to the beach, or go on a camping trip." While they want us to have worldly happiness, they do not consider future lives, lack an understanding of karma, and believe the purpose of our lives is to have pleasure, make a name for ourselves, and be successful according to societal standards. They do not understand either the rarity and value of a precious human life or its ultimate meaning and purpose.

Although they wish us well, their advice is unwise. If we seek them out when we are upset, they will take our side and say, "You are right. That person is treating you horribly, and you have every right to be angry. Go tell that person off." Because they encourage us to create the destructive karma of harsh speech, we say these people are "bad friends."

As we learn the Dharma and understand more about karma, our perspective shifts regarding the purpose of friendship and the qualities we look for in friends. Some people go through a difficult period at the beginning: "My friends often drink and take drugs (gossip, backbite, make fun of others, or whatever activity you are losing interest in that was the basis for your friendship). I'm trying to stop, but if I don't do that with them, there's no basis for our being together. They'll think I'm prudish if I don't do what I used to do with them. They'll think I'm conceited and standoffish. Yet I care about them, so what do I do?"

At that point people are comparatively new in the Dharma, and their attachment to old friends and familiar activities is strong. Some people have a mistaken sense of loyalty and stop attending Dharma class in favor of continuing the relationships with their old friends. This is a big loss. Other people decide the Dharma is more important, and not wanting to be adversely influenced by their old friends, they begin new friendships with people who have Dharma values. While we *give up negative friendships,* we do not inconsiderately reject our old friends. We can still be friendly and compassionate toward them, but do not get involved in the same activities as before. If our old friends can adapt to this, the friendship will continue, but if we see that our interests have changed, we can let the relationship gradually fade and cultivate new friends with good values. We become wiser in terms of whose advice we follow and whom we trust to discuss our problems with.

Following friends who have worldly values causes us not to meet spiritual teachers or, if we meet them, to have difficult relationships. Being cautious in this regard is important, because meeting qualified spiritual teachers is essential on the path. If we are enamored with spiritual teachers who are not qualified, we receive incorrect instructions and go down a wrong path. If we learn from and serve qualified spiritual mentors, they will guide us in purifying our negativities and cultivating our good qualities.

17

When others assail me with exaggeration, denigration, and so on,
It is the weapon of destructive karma turning upon me
For disparaging the sublime beings;
From now on I will never belittle others with disparaging words.

This verse concerns people falsely accusing us or insinuating to others that we have, for instance, transgressed our precepts or acted unethically. Due to jealously, they may *assail us with exaggeration, denigration, and so on* by putting us down or scapegoating us for others' misdeeds. When this happens, instead of becoming upset and depressed, we have to recognize that this is due to our previously having *disparaged sublime beings*.

These lines make me think of the false accusations the communist Chinese throw at His Holiness the Dalai Lama, calling him the "splitter of the motherland." Although these communist leaders have much worldly power, they use it to create massive destructive karma. Another great Buddhist monk, Thich Nhat Hanh, refused to side with either the North or the South during the Vietnam War, so both sides criticized him and he could no longer remain in Vietnam. He loved his country and wanted peace, but not seeing that, people disparaged him.

Engaging in destructive actions against holy beings often results in hellish rebirths. Even when people are born as human beings in the future, it is difficult for them to meet the Dharma and to find a qualified teacher. With little provocation, others blame, criticize, and denigrate them. This is *the weapon of destructive karma turning upon* them.

To avoid these unwanted results, we resolve *from now on to never belittle others with disparaging words.* Instead, we train ourselves to recognize and praise others' wholesome deeds and to point out their good qualities.

Whenever we are denigrated or our faults exaggerated, it is helpful to remember, "This is a result of my own harmful actions. There is no sense getting hurt, angry, or depressed." We become adept at recognizing the state of things: "This is the fault of my own self-centeredness, and I'm glad this karma is ripening as the present problematic circumstance rather than in a horrible rebirth." We resolve to avoid such behavior in the future.

For those of us who are particularly sensitive when our faults are exaggerated and our good qualities denigrated, doing the taking-and-giving meditation when we are put down or disparaged is very effective. It forces us to think of the feelings of others who face this situation, and that pulls us out of the self-centeredness that thinks, "I'm the only one who is treated unfairly like this." In addition, we have to develop a strong mind to think of taking on all the suffering of others who are criticized and to give them our happiness.

18

When my material resources waste away
It is the weapon of destructive karma turning upon me
For being disrespectful toward others' resources;
From now on I will help others find what they need.

It happens that sometimes we may not be able to get the things we require to stay alive—food, shelter, clothing, and medicine—or if we have them, they are stolen or destroyed before we can use them. An earthquake or fire destroys our home; war destroys crops or makes it dangerous to leave home to go to the store. Insurgents prevent humanitarian relief from reaching those in need. Meanwhile, grain in silos in some countries rots either because people won't sell it or obstacles prevent its distribution.

The karmic cause for such unfortunate situations is *being disrespectful toward others' resources.* We did not care when others needed things and did not share what we had with them. In other situations, we stole others' possessions or deceived people so that they gave us ownership of things that rightfully were theirs. In the past we did not pay fair wages, exploited workers, or incited a crowd to destroy the property of those we didn't like.

In short, when we lack what we need, our resources go to waste, or we cannot access them; this is a karmic result of thinking only of ourselves: *I want. I need. This is mine.* To change this behavior, with a heart that genuinely cares about others and to the best of our ability, we practice *helping others find what they need.* As Shantideva, the eighth-century Indian sage, said, "May people think of benefiting each other."

As I was writing this book, a friend wrote me about an experience he had and how he applied thought training to it:

> I was helping some Tibetan nuns get their visas at the Indian embassy, and left my bicycle outside. When I returned, it had been stolen. There is a lot of desperation and suffering in that part of town, and from my side this was a good check on how I'm doing in my practice. Unlike if this had happened prior to meeting the Dharma, now I didn't experience any strong afflictive emotions. Instead, I immediately started watching my mind and processing the theft by seeing it in a broader perspective as negative karma ripening in a way I am fortunate enough to be able to shrug off.
>
> Later, while doing the practice of Chenrezig [the buddha of compassion], I remembered to offer the bike to the thief and to assume responsibility for the harmful action myself by offering the fruits of my own amazing fortune to him. I also went to the Asian Art Museum to visit my favorite deity there, a stone Vajra Tara, and we had a good laugh about it. I think the fact this happened while I was doing something virtuous with good intentions is auspicious. Maybe if it hadn't happened, I would have been hit by a car on the ride home.

19

When my mind becomes unclear and my heart unhappy,
It is the weapon of destructive karma turning upon me
For making others accumulate negative karma;
From now on I will shun enabling others' destructive actions.

We sit down to meditate or study, and our minds are moody, heavy, or unhappy. We lack energy, and even though we have the opportunity to practice the Dharma or even do an ordinary task that requires concentration, we doze off. We may have many good things going for us in our lives, but all we see is what we lack and complain that life is unfair. Whatever we have, it's not good enough. We're envious of those who have more and better. In Dharma circles we call this "thinking the chanting is better on the other side of the temple."

An *unclear* mind and *unhappy* heart are due to having made unwise choices in the past. Instead of encouraging others' good qualities and virtuous activities, we drew them into our illegal schemes, vengeful actions, and dirty business deals. Perhaps in a previous life we were an army general who commanded troops to kill the enemy. We asked family members to lie for us or encouraged them to report they worked more hours than they did so that the family would have more money.

Seeing the unhappiness we experience due to these actions, we make the determination to *shun enabling others' destructive actions.* We decline to get entangled in their nonvirtuous activities and don't dream up ones of our own that we get them involved with. In fact, we do the opposite and encourage others to do constructive actions and to use their talents to benefit others.

People often ask me how to benefit their deceased relatives and friends so that they will have a good rebirth. The best way to do that is to encourage them to engage in virtuous deeds while they are alive: inspire them to be generous, to live ethically, to be tolerant and get along well with others. Don't feed their rancor; discourage their harmful actions. The more we can help them live a wholesome life, the more they will create constructive karma that will ripen in their future happiness. When they die, we will not have to worry about them, and our prayers will be more effective because there will be the seeds of constructive karma on their mindstreams that can be activated.

20

When I fail in my endeavors and feel deeply perturbed,
It is the weapon of destructive karma turning upon me
For obstructing the work of sublime ones;
From now on I will relinquish all obstructive deeds.

This verse concerns failing in the projects we try to accomplish. We try to encourage people in our workplace to recycle, but they aren't interested. We try to create a Dharma website, but the causes and conditions don't come together. We want our children to join the family business, but none of them are interested. Despite our creative ideas and efforts, our goals, either spiritual or worldly, aren't actualized, leaving us feeling feel stymied and frustrated.

When this happens, rather than complain or feel sorry for ourselves, let's recognize that this is due to *obstructing the work of sublime ones*—the Three Jewels and our spiritual mentors, who are intent on virtue. In the past, we may have disturbed meditators by talking loudly, playing music, or taking their food. We may have interrupted the efforts of Dharma students by asking them to do trivial activities or created obstructions for a charity doing good work in the community. Perhaps we were government officials who interfered with the activities of a temple, or in the case of the Cultural Revolution in China, they destroyed temples and Buddha statues, forced monastics to disrobe, and burned Dharma texts.

Recognizing the damaging effects of such actions, we make a resolution: *from now on I will relinquish all obstructive deeds.* When holy beings or ordinary people build hospitals and schools to benefit society, when they start drug and alcohol recovery programs, bring meals to the elderly, or tutor disadvantaged children, we support their efforts and avoid creating problems and obstacles for them. To the contrary, we do our best to encourage people in their wholesome attitudes and actions and to facilitate the conditions to bring these aspirations to fruition.

With all these verses, remember to do the taking-and-giving meditation. In this verse, we take on the suffering of people who fail in their endeavors and feel deeply perturbed, frustrated, and misunderstood. We transform our body, possessions, and merit into what they require to actualize their virtuous aims and take delight in envisioning their success, including their successful Dharma practice, which brings them lasting happiness.

21

When my gurus remain displeased no matter what I do,
This is the weapon of destructive karma returning on me
For acting duplicitously toward the sublime Dharma.
From now on I will be less deceitful with respect to the Dharma.

When our spiritual mentors are displeased with our behavior, we feel uncomfortable inside. We may blame our spiritual mentors, thinking they are insensitive and do not respect, appreciate, and understand us. We may also believe they are trying to control us, or we may withdraw inside ourselves, telling ourselves that we are deficient in one way or another. All these emotional reactions keep us caught up in the turmoil of self-preoccupation and make it hard for us to accurately understand the situation.

In fact, our spiritual mentor is displeased with us because of our inappropriate behavior in this or previous lives. We may have been rude, unreliable, or deceitful, seeming to be an excellent student while in our spiritual mentor's presence but acting recklessly when we're not. Such behavior does not help our practice at all. We may believe we are doing the right thing, being well behaved with our teachers, but we need to be courteous and kind all the time, with everyone. We cannot deceive the functioning of karma and its effects. The real issue is our motivation, not whether our teachers are watching. Our hypocrisy, as well as our boasting of good qualities we lack and hiding our faults, separate us from our spiritual mentors. They cannot help us when we are not truthful with them or when we arrogantly resist their advice.

Sometimes we pick and choose what advice we listen to, following only what pleases our ego. Or we may agree to do something when we are with our teacher and then not follow suit afterward. Or we go from one spiritual mentor to another, asking for advice, and we don't listen to any of it. Such behavior only creates more obstacles for us on the path.

Being straightforward and honest with our spiritual mentors opens the door to receiving benefit from them. Because we got to know someone before accepting him or her as one of our spiritual mentors, we have already decided that this is a knowledgeable and trustworthy person who cares about our spiritual progress. Thus, when things come up between us, instead of blaming our mentor or withdrawing, we examine our own thoughts and behavior until our error becomes clear. We can then remedy our mistake and restore the relationship with our spiritual mentor to its previous level of comfort and closeness.

To get the outcomes we seek in our relationship with our spiritual mentors, we resolve *from now on to be less deceitful with respect to the Dharma.* We do our best to keep the precepts we take from our spiritual mentors. We are truthful in both word and deed and are reliable in serving our teachers. Humbly admitting our mistakes, we are neither deceitful nor pretentious.

22

When everyone challenges what I say,
It is the weapon of destructive karma turning upon me
For disregarding integrity and consideration for others;
From now on I will refrain from troubling behavior.

We experience situations where people do not believe us, lack confidence in us, or doubt the wisdom of our decisions. Sometimes there is good reason for this; other times we may know what we're doing, but others question our recommendations. We may be in positions of responsibility, but our followers constantly contradict and challenge our goals, plans, and ways of enacting them. It is helpful to realize that this is due to our *disregarding integrity and consideration for others.*

Integrity is a mental factor that prevents us from acting negatively because we have a sense of our own dignity and values. For example, when faced with the opportunity to lie, manipulate, or deceive someone, we think, "I value the Dharma and want to act according to it, so I won't do that." Consideration for others is a mental factor that restrains us from acting destructively because we don't want our bad behavior to have an adverse effect on others, especially by making them lose faith in the Dharma or in humanity in general. For example, knowing that other people will lose faith in the sangha, monastics wear their robes, act with decorum, and stop themselves from gossiping. In addition, knowing the buddhas and bodhisattvas will not be pleased if we are boisterous and rude or if we harbor grudges and wrong views, we refrain from such activities. These two mental factors—integrity and consideration for others—are the root of abandoning negativities. Without them, we would be completely reckless and act without conscience. They are the keys to ethical living and inspiring behavior.

Seeing how the lack of integrity and consideration for others has led to the karmic boomerang—our experiencing something similar to what we have caused others to experience—we make a resolution. Employing integrity and consideration for others, we *refrain from troubling behavior,* such as the ten unwholesome paths of action. We will do our best not to transgress our precepts or act in ways that will cause others to lose faith in the Three Jewels. As Dharma friends, we should draw each other's attention to our inappropriate behavior, and when others make us aware of it, let's not react with defensiveness, but listen to their words.

Attachment to reputation and consideration for others are "close enemies." In other words, in some respects they look similar, but they are actually very different. Attachment to reputation and praise is completely self-centered—we want to look good—while consideration for others is genuinely caring about them. If our motivation is to be a "people pleaser" so that we will receive praise, approval, and have a good reputation, when we do not succeed in getting these, our attitude sours and we get angry. When we have genuine consideration for others, we do what we know is best without attachment to reputation.

23

When disputes arise as soon as my companions gather,
It is the weapon of destructive karma turning upon me
For peddling my destructive, evil character in all directions;
From now on I will maintain good character wherever I am.

When our family, friends, or colleagues come together, they argue and bicker. We live in a monastery, and our students or fellow monastics cannot get along. It's unpleasant being around people who are difficult to get along with and constantly quarreling.

When we encounter this disagreeable situation, let's recall that this is due to *peddling our destructive, evil character in all directions.* Sometimes it is hard to acknowledge that one part of us likes to stir things up or be demanding, controlling, and uncooperative. By having acted in this way and disturbing the minds of others, we now find ourselves surrounded by people who disturb our minds. There is no reason for us to complain: we created the causes for this experience by the way we acted.

After 9/11 the US government sent troops to Afghanistan and later to Iraq. Personally speaking, I didn't want to be involved in wars in these countries. My way of dealing with harm or with dictators is different. I felt trapped: without a choice, I was stuck in the middle of others' quarrels.

I thought, "While I disagree with the policies of Osama bin Laden, Saddam Hussein, and George Bush, I cannot blame them for my uneasiness. The karmic causes lie in actions I did in previous lives. I was rude, quarrelsome, disagreeable, and uncooperative. I incited violence and started fights. Perhaps as a governmental leader in a previous life, I started a war or refused a cease fire or violated treaties. Though it is unpleasant to think I did such things, this can't be ruled out. After all, it is said that we have been everyone and done everything in our beginningless cyclic existence."

We make a determination: *from now on I will maintain good character wherever I am.* No matter where we are or who we are with, we will try to listen sincerely to others' feelings and needs, to be earnest in resolving conflict, and to act with mindfulness and kindness. We pay attention to and respect cultural differences. We discuss options and brainstorm instead of forcing our ideas and behavior on others.

24

When all who are close to me arise as enemies,
It is the weapon of destructive karma turning upon me
For harboring harmful, evil intentions within.
From now on I will diminish deceit and pretension.

Human beings are social creatures, so close friends and relatives are important to us. Strife and misunderstandings arising in our relationships can be painful and difficult as the people we value and depend on transform into enemies. Spouses cannot get along; Dharma friends clash; parents and children cannot tolerate being near each other.

Instead of blaming others for the situation, we recognize that this is due to our *harboring harmful, evil intentions within.* In the past, we were spiteful, undermined others' projects, and sought revenge for small offenses. We pretended to have good qualities and skills that we didn't and hid our faults, misgivings, and past misdeeds from others. Due to this, those who are close to us do not trust us; they back away and may even shun us.

Learning from our previous mistakes and seeking to prevent creating the causes for this to happen in the future, we make a resolution: *from now on, I will diminish my deceit and pretention.* These two mental factors are often coupled together: deceit involves a type of dishonesty that covers up our bad habits that we don't want others to know, and pretension involves feigning good qualities that we lack. Attachment to the eight worldly concerns is definitely at play here, as we pompously present ourselves as someone we are not in order to get others to like us or do something for us.

Such intentions and behaviors motivated from them are forms of lying, pretending to be what we aren't. After a while, we become impervious to our errors and deficiencies. Animals may lack a precious human life, but at least they are honest, and we know what's going on with them. Human beings are not—we put on shows to impress others. Acting with deceit and pretention creates many impediments to meeting with fully qualified spiritual masters in the future. If we cannot be honest and transparent with our teachers, how can they teach and guide us? Our behavior cuts off our lifeline to the Dharma. Thus, for our own benefit, as well as that of others, we want to cease such deceptive intentions and actions.

5

Woe Is Me

DEALING WITH SICKNESS, LAZINESS, AND DISTRACTION

25

When I am sick with chronic ulcers or edema,
It is the weapon of destructive karma returning on me
For wrongfully and with no conscience using others' possessions;
From now on I will renounce such acts as plundering others' possessions.

WE MAY HAVE a chronic illness or health problem we cannot shake. This isn't simply bad luck; it is related to our past actions. We *wrongfully and with no conscience used others' possessions.* Perhaps we stole others' belongings, used them without asking permission, borrowed others' possessions and did not return them. We may have misused what others loaned us or taken what is shared property as our own. Financial advisors, bankers, and stockbrokers must pay special attention to this. Misusing others' money or challenging the economic well-being of the country due to greed is irresponsible. Although one may temporarily be rich in this life, such behavior will lead to having chronic health problems or living in dire poverty in future lives.

Stealing from the Three Jewels is a particularly heavy destructive karma. Someone may take food, money, or jewelry on the altar that was offered to the Buddha. Misusing possessions of the monastic community—for example, borrowing books from their library and not returning them or wastefully using resources when we do a task for the sangha—is heavy destructive karma because this is a large group of people who are intent on virtue. To purify this karma, we must return the object to the same group of people.

Monastics misuse offerings made to them by accepting food, cloth-ing, shelter, medicine, and other items but not keeping their precepts properly. Since these offerings were made with respect and faith in the Three Jewels, it is important to use them wisely, without wast-ing them or using them frivolously. For this reason, before each meal monastics contemplate the causes and conditions and the kindness of others entailed in receiving the food they eat. We eat mindfully, with-out complaining about the food, and dedicate our merit for the donors' well-being afterward.

From now on I will renounce acts such as plundering others' possessions. If we keep accounts for a business, we need to be scrupulous. If someone donates money to a Dharma center, monastery, or temple, it must be used for the purpose the donor indicated. If a donor gave money for the medical needs of the monastics, it must be used in that way. If we want to change the purpose, we must explain the situation to the donors and ask their permission to do so. Respecting others' possessions creates peace and trust among people.

26

When my body is struck suddenly by contagious disease,
It is the weapon of destructive karma turning upon me
For committing acts that undermine my solemn pledges;
From now on I will renounce nonvirtue.

The previous verse referred to chronic illness, while this verse con-cerns acute diseases that arise suddenly and forcefully, for example, con-tracting Ebola or SARS, or having an accident. This is due to *committing acts that undermine our solemn pledges.*

Solemn pledges refer specifically to tantric precepts and commitments, but they also include the five precepts, monastic ethical restraints, and bodhisattva ethical restraints. When we take precepts and commit-ments, we make a promise in the presence of our spiritual mentor and the Three Jewels, and try to honor our word as best we can. Of course, if we could keep the precepts and commitments perfectly, we would not need to take them. Being sentient beings with afflictions, we will commit infractions, but we should do our best to keep our precepts and commitments well and to purify any transgressions.

In his treatise *Bodhisattva Bhumi* (Bodhisattva Stages), the third-century Indian sage Asanga described four doors through which downfalls occur: (1) ignorance, not knowing the boundary of what does and does not constitute a downfall; (2) lack of respect for the precepts and commitments, the Three Jewels, and so forth, even if we know the boundaries; (3) lack of conscientiousness, mindfulness, and introspective awareness, even if we have respect; and (4) being overwhelmed by strong afflictions, even when we know the precepts and commitments, respect them, and and are conscientious. Thus it is important to (1) study, so we know the precepts and commitments as well as what constitutes a downfall; (2) develop respect for them and for ethical conduct in general by considering the advantages of keeping our precepts and commitments, and disadvantages of transgressing them; (3) cultivate conscientiousness, mindfulness, and introspective awareness, so we will remember our precepts and commitments; and (4) practice the antidotes to the various afflictions, so we'll be able to counteract them when they arise.

Sometimes we transgress our precepts. It is important to confess our misdeeds and purify them by means of the four opponent powers in order to prevent or lessen the unpleasant result we will experience as a result of doing them. As mentioned before, the four opponent powers are (1) having regret (not guilt) for our harmful actions of body, speech, and mind; (2) taking refuge and generating bodhicitta to transform our attitude toward those whom we have harmed, holy beings and sentient beings, and in this way strive to restore the relationship with them; (3) making a determination to avoid doing the action again; and (4) engaging in remedial actions, such as making prostrations or offerings, reciting mantras or the names of buddhas, meditating on bodhicitta or on the emptiness of inherent existence, offering service and volunteering at charities, and so forth. Another way to purify is to do the taking-and-giving meditation. Instead of pushing suffering away, what better way to purify our self-preoccupation and self-grasping than to take on the suffering of others and to give them our joy and happiness?

In particular, many monastic precepts can be restored by the fortnightly *posadha* practice. Bodhisattva precepts can be retaken in the presence of our spiritual mentor or by visualizing the buddhas and bodhisattvas and reciting the verse of engaging bodhicitta. Tantric precepts and commitments can be restored by taking the empowerment again, doing the self-empowerment practice after doing the retreat and concluding practices, or reciting the Vajrasattva mantra one hundred thousand times.

Before adopting any ethical restraint or commitment, we need to be properly prepared and think carefully about whether we are ready to assume these. Nowadays some people want to receive tantric empowerments but do not know that receiving empowerments entails taking certain precepts or commitments. They want to receive high practices and advanced teachings but do not want to relinquish killing, stealing, unwise or unkind sexual behavior, lying, or taking intoxicants—five activities that even secular people can see the disadvantages of doing. This is like constructing the roof of a building before the foundation and the walls. We'll waste a lot of energy and only have a mess to show for it.

Some people feel pressured to take tantric empowerments when their friends say, "You must take it, because you never know when you'll have this opportunity again!" As a result they take precepts and commitments that that they are unprepared to keep. After a while, they say, "I've taken tantric precepts and commitments but don't want to keep them anymore. Tantric practice is too advanced for me at this moment. Can I give them back?" This is difficult, because they have taken these from now until full awakening.

We can make a resolution: *from now on I will renounce nonvirtue.* We should do our best to keep our precepts and commitments, including our refuge guidelines and the five lay precepts. Following them improves our practice, enables our relationships to be harmonious, and prevents guilt and regret. We should not regard precepts, commitments, or guidelines as an unwanted tax that we have to pay, but as something that furthers our practice. They bring to our attention aspects of behavior that we may never have considered before. Keeping them well protects us from engaging in behavior that we have already decided we do not want to do.

27

When my intellect becomes ignorant in all fields of knowledge,
It is the weapon of destructive karma turning upon me
For persisting in activities that must be cast aside;
From now on I will cultivate the insights of learning and so on.

Sometimes when we sit down to study, our mind is dull, drowsy, or distracted, and nothing goes in. We listen to teachings or read texts but cannot remember the points, and when we do analytic meditation, we don't reach the proper conclusion. This is due to *persisting in activities that must be cast aside,* such as procrastinating in our Dharma practice or not taking the teachings seriously. We may think, "I've heard this teaching before, so I don't need to hear it again," "I'm tired and will meditate tomorrow," or "I'll start the preliminary practices when I have a better situation." Meanwhile we seek entertainment and get distracted by our smartphones, the Internet, and the latest computerized widget. Numbed by information overload, our ability to engage in critical thinking declines. This leaves us no interest or time to listen, reflect, and meditate on the Dharma, increasing our ignorance while cluttering our mind with useless information about things that lack enduring meaning or purpose.

As Dharma practitioners, we need to know something about current events and how the world operates so that we can be responsible global citizens. It is also helpful so that we can give examples relevant to people's lives when discussing the Dharma. We can apply the *lamrim*—the stages of the path to awakening—to current events. For example, contemplating the causes of war, we see that attachment and anger play major roles. Self-centeredness that focuses on our immediate happiness makes us ignore the future results of not caring for our environment now. The changing relationships among countries is an excellent example of the foolishness of having attachment to friends, hostility toward enemies, and apathy for strangers. It reminds us that having care and concern for all parties equally makes much more sense in the long term. Witnessing the misery in the world reminds us of the importance of observing karma and its effects.

Looking closely, we may see that we're involved with many *activities that must be cast aside.* For example, we may make decisions according to worldly values: How can I make the most money? Which situation will be the most comfortable for me? We may neglect the Dharma in order to advance our career or to have a relationship. In short, we get distracted and engage in actions that will not bring us ultimate happiness, thus relinquishing the opportunities that Dharma study and practice bring us.

This doesn't mean we're "bad" people or "failures." We're doing the best we can. However, we need to be responsible for our choices and our actions. No one else makes us ignorant. By making decisions and engaging in activities with a worldly perspective, we bring obstacles upon ourselves. Confusion about how to live a meaningful life is the result of not having studied and thought about the Dharma in the past. The recommendation to solve this problem is to *cultivate the insights of learning and so on.* We begin with learning—hearing Dharma teachings and studying texts. Then we reflect on what we have learned to eliminate doubts and misconceptions and to understand it correctly. Third, we meditate on the material, integrating it with our mindstreams so that it effects a stable change in us.

Understanding what is and is not Dharma is important in order to engage in learning, reflecting, and meditating. We may think somebody who is studying Dharma day and night, memorizing scriptures, and debating their topics is practicing Dharma. However, if his motivation is to learn the Dharma in order to become a famous, wealthy, or influential teacher, that person is not practicing Dharma, no matter how many students she has.

Creating the causes for a fortunate rebirth, aspiring for liberation, or aiming for full awakening in order to benefit all sentient beings most effectively are genuine Dharma motivations. It takes time and practice to cultivate and stabilize these motivations so that they arise spontaneously. In the meantime we consciously cultivate bodhicitta each morning and before beginning new activities during the day by either briefly recalling the meditations to generate bodhicitta or by contemplating the meaning of a verse such as the following:

> I take refuge until I am awakened in the Buddha, the
> Dharma, and the Sangha.
> By the merit I create by practicing generosity and the other
> perfections, may I attain buddhahood in order to benefit
> all sentient beings.

28

When I am overwhelmed by sloth while practicing the Dharma,
It is the weapon of destructive karma turning upon me
For amassing obscurations to the sublime Dharma;
From now on I will undergo hardships for the sake of the Dharma.

Many people have had the experience of sitting down to meditate and starting to nod off. For others, laziness prevents getting to the meditation cushion. We may have had a good night's sleep, but our mind is dull and cannot focus on the meditation object.

This is related to *amassing obscurations to the sublime Dharma* by looking down on learned people and sincere practitioners. In particular, we denigrated the sangha, not appreciating what they do and their importance in preserving and spreading the Buddha's teachings. For example, sometimes we hear people say, "The sangha is patriarchal, hierarchical, and rigid; we don't need it anymore. Monastics don't want to work and expect us to support them." Disparaging those who are earnestly trying to practice the Dharma obscures our mind and in future lives prevents us from being born where the sangha is present.

We also amass obscurations with respect to the Dharma by not respecting the texts that describe the true cessations and true paths to awakening. We put our Dharma books on the floor, set our coffee cups on top of them, and step over them. We would never treat our paycheck that way! We put it in a clean place and take good care of it. It seems we respect and appreciate money, credit cards, and checks much more than scriptures containing the Buddha's liberating words.

Think about how difficult it is to find Buddhist scriptures in many places in the world. Imagine having a keen interest in the Dharma but not having access to spiritual mentors, scriptures, or others who know the teachings. Perhaps we live in an impoverished country or a place where there is constant warfare or a country that doesn't allow freedom of religion. Disrespecting the sangha, scriptures, statues of the Buddha, or our spiritual mentors is the kind of action that causes us to be reborn in that situation.

To purify this destructive karma and establish new patterns of behavior, we resolve to *undergo hardships for the sake of Dharma.* We are willing to undergo whatever hardships we encounter along the path, using the thought-training teachings to transform adversity into the path and to eliminate our *obscurations to the sublime Dharma.* Siddhārta Gautama and Atisha gave up luxurious lives in royal palaces to become renunciates and practice the Dharma. To have the freedom to study and practice the Dharma, my own teachers fled Tibet and became refugees in India, enduring the drastic change of climate that sickened and killed many of their friends and relatives. They cleared jungle land inhabited by elephants and tigers in South India in order to reestablish their monasteries and continue their studies.

In Tibet before 1959, people from outlying areas walked for months, risking bandits and cold, in order to study at the three great monasteries in central Tibet. There were no covered wagons, let alone cars, trains, and planes. People were willing to walk, ride a yak, or even prostrate the entire way to Lhasa.

Since there weren't any Tibetan Buddhist centers in the United States when I met the Dharma, I had to move to Nepal and India. The monasteries were extremely poor in those days, with no running water or indoor plumbing, poor food, and limited medicine. The Kopan meditation course was held in a tent with flea-infested straw mats covering the dirt floor. We lived in rundown buildings and got sick with hepatitis, dysentery, and flu. Visa problems interrupted our studies and retreats. But those of us who turned up really wanted to learn and practice the Buddha's teachings. The Dharma rang true in our hearts, and we wanted to become like the remarkable teachers we met.

This ability to undergo hardships for the Dharma is important. It makes our mind strong, and we come to appreciate our opportunities and use them wisely. When things are too easy, we often take them for granted and become lazy. Nowadays, we are pampered and spoiled. We complain that it takes too long to drive half an hour to the Dharma center or that we'll have to miss a social event to go to Dharma class or wake up fifteen minutes earlier to meditate in the morning.

We lead such busy lives that we want the Dharma to come to us on our terms, when it is convenient and for the right amount of time. Our teachers should come to where we live; they should start and finish on time because our calendar is full; someone else should prepare the site before teachings.

When we cherish the Dharma, we are willing to undergo hardship because we know it is for a good purpose. What keeps us from undergoing hardships for the sake of Dharma? It is attachment to the happiness of this life, self-centered thought, and self-grasping ignorance. Realizing these are the real enemies that keep us trapped in cyclic existence, we learn and practice the antidotes to them. When we are not fixed on the happiness of only this life, undergoing hardships becomes easy. In fact, we cease seeing circumstances that we can't tolerate as uncomfortable or inconvenient because now our mind is filled with joy and enthusiasm for the Dharma.

Many years ago, I went to the place in Tibet where Je Tsongkhapa did 3.5 million prostrations, and saw the imprint of his body, which is visible on the rock. When we prostrate, we put carpet and pillows under our knees to make ourselves comfortable or have a nice prostration board. Je Tsongkhapa made mandala offerings using a rock as the base plate. As a result, his forearm became raw and bled. You can see outlines of flowers and sacred syllables that appeared spontaneously in that rock.

Thinking of practitioners who were willing to undergo that level of hardship gives us more energy to practice the Dharma purely. However, we should not go to the opposite extreme and deliberately inflict suffering on ourselves, thinking we are macho Dharma practitioners. That is just ego. Whenever someone at Kopan Monastery tried to do that, Lama Yeshe would stop them. One Western monk slept on the cold brick floors. When Lama saw this, he scolded the monk, "Stop going on a Milarepa trip! Get a mattress!"

What is hardship for one person is not hardship for another. We need to be flexible to deal with whatever we encounter. For some people, being alone is easy; for others, it is difficult. For some people, living in community is easy; for others, it is hardship. Whatever is hardship according to our own personal karma is what we need to be willing to work with.

29

When I delight in afflictions and am greatly distracted,
It is the weapon of destructive karma turning upon me
For not contemplating impermanence and the defects of cyclic existence;
From now on I will increase my disenchantment with cyclic existence.

When we meditate, read, or listen to teachings, memories and daydreams sometimes pop into our minds. Afflictions then arise and take us away from our virtuous activities. Distracted by attachment, we imagine being wealthy, famous, loved, and honored. Mixing attachment in with the Dharma, we daydream about the retreats we're going to do, the extraordinary meditation experiences we'll have, and the respect others will give us afterward. Distracted by anger or revenge, we mull over our problems, mentally enumerate others' faults, and plan how to get even for a wrong done to us. When we're doing socially engaged work in the community, doubt distracts us, making us wonder if what we're doing will bring good results.

When these hindrances erupt, it is due to *not contemplating impermanence and the defects of cyclic existence* and consequently still nurturing the hope that samsaric enjoyments will bring us lasting joy. Meditating on *impermanence and the defects of cyclic existence* deflates these unrealistic daydreams, making our mind sober and clear and increasing our *disenchantment with cyclic existence.*

Many people avoid hearing teachings and meditating on impermanence and the faults of cyclic existence. They would rather meditate on love and compassion, which makes them feel good. They prefer to meditate on Chenrezig or another deity, doing a beautiful visualization and reciting mantras. Some people first turn their energy toward *dzogchen* or *mahamudra* meditation because they are said to lead to the highest meditative states. Our self-centeredness prefers to do meditations that leave us feeling light and blissful.

Yet, the reality is that without understanding gross and subtle impermanence—death and the momentary nature of all things—insight into the nature of reality will evade us. Why? Without awareness of our own mortality, our priorities remain murky and our Dharma practice lacks strength and consistency. Contemplating our own transient nature clarifies our purpose in life. It also begins to tear down the ego structure we have spent our life creating, maintaining, and protecting. Meditation on death and impermanence prepares us for the time when we will have to separate from our relatives, friends, bodies, and possessions.

Personally, I find the sobering effect of meditating on impermanence, death, and the disadvantages of cyclic existence a relief. These reflections enable us to see the reality of our lives, and the more our minds are in accord with reality, the greater their clarity, calm, and enthusiasm. For example, creature comforts may be nice, but they do not bring ultimate happiness. The same applies to fantastic personal relationships, marvelous possessions, and fame, praise, and honor. Not only do these things disappear later on, but having them doesn't guarantee happiness right now. Our experience shows us that: We fear losing the good things we have and worry that someone else may have more and better. Anxiety lurks in the back of our mind; we are apprehensive that our lives will fall apart. Even when we are in good situations, we cannot relax and enjoy them. When they end, we get angry and upset, claiming that life is cruel to us.

Cyclic existence is like a prison, but as long as we see it as a luxury hotel complete with spa, sports, and entertainment, we will not want to leave. When we see the prison as prison, we want to get out. The aspiration for liberation from cyclic existence is an essential motivation on the path. Without it, generating bodhicitta is impossible. Thus, to progress spiritually we have to be willing to do these initial meditations that shake up our solid notion of the world and our place in it. But the more we do them, the more we see the truth in the Buddha's teachings and want to cultivate our good qualities and counteract our bad habits.

30
When I continue to regress despite all my efforts,
It is the weapon of destructive karma turning upon me
For defying karma and the laws of cause and effect;
From now on I will strive to accumulate merit.

Sometimes we find ourselves in situations that get worse no matter what we do. We work hard to run a business but go bankrupt. We save our money for retirement, and then the stock market falls. Despite our efforts, our personal growth doesn't coincide with that of the people we love. Treasured relationships disintegrate. We do not get the recognition we think we earned or the love we believe we deserve. Spiritually, we start to make some progress, and then laziness overwhelms us and we abandon our daily meditation practice; or our minds become foggy, and we cannot concentrate.

When this happens, instead of lamenting, we can recognize that in the past we did not take karma and its effects seriously. We may have intellectually understood how karma operates, but living our lives as if we really believed that our actions have an ethical dimension and condition our future experiences would challenge many of our habits and preferences.

If we really took the teachings on karma to heart, we would be more generous with our possessions and finances. We would not be so eager to retaliate when people harmed us. We would make an effort to meditate daily, because we would be certain of the benefits. We would make decisions based on sounder criteria: "Which option would enhance my ethical conduct? Which option would facilitate generating bodhicitta and enable me to be of greater benefit to others? Which option would have more conducive circumstances for understanding emptiness and its compatibility with dependent arising?"

To rectify the situation, we make a determination: *from now on I will strive to accumulate merit*—constructive karma. To do this, upon waking each morning, we generate the positive motivation not to harm others, to benefit them as much as possible, and to hold bodhicitta as our long-term motivation. Throughout the day, we continue to remind ourselves of this motivation and act according to it. It can be helpful to use an event that happens frequently during the day to remind us of our positive motivations. For example, every time before you read a text, recall the aspiration to benefit others, and every time you get in a vehicle recall the wish not to harm anyone. One woman told me that every time her child cried out, "Mommy, come here!" she paused and reminded herself not to get stressed. If we practice like this, then if somebody cuts us off on the highway, instead of jamming the horn and swearing at the person, we say, "Please go ahead." We get there one car later; it does not matter.

To make our practice effective, we must be willing to wrestle with our stubborn self-centeredness and the wrong conceptions we hold so dearly. We have to see the benefits that come from applying Dharma antidotes to our anger and attachment, instead of simply caving in to these afflictions. Undergoing hardship is not about living in a cave and eating nettle soup, like Milarepa. The hardship of working with our obstinate minds can sometimes make living in a cave look easy! But with consistent mind training, our compassion and wisdom will overcome all obstacles.

6 Don't Create Problems for Yourself

OVERCOMING SPIRITUAL OBSTACLES

31

When all the religious rituals I perform go amiss,
It is the weapon of destructive karma returning on me
For investing hope and expectation in forces of darkness;
From now on I will turn away from forces of darkness.

MANY PEOPLE DO religious rituals for health, long life, or wealth, or they request the sangha to do these rituals for them. While some people do these rituals with a Dharma motivation—meditators need a long life to have more time for practice, and a monastery needs funds to build a temple where others can practice—other people do these rituals with worldly motivations, for the happiness of only this life. When these rituals don't bring the effects we wish, it is not because the buddhas and bodhisattvas have let us down; it is due to *investing hope and expectation in forces of darkness.*

Relying on *forces of darkness* has several meanings. It may mean relying on worldly spirits for success, instead of the Three Jewels. Here, instead of observing the law of karma and its effects, people propitiate worldly spirits. Another force of darkness is our wrong conceptions and disturbing emotions that cause us to create destructive karma. Even though we do rituals, they will not bear fruit because our destructive karma creates obstacles. Forces of darkness can also refer to bad friends. Instead of relying on our spiritual mentors and the teachings they give, we follow friends who encourage us to retaliate against people who harm us, to have extramarital affairs, or to cheat others to accumulate wealth. To avoid again creating karma that brings these undesirable results, we resolve to *turn away from forces of darkness* and to maintain our refuge in the Three Jewels purely.

32
When my prayers to the Three Jewels remain ineffectual,
It is the weapon of destructive karma turning upon me
For not entrusting myself to the Buddha's way;
From now on I will rely solely on the Three Jewels.

When our prayers to the Three Jewels do not bear the fruit we want, we should not blame the Buddha, Dharma, and Sangha. Instead, let's acknowledge that we have not entrusted ourselves to the Buddha's path. Instead of listening to the Buddha's teachings with respect and putting them into practice, we may have been critical of the Buddha, Dharma, and Sangha; we may have criticized them or stolen from them. We may have not abided by the refuge guidelines, the chief of which is to help others as much as possible and, if we can't do that, at least to stop harming them.

Initially our faith in the Buddha and his teachings is not based on conviction. As a result, we may be able to talk about karma and its results intellectually, but we do not want to change our emotional, verbal, or physical habits. We'd rather listen to people who encourage our self-centered activities: those who tell us there's no problem if we drink and take drugs, who help us justify spending the family's money on our shopping or gambling addictions, who encourage us to lie or to drive recklessly.

When we put the Dharma teachings into practice sincerely, we discover that they actually work. Our mind becomes clearer and more peaceful. This firsthand experience increases our faith in the Buddha's teachings. Faith is not blind belief. The Buddha advised us to examine his teachings like a goldsmith testing gold—by burning, cutting, and rubbing it. In the Kalama Sutra, he encouraged us to scrutinize the teachings by using reasoning and by practicing them to see if they work. If we do, then if we encounter someone who puts forth opposite views, our faith in the Buddhist path will not be shaken. In fact it will be strengthened because we'll be able to see the faults of their wrong views.

By deciding to *rely solely on the Three Jewels,* we turn to them for guidance both when our lives are relatively calm and when we face difficulties. Turning to the Three Jewels for refuge does not mean we pray, "Buddha, please make this situation turn out well for me," and think Buddha will do all the work while we drink tea! Rather we request inspiration to remember the teachings we've heard and to be able to practice them and transform our minds so that we can deal with the situation wisely.

For example, when we are sick, we may pray to the Buddha to recover so that we can continue our Dharma practice. However, in doing so, we should not see the Buddha as an omnipotent being who can cure us at will. The Buddha is not a god who controls or wills what happens to us. If there were such a god, he or she would be the cause of our misery. But in Buddhism, we say that our destructive actions are the primary cause of our suffering.

It is much more effective to pray to the Buddha for inspiration to transform the experience of being ill into the path to awakening by applying the thought-training practices. We should also pray for inspiration to engage in purification practices so that we can neutralize the destructive karma that is causing our suffering. In brief, the best way to change our situation is by changing our actions.

Each verse in *The Wheel of Sharp Weapons* gives us clues about the specific karma causing different situations. We can then think, "I will reflect on my life and acknowledge when I've done that type of action. I have probably done that action in previous lives as well. Now I regret such harmful behavior, and I want to make preparations by studying and practicing thought training so that when similar situations arise in the future, I will not act according to the same dysfunctional, habitual behavior. Instead I will know how to see the situation in a different light and transform it into the path."

This is a wonderful way to take refuge in the Three Jewels. Based on this, visualizing Vajrasattva or Chenrezig and doing the four opponent powers will have a deep spiritual impact on us.

33
When my imagination rises as veils and possessor spirits,
It is the weapon of destructive karma returning on me
For accumulating negative karma against deities and their mantras;
From now on I will vanquish all negative conceptions.

Imagination—*namtok* in Tibetan—refers to misconceptions, preconceptions, false assumptions, and fabricated stories and beliefs that our
minds create. Some of these, such as the four distorted conceptions—
seeing impermanent things as permanent, impure things as pure,
things that are unsatisfactory in nature as pleasurable, and things that
lack a self as having a self—are deeply rooted. (See verse 91 for more
on the four distorted conceptions.) Others are grosser: they are the mistaken interpretations we have of events around us, our projections on
others, and our assumptions about their motivations.

In cultures where belief in spirits is strong, *veils* refer to demons
or spirits that possess others. People attribute falling unconscious,
strokes, and mental illness to interference from spirits. It is hard to tell
what is actually due to outside forces and what is caused by medical or
psychological ailments. His Holiness the Dalai Lama points out that
many maladies or harmful events that Tibetans attribute to spirit interference are in fact due to other causes.

This verse points out that our misconceptions are ultimately responsible for such difficulties. While meditating, the great Tibetan yogi
Milarepa was disturbed by spirits. He questioned them, "Why are
you bothering me?" They replied, "Your *namtok* invited us to come."
In other words, these spirits were created by his misconceptions or
invoked by them.

When we face interference, let's recall that it is due to *accumulating
negative karma against deities and their mantras.* In previous lives, we may
have taken empowerments and not kept our precepts and our commitments. We may have promised to do the Six-Session Guru Yoga daily
but not followed through. Our actions boomerang back to us as our
experiencing mental difficulties or inexplicable illnesses.

The remedy is to *vanquish all negative conceptions.* In addition to the above description, *negative conceptions* also refer to what in tantra are called "ordinary appearance and ordinary grasping." That is, things appear to us as ordinary and truly existent, and our minds assent to that appearance and grasp things as being ordinary and truly existent. For example, we appear to ourselves as being someone who is a truly existent person full of faults, lacking in love and compassion, and incapable of changing our bad habits.

In tantric practice, this view is opposed by a practice called "clear appearance and divine identity." By means of clear appearance, those who have received tantric empowerment practice seeing themselves and their companions as deities, their environment as the deity's mandala, their actions as the compassionate activities of buddhas, and the objects they use as pure objects of use. They also practice viewing all these as empty of inherent existence and existing dependent on terms and concepts. Doing this is the practice of abandoning ordinary appearance and ordinary grasping through cultivating clear appearance and divine identity.

When our preconceptions proliferate—"I know everyone dislikes me. They're talking about me behind my back"—how do you use clear appearance and divine identity to counteract that? Someone who has received tantric empowerment sees himself or herself and the other person as deities, and the words that are spoken as mantra. As Chenrezig, you certainly won't think, "Tara doesn't like me; Manjushri doesn't want to speak to me; even Vajrapani is talking behind my back!" Changing our view in this way counteracts the habitual, self-centered, mistaken conceptions that see others as enemies.

34
When I am lost and wander about like a powerless person,
It is the weapon of destructive karma returning on me
For driving others, such as my guru, from their abodes;
From now on I will expel no one from their home.

People are displaced from their homes and countries due to a variety of reasons: natural disasters, wars, terrorism, epidemics, political problems, poverty, environmental disasters, or family conflicts. Here, you are homeless and lack the ability to engage in meaningful activity to change the situation. You are exiled from your home, distanced from people who could help you, and living in foreign places where you do not wish to stay.

What did we do in past lives or even in this life to create the causes for this? We *drove others, such as our gurus, from their abodes.* We may think, "I would never do this, even in my previous lives!" Consider what happened during the Cultural Revolution in China. People who were ordinarily decent and trustworthy turned on each other. Disciples turned in their spiritual mentors, accusing them of being counterrevolutionaries. Poor peasants joined the People's Liberation Army with the thought to earn some money for their families and turned entire villages upside down, forcing people to flee. Or perhaps we were a landlord who evicted people from their homes, forcing them to live on the streets because they were in arrears in paying their rent. Maybe we were a greedy child who forced our elderly parent to leave the family house, or we were a roommate who made problems for a fellow roommate, so that he had to move out. Such actions bring about the result of having to wander about as a powerless person.

The antidote to that is to make a resolution: *from now on I will expel no one from their home.* Instead, we care about others and want them to feel secure and live in a safe place. We help build houses for Habitat for Humanity, work in a homeless shelter, or help homeless teens to stay in school.

35
When calamities such as frost and hailstorms occur,
It is the weapon of destructive karma returning on me
For failing to properly observe my pledges and ethical precepts;
From now on I will keep my pledges and precepts pure.

In chapter 2, we spoke about karma and the results that a complete action brings. One of these is the environmental result, the place we live in. Situations where frost and hailstorms destroy crops and livestock, or where there is turmoil caused by climate change or out-breaks of disease are environmental results of karma, specifically, *failing to properly observe our pledges and ethical precepts.* This happens when we take the five precepts, bodhisattva ethical restraints, or tantric precepts and commitments but don't live according to them. In the same way that frost and hailstorms destroy external crops, poor ethical conduct destroys the crop of spiritual realizations. This environmental result is the external manifestation of an internal process.

How do we remedy this? *From now on I will keep my pledges and ethical precepts.* Having experienced the faults of being negligent in our ethical conduct, we make the determination to keep them well henceforth.

I recommend people to go slowly in terms of taking precepts, pledges, and commitments. Take these when you know the benefits of keeping them and have some confidence in your ability to keep them reasonably well.

Before people take refuge and the five lay precepts, I suggest they participate in a refuge study group where you learn the meaning of taking refuge in the Three Jewels, study the five precepts, and make examples of how to keep them in your life. Discuss with others which precepts you will have the most difficulty keeping, the circumstances in which you could easily transgress them, and the attitudes you want to cultivate that will help you maintain them well. In this way, you will understand what you are doing when you take refuge and precepts. Your mind will be happy and confident when doing so, and there will be no regret or confusion afterward. Along this line, it is helpful to prepare in a similar way before taking monastic ordination, bodhi-sattva ethical restraints, or the tantric precepts and commitments. In this way, we are well informed, confident, and joyful about what we are doing.

36

When I am greedy but bereft of material wealth,
It is the weapon of destructive karma returning on me
For failing to give charity and make offerings to the Three Jewels;
From now on I will exert effort in giving and offering.

In this situation, we are poor but full of greed. We have strong ambitions to possess wealth and status, but we cannot afford what we want. Rather than feeling like a victim, blaming others, and making a ruckus about how life is unfair, we need to realize this is the ripening of our own karma. It makes no sense to get angry at others when our suffering originates in actions we did under the influence of ignorance and self-centeredness.

In particular, here we *failed to give charity and make offerings to the Three Jewels.* Giving charity is done by aiding the "field of compassion"—those who are sick, poor, needy, and cannot take care of themselves; and those who are enmeshed in difficulties, are mentally depressed or physically incapacitated. Previously, when we had the opportunity to help these people, we were stingy or arrogant and turned our back on them. Perhaps we thought, "These people are poor because they don't work hard. I'm not going to give them anything because they don't deserve it."

We have also *failed to make offerings to the Three Jewels*—also called the "field of merit" because making offerings of resources, service, or our practice to them creates great merit. We make offerings to the Three Jewels because they are endowed with so many good qualities. Offering to them forms a connection with them and creates the constructive karma that will enable us to have conducive circumstances to encounter and practice the Buddha's teachings. Perhaps we justified our miserliness by cynically thinking, "The monastics should go out and get a job like everyone else, instead of just sitting there meditating and pretending to be holy." In addition to creating the cause to be bereft of material wealth as human beings, miserliness also causes rebirth in the hungry ghost realm.

The remedy is to make a determination: *from now on I will exert effort in giving {to sentient beings} and offering to the Three Jewels.* It is important not to hoard our possessions and then claim that we are too poor to give to those who are lacking. Many of us have drawers full of extra things we don't use. We fear that if we give them away, we won't have them later when we need them. In the meantime, others need them now, but our miserliness prevents us from extending our hands to fellow human beings.

When making offerings to the Three Jewels, give things of good quality. For example, avoid putting the bruised fruit on the altar as an offering to the Three Jewels, while keeping the good fruit for you to eat. Whether making offerings or giving charity, our attitude should be one of delight in giving, free from the expectation of honor or reward in return. When giving to a Dharma teacher, temple, monastery, or Dharma center, we shouldn't think, "I made a large donation, so they should pay more attention to me and give me a good seat." When giving to those in need, we should avoid thinking, "Now they owe me something in return." Such thoughts pollute our motivation and risk making our generosity just another activity done for the happiness of only this life. Instead, let's ensure our motivation is aligned with the Dharma, at least aiming for a fortunate rebirth in the future. Better yet is the motivation to attain liberation, and even better than that is the intention to attain full awakening for the benefit of all sentient beings. What we give may be the same in these three cases, but our motivation is the dominant factor in determining the benefit and result of our action.

By giving with a good motivation, we immediately experience a happy mind that feels connected to others. Studies have indicated that people experience more happiness in sharing with others than in keeping things for themselves. Giving with delight creates so much good karma, and that gladdens our hearts. Generosity in this life brings wealth in future lives. Furthermore, even in this life, people are drawn to those who are generous and help them when they are in need.

In addition to giving money and possessions, we can give our time to offer service to those needing help to complete a project. We can give affection and support to those in need of emotional comfort or confidence. Protecting people, animals, or insects in danger is a form of generosity. The best generosity is the gift of the Dharma, giving teachings with the motivation to lead others on the path to awakening. Although we may not be capable of teaching others at this moment, we can share Dharma books with them, answer basic questions, and invite them to attend teachings or ceremonies with us. When friends have problems and ask us for advice, we can share the Dharma with them using everyday language without any Buddhist jargon. After all, so much of Buddhadharma involves changing our perspective, and this does not depend on any philosophy or theology and can be shared with secular people and those of other faiths as well.

37
When I am ugly and mistreated by my companions,
It is the weapon of destructive karma returning on me
For constructing ugly images while in the turmoil of anger;
From now on I will be patient when creating sacred images.

We experience physical and mental suffering when we are born with a deformity or a handicap, or have an unattractive body. We also suffer when we are old and others shun us as useless or when we are very ill and people don't want to be near us. While education is needed to counteract such discrimination and uncompassionate actions, we still need to deal with our feelings in that moment.

When we experience the pain of others' reactions toward our body, instead of getting angry with them, we recall it is due to *constructing ugly images while in the turmoil of anger.* We may have destroyed stupas or statues with anger—like the communists did in Tibet and China—or made ugly images of the Buddha while we were angry. Having an unattractive body is, in general, a result of anger. It is easy to see the causal relationship. Right in the moment when we are overcome with anger, we become not only emotionally vile, but also physically ugly, with a red face, bulging eyes, and shrill voice. That angry state of mind also causes us to be unattractive in future lives.

There is a story about a monk who had an extremely ugly body but a beautiful voice. People loved to hear him chant but recoiled when they saw him. Someone who had clairvoyant powers saw that in a previous lifetime, while constructing a stupa—a monument representing the Buddha's mind—he continually complained and showed an ugly face.

When the stupa was completed, he had a change of heart and offered a bell with a charming and elegant sound to the stupa. His ugly body was a result of his anger while making the stupa, and his beautiful voice was the result of having later offered the lovely-sounding bell to the stupa.

We now resolve to *be patient when creating sacred images.* If we make *tsa tsas,* the small clay or plaster images of buddhas and deities, let's do it respectfully with a happy heart, taking our time to ensure the image is beautiful and made correctly. When looking at buddha images, we don't say, "This buddha is ugly." A fully awakened being can never be ugly! However, the artistry may be poor.

Although being good-looking is not our principal aim in life, if we want to benefit sentient beings, having a pleasant appearance is helpful so that people will be drawn to us. That then gives us the opportunity to share the Dharma with them. However, if you are a monk or a nun who is very attractive, it is much more challenging to hold your precepts! It is better to be somewhere in the middle, where we are pleasant looking, but not somebody others will ogle.

People often ask why monastics shave their heads. Aside from it being a symbol of our effort to renounce the three poisonous attitudes of attachment, anger, and confusion, it removes one of the chief things we associate with physical beauty—our hair. When I tell teenagers that I want to cultivate inner beauty—kindness, love, forgiveness, and so forth—rather than external beauty, their mouths drop open. I explain that people attracted to me because of inner beauty will be better friends than people attracted to me due to my looks, and they are surprised. In a society where physical beauty and sex are used to sell everything, the idea of cultivating our inner beauty and valuing others due to their inner beauty is a unique idea.

38

When attachment and anger erupt no matter what I do,
It is the weapon of destructive karma returning on me
For allowing my untamed negative mind to become rigid;
From now on I will root out you, the "I."

Sometimes our minds are overcome with neediness or hostility, and no matter what antidote we apply, these afflictions don't seem to decline. We notice we are getting angry and try to meditate on fortitude or love, but our anger only declines a little. Or we meditate on the insides of the body, but the mind is still filled with lust. Our *untamed negative mind is rigid* and obstinate.

Why is this? In the past we had similar lust, hatred, jealousy, and arrogance and allowed them free reign in our minds, where they subsequently became well entrenched. Although we have heard many teachings on the disadvantages of self-centeredness and benefits of cherishing others, we have stubbornly hung onto "me," "I," "my," and "mine." If we did bother to curb them at all, it wasn't because we cared about others; it was because we selfishly wanted to avoid criticism or a bad reputation.

The antidote is to *root out you, the "I."* Here, *the "I"* refers to grasping an inherently existent self and to self-centered thought. We make a strong determination to note when self-grasping and self-centeredness arise and to counteract them. This is hard to do because we are so habituated to them that when they arise, we do not even notice them, let alone be aware of the havoc they wreak. Instead, we believe that their viewpoints are reality: there is an independent "me," and we are the most important ones in the universe.

Courage, fortitude, enthusiastic perseverance, and deep understanding of the horrors of cyclic existence are necessary to chip away at these. We have to be willing to endure the temporary discomfort of facing our ignorance and self-centeredness in order to gain the long-term benefit of being free from them.

In general, if a particular action brings benefit in both the short term and the long term, we should do it. If it brings problems in both the short term and the long term, we should avoid it. If an action brings benefit now but problems later on, it's best to avoid it, and if it brings difficulty now but benefit later on, we should do it. The last two are more difficult to do because, due to self-grasping and self-centeredness, we cling to our immediate happiness and pleasure. However, when we meditate strongly on the defects of cyclic existence and the limitations imposed on us by self-grasping and self-centeredness, our determination to be free from them and to attain full awakening increases.

The actual antidote to ignorance and the afflictions is the wisdom of directly realizing ultimate reality—the emptiness of inherent existence of all persons and phenomena. The antidote to self-centeredness is love, compassion, and bodhicitta. To cultivate the latter, we rely on two methods: the seven-point cause-and-effect instruction and equalizing and exchanging self and others. Rather than go into these in depth in this book, I will refer you to *Transforming Adversity into Joy and Courage,* by Geshe Jampa Tegchok. It is a commentary on the "Thirty-Seven Practices of Bodhisattvas," another thought-training text. While we have this precious human life, let's take its essence by practicing these methods taught by the Buddha to purify all defilements from our minds and bring all good qualities to their utmost development.

39

When all meditative practices fail in their aims,
It is the weapon of destructive karma returning on me
For allowing pernicious views to enter my heart;
From now on whatever I do will be solely for others' sake.

We do analytic meditation on the stages of the path to awakening (*lamrim*), but our minds feel like a dry desert; we meditate on a tantric practice, but uncertainty about the effectiveness of visualization floods our mind; we try to develop serenity, but we become drowsy instead. At this time, instead of allowing doubt and frustration to threaten our practice, we need to remember that these obstacles are due to *allowing pernicious views to enter our hearts.*

Pernicious views are wrong views we held in previous lives or in this life. They include thinking Dharma practice is unimportant, attaining full awakening is impossible, our actions have no ethical dimension, and being self-centered is useful to prevent people from taking advantage of us. Pernicious views also refer to the eight worldly concerns, bad motivations, and rebelling against our spiritual mentor's wise instructions.

How do we ameliorate this? *From now on whatever I do will be solely for others' sake.* We make a determination to turn our motivation around completely. Working for the benefit of others does not mean becoming a people pleaser, being kind only to avoid something unpleasant ourselves or to get what we want. Acting solely for others' sake means considering others as equal to or more important than ourselves. In its purest form, it is bodhicitta, the aspiration to gain full awakening for the benefit of others.

Some people mistakenly believe that love, compassion, and bodhicitta entail making everyone happy, something that is impossible to do. Beings in cyclic existence are never content! However, we do wish them to be happy and do what we are capable of to bring that about with a kind attitude, when it does not involve harming someone else.

Other people believe that working for the welfare of others entails ignoring ourselves. This, too, is incorrect. We have to take care of ourselves wisely, keeping our bodies healthy and our minds content and eager to learn. This is done without self-indulgence, but for the sake of maintaining our precious human life as the best vehicle for Dharma practice.

By now, you may be thinking, "Can't Dharmarakshita go easy on me for a while? Does he have to keep saying that everything is my fault?" Actually Dharmarakshita isn't attacking us. He's simply pointing out that the self-grasping ignorance and self-centered thought that we previously thought were our friends are actually the cause of our misery. He isn't blaming us, because he understands that these two mental attitudes are not who we are; they are adventitious factors that we can oppose and eliminate through cultivating wisdom and compassion. In fact, Dharmarakshita has full faith in our ability to abandon these obscurations and attain full awakening. For that reason, he put time and energy into writing this poem. So don't become discouraged when recognizing the machinations of our confused minds. Instead feel relieved because now you know what to do to bring about a state of lasting peace and fulfillment for yourself and others.

40
When my mind remains untamed, despite my spiritual practice,
It is the weapon of destructive karma returning upon me

For eagerly pursuing mundane ambitions;
From now on I will concentrate on aspiring for liberation.

This situation is familiar to most of us. Our mind is rough, unruly, and rebellious. Despite our efforts to practice, disturbing emotions continue to arise, and we find ourselves again doing the very action we vowed not to do. We do prostrations, but rather than become more humble, our arrogance increases: "I'm such a spiritual person!" We do Vajrasattva to purify negativities and become jealous of others who finish the retreat before we do.

This is caused by our "constant companion," the eight worldly concerns, especially attachment to being important and having a good reputation. We want to be president of the company or director of the Dharma center. We would like to be featured in a magazine as an excellent horse trainer, gardener, rock climber, or executive. We may go through the motions of doing pure Dharma practice, but due to a corrupt motivation seeking fame, approval, offerings, and praise, we are not able to transform our mind.

A few centuries ago, a Tibetan monk heard his benefactor was coming to visit. He proceeded to set up his altar nicely with beautiful offerings to impress his benefactor in the hopes the benefactor would then make an offering to him. Suddenly he realized what he was doing and threw dirt on his altar to foil the plot his self-centered mind had invented. His teacher, who had clairvoyant powers, noticed this and commented, "This monk just made a pure offering by countering his self-centered thought."

Instead of seeking worldly gain, which results in our continued rebirth in cyclic existence with the same untamed mind, we need to learn and practice the meditations that will transform our motivation into a genuinely spiritual one. Topics to meditate on are impermanence, the unsatisfactory nature of cyclic existence, the conditions for afflictions to arise, and the process of taking rebirth in cyclic existence through the twelve links of dependent arising. Getting a feel for what it means to be under the influence of ignorance, afflictions, and polluted karma, and how these bring us and others repeated misery turns our mind toward liberation and full awakening. When our mind is intent on liberation or awakening, our motivation is upright because it is focused on a spiritual goal. It is impossible for the eight worldly concerns to be present in our minds when at the same time our motivation is pure.

When we are convinced that the glitter of the eight worldly concerns will not make us happy, it's easier for our minds to generate renunciation of cyclic existence and the determination to be free from it. Such a motivation makes our minds much more peaceful because instead of fretting about irrelevant things, it is focused on something meaningful. This motivation must be cultivated with effort. Then, if somebody criticizes us or blames us, we don't care much because we are focused on liberation. If you are in prison and want to get out, you don't worry about dust in your prison cell because you're focused on how to escape.

41

When I feel remorse the moment I sit down and reflect,
It is the weapon of destructive karma returning upon me
For being shamelessly fickle and clamoring for high status;
From now on I take my associations with others seriously.

Sometimes we sit down to study or reflect on the teachings and instead of feeling inspired and eager, we feel remorse that we may be missing out on another interesting activity, social event, or opportunity to advance our career. Wondering if our practice will bring the desired results, we get confused and agitated. Or we have great expectations—we meditate a little and think we will have great realizations and visions of the Buddha. When this doesn't happen, we get discouraged, regret that we even tried, and want to give up. We think, "I could have gone to the beach with this great guy instead of doing retreat."

This boredom, disappointment, and remorse are the results of being *shamelessly fickle and clamoring for high status.* Seeking fame and recognition, we buttered people up in the hope that they would do something for us. But as soon as another person could do more for us, we deserted our previous companions and took up with new ones. Similarly, we might go "guru-hopping"— forming a relationship with one teacher, but when he or she doesn't tell us what we want to hear, we leave and find another teacher who does. In short we don't know how to be a good friend to our friends or a good student to those who kindly teach us the Dharma.

We may have boasted of doing great practices that we cannot accomplish because we haven't yet established the firm foundation necessary to do them. We may have a lot of ambition, wanting to make a name for ourselves as a great teacher or practitioner, and so take one empowerment after another but do not do the corresponding practice. Or if we do it, we get bored and jump to another practice, another Dharma center, or another spiritual mentor. In our daily life, we go from one friend to another friend, from one job to another job, all due to having a fickle mind that is trying to eke out the most possible pleasure for ourselves.

The remedy for this is to *take all my associations with others seriously* and to be vigilant in forming and nurturing beneficial relationships. Before making a commitment, we should determine whether we'll be able to follow through on it. If something unexpectedly comes up, we communicate well with others instead of leaving them high and dry. We take our connections seriously and try to create long-term, durable relationships with mutual respect.

I observe my spiritual mentors' behavior in order to learn from it and am continually impressed with their peaceful, humble, and compassionate manner in all situations. These are the kind of people I want to be around in this and future lives. I want to form strong relationships with them so that they will continue to influence me in positive ways. By making sure our motivation for Dharma practice is sincere and by following our teachers' instructions in this life, we'll create the causes to meet them and be their disciples again in future lives.

When I first met the Dharma, I was young, foolish, and lacked the ability to discriminate between authentic and false spiritual mentors. I was extremely fortunate in meeting my teachers. This was not due to luck, but to prayers made in a previous life. Knowing this reminds me to create merit and make similar dedications, because I want to meet qualified teachers and have good Dharma friends in future lives.

41

When I am deceived by others' treachery,
It is the weapon of destructive karma returning upon me
For being conceited and greedy;
From now on I will minimize attachment to everything.

It may happen that others take advantage of us without our realizing what is happening. Perhaps we gave people money to use for great projects, but they squandered it. Perhaps someone pretended to have excellent qualities he lacked and hid his faults, and we fell for it. We thought that person was marvelous, followed their suggestions, and ended up in a predicament. Our self-centered, unclear mind thought there was something to gain from getting involved with this person, but it backfired.

Why are we susceptible to such deception? It is the result of *being conceited and greedy.* We can see that having such mental states in previous lives creates the karma for this to happen now and that our present self-centeredness provides the condition for that karma to ripen. For example, we may have taken advantage of others in previous lives by returning their kindness with ingratitude or deceiving them with our ploys. Full of ourselves, we thought we could conquer anything or anyone that got in our way. Such attitudes and behavior ripened in the causally concordant experiential result; that is, we experience something similar to what we caused others to experience.

We blame others for deceiving us, but we also need to look at why we fall for their schemes. Why did we naively believe this person? Often we find there was some kind of selfishness, arrogance, or greed in our mind that led us to follow him or her. We were looking for a shortcut or had inflated expectations of gain and fame. To remedy this we must *minimize attachment to everything* and be more discreet and honest.

Doing the taking-and-giving meditation will help us in this situation. In this case, with compassion, we take on the pain and difficulties of others who are being used and deceived, and whose trust is betrayed. This will decrease our selfishness, conceit, and greed and make us more attentive so that we will quickly notice these emotions and apply the antidotes when they arise in our minds. Then we imagine giving our body, possessions, and virtue—plus whatever we have procured due to deceptive and treacherous behavior—to others and imagine all their needs being fulfilled. Having all conducive conditions for Dharma practice, they generate renunciation, bodhicitta, and wisdom; they enter the Vajrayana path and attain full awakening.

43

When my studies and teaching fall prey to attachment and anger,
It is the weapon of destructive karma returning upon me
For failing to contemplate the ills of the demons in my heart;
From now on I will examine these hindrances and eliminate them.

We may have faith in the Buddha's teachings, but when we sit down to study them, our minds wander to objects of attachment and anger, such as the good-looking person we'd like to get to know or the colleague who insulted us. We are jealous of those who receive teachings we have not; we scheme to get invited to give a talk to people who will certainly give us a hefty offering afterward.

Such situations are due to *failing to contemplate the ills of the demons in my heart.* The *demons* refer to afflictions, and the *ills of the demons* refer to their disadvantages. Self-centered thought and self-grasping ignorance, in particular, are the real demons. There is no external demon or devil. Instead of letting afflictions distract us or influence how we study and who we teach, we must focus on the teachings themselves and use them to counteract our afflictions.

While we may not believe in an external devil, we still blame others instead of understanding the faults of our inner afflictions and selfishness. When self-centered thought speaks, we are at its beck and call. We do not realize this is the demon that has been cheating us all this time. In fact, we may have a great deal of fear about giving up our self-centeredness: "If I do not look out for myself, I will be left behind and nothing good will come to me."

In fact, our self-centeredness has gotten us into one jam after another, whereas all of our knowledge and possessions come due to the kindness of others. Others grew our food, sewed our clothing, built our homes, constructed the roads we drive on and vehicles we ride in. Others taught us and encouraged our talents. We have so many advantages in life not because we selfishly took care of ourselves, but because others helped us. Examining how this functions in our own lives, we realize we have been the recipient of tremendous kindness. We can relax and trust the universe a little, instead of thinking we have to control everything.

Let's challenge our fear of letting go of self-centered thought. Other sentient beings have been protecting us and caring for us all these years, while our suffering and problems have come from self-centered thought. Others taught us how to read and write, as well as the skills we use to earn our living. Our financial problems are due to our greed and ignorance. When we see that everything we have comes due to the kindness of others, the fear that giving up our self-centered thought will make us vulnerable seems totally ridiculous!

What do we do to counteract the blindness that prevents us from seeing the defects of the afflictions? *From now on I will examine these hindrances and eliminate them.* That is, we identify our afflictions and then apply the antidotes to counteract them. It is important to see ourselves as a patient suffering from the disease of cyclic existence, caused by the virus of self-grasping ignorance and self-centered thought, and then turn to the Buddha, Dharma, and sangha for guidance on the way to attain good health.

44

When all the good I have done turns out badly,
It is the weapon of destructive karma returning upon me
For repaying others' kindness with ingratitude;
From now on I will respectfully repay others' kindness.

Sometimes we do a project with a kind motivation, but all sorts of problems and competitiveness result, or we undertake an ingenious project to help others but experience obstacles. We reach out to assist someone, and they scream that we're interfering in their lives. Our temptation, then, is to feel hurt, angry, and defensive: "Look how hard I worked for these people and they treat me so badly!"

Instead of falling into self-pity or self-righteous anger, we need to recognize this is due to previously having *repaid others' kindness with ingratitude*. In the past, we have done exactly what we are accusing others of doing. To remedy this, we should spend some time thinking about the kindness others have shown us and how we have responded. Many times we were ungrateful, or we misinterpreted their actions and criticized them. For example, our teachers gave us some good advice, but we got angry because the advice did not match what our ego wanted to hear.

In Chinese and Japanese Buddhism, one meditation to help us cultivate bodhicitta involves considering our relationships with different people: parents, teacher, older and younger siblings, managers, colleagues, employees, and children. With each we contemplate how they have helped us, our responsibility toward them, and how we treated them. This meditation is very humbling, because we often discover that others have benefited us, but we have responded in inappropriate, ungrateful, or even negligent ways. We have accepted their affection, care, and kindness without any thought of helping them in return.

The remedy is to *respectfully repay others' kindness.* Instead of keeping a balance sheet—"I've done this for you, so you owe me this"— we need to recognize our interdependence with others and make an effort to repay their thoughtfulness with appreciation and gratitude by both extending kindness to that person and by "paying it forward" by helping someone else. In this way, we cultivate the attitude that takes delight in giving. Doing the positive action is the reward in itself. We do not need somebody to notice it, thank us, or praise us.

Our constructive actions should always be done respectfully: we offer a gift with both hands. We point out someone's good qualities with a smile. We stand up to greet others, give them the best seat, fill their glass with water. There are so many small actions we can do with respect that make people feel cared for.

This poem is not theoretical. We can see ourselves in these situations, think about the kind of actions we may have done, do the taking-and-giving meditation, and resolve to act differently in the future. This mental spring cleaning will benefit us. We have to start looking under the rugs and behind the furniture, hauling out stuff that we have tried to ignore for a long time. A lot of rubbish has been stored in our mental house. It smells awful, but until now we've tried to cover it up with the scent of Internet, shopping, and fun. Now, instead of trying to cover up our dirty motivations, we decide to clean the house, to clean our hearts and minds. This process is liberating and refreshing, and the result is joy and peace.

In this section, each verse has a similar structure. It begins with an undesirable situation that we are experiencing, which prompts us to question, "Why is this happening?" The middle two lines answer that question, saying it is the *weapon of destructive karma returning* full circle upon us and explaining the karmic causes of that kind of situation— what we did in previous lives or even earlier this life that brought it about. The last line presents the attitude to cultivate or action to do to avoid creating the causes for these undesirable situations in the future and to instead create the causes for happiness. Now Dharmarakshita will summarize the chief points that he has made so far.

45
In brief, when calamities befall me like bolts of lightning,
It is the weapon of destructive karma returning upon me
Just like the ironsmith slain by his own sword;
From now on I will be heedful of nonvirtuous acts.

When we fall ill, when someone dies, when plans created with pains-taking care don't work out, we are surprised—it seems like *calamities befall me like bolts of lightning*—because we believe life is not supposed to be like that. Especially when we live in a wealthy country that is relatively peaceful, it's easy to take our good circumstances for granted. However, as long as we are in cyclic existence, unsatisfactory experiences and outright suffering will naturally come to us. Suffering is not a punishment, and it does not indicate failure. It is simply *the weapon of destructive karma returning upon us like an ironsmith slain by his own sword.*

The smith crafted the sword in order to earn a living but was killed by his own creation. Similarly, we do harmful actions thinking they will further our ambitions, but they plant the seeds for our misery.

No one else is to blame for this situation. We made the weapons. If we did not make the weapons, nobody could take them and throw them at us. If we did not create the karma, pain and frustration would not come our way. Rather than accusing others of being the source of our misfortune, we need to investigate our situation well and see that we are being slain by the weapons we created through the force of our own self-grasping ignorance and the afflictions it nourishes. In this way, we begin to take responsibility for our experiences. That gives us real power, because we see that we can change our experiences by changing our attitude and actions.

This is one aspect of the satisfaction I find in working with the incarcerated. Prison inmates who write me are interested in the Dharma and are usually ready to take responsibility for their lives. They have done things they deeply regret, and they do not blame others, cover it up, or rationalize their mistakes. They own their misdeeds and go about the hard work of releasing anger and resentment.

One prisoner I correspond with murdered someone when he was seventeen. When he told me the story, he said, "I was sentenced for first-degree murder, and rightly so." He did not try to shirk responsibility or blame anybody else. This is the first step in doing powerful purification, for the degree of purification corresponds to the intensity of our regret. When we take responsibility, we have genuine regret and a strong determination not to repeat the action.

Learning from our mistakes, we pledge *from now on I will be heedful of nonvirtuous acts.* This involves developing the conviction that suffering arises from self-centeredness and happiness springs from cherishing others, instead of the other way around. Making many examples from our lives will help us understand this.

Now we practice *being heedful of nonvirtuous acts.* This means we cultivate conscientiousness, an attitude that cherishes virtue and guards the mind from defilements. To do this, recall a time in your life when you cherished noble aspirations and virtuous intentions. Recall how happy you felt then, and notice that your mind was free from afflictions at that time. The attitude that cherishes virtue prevents ignorance, anger, and attachment from arising. And if they do start to arise, we immediately recognize this and direct our attention back to our positive intention. Conscientiousness is the root of all the paths and grounds leading to awakening. One condition of our precious human life is having interest in the Dharma, and we are interested in the Dharma because we are conscientious; we cherish virtue.

46

When I undergo sufferings in the lower realms,
It is the weapon of destructive karma returning upon me
Like a fletcher slain by his own arrow;
From now on I will be heedful regarding destructive actions.

When the seeds of our destructive actions ripen, we find ourselves in unfortunate realms of existence. While some people think of these as psychological states, when born there, they are just as real to us as our human life is now. In the hellish rebirths, there is not just the physical suffering of extreme heat and cold, but also the mental suffering of not knowing where to turn for help. Our minds are immobilized by fear and animosity, and although we want happiness, our suspicion blocks us from seeing a trustworthy person who can help us. We can see that same mechanism at work in our current lives. There may be a lot of kindness around us, but our mental state or our karma prevents us from seeing it.

In the hungry ghost realm, beings are totally dissatisfied. The mind that is tight, greedy, and stingy becomes our whole life. There is constant dissatisfaction and frustration because we can't get what we want. On a physical level, there is the suffering of hunger, and on a mental level there is a feeling of insatiable craving.

In the animal realm, beings suffer physically from being hunted or eaten, but what may be even more torturous is the deep stupidity and ignorance that overwhelm their minds. Imagine being in a body when your biological structure restricts the functioning of your intelligence. To me, this is very frightening.

In previous lives, we have been born in such rebirths numberless times. It is remarkable that we have the opportunity we have right now with our present precious human rebirth with all its conditions to learn and practice the Dharma. All the suffering we experienced in unfortunate realms is *the weapon of destructive karma returning upon us like a fletcher slain by his own arrow*. We put negative energy into the environment through our distorted thoughts and harmful actions, and it comes right back to us as our experience, like the fletcher killed by the arrow he made.

The conclusion is *from now on I will be heedful regarding negative actions.* We will be conscientious by treasuring ethical conduct, mindful of our precepts and values, and use introspective awareness to continuously be aware of our thoughts and actions.

Many people do not understand the purpose of precepts or monastic vows and see them as rules imposed from outside. In fact, they are tools to help us be aware of our thoughts, emotions, words, and deeds. We may notice that we want to drink or take drugs "to relax." Remembering we have a precept regarding this, we recall the precept's purpose: we don't want to numb our mind but to keep it alert so that we can make wise decisions, connect with people on the heart level, engage in wholesome deeds. Then we investigate our mind: "Why do I want to drink or take drugs? What do I think I'll get out of doing this?" This puts us in touch with our internal restlessness, our feelings of being socially awkward, our desire to fit in, or our wish to zone out and not have to deal with life. In this way, precepts act as a mirror that helps us to see what we are actually feeling and thinking inside ourselves. Then we can ask ourselves, "What do I actually need at this moment? Is it communication? Connection? Creativity? Exercise?" By determining what our actual emotional need is at that moment, we can offer ourselves empathy and think creatively about how to fulfill that need in a way that harms neither ourselves nor others.

Instead of continuing to be like an ironsmith slain by the sword he made or fletcher killed by his own arrows, we realize that we can do something about our situation. We cultivate a mind that cherishes others and wants to aid them, creating an "arrow" of bodhicitta that will pierce our self-centeredness. We develop wisdom that understands dependent arising and emptiness and use it as the sword to cut off the ignorance that is the root of our cyclic existence.

47
When the sufferings of householders befall me,
It is the weapon of destructive karma returning upon me
Like parents slain by their own cherished children;
From now on I will rightly renounce worldly life.

The *sufferings of householders* refer to relationship problems, financial difficulties, problems with your children, parents, or siblings. You fall in love, but the other person either does not pay enough attention to you or is too possessive. You suffer when there are hindrances to having children, but when you have them, you have other problems. You have so many hopes and aspirations for your children but cannot make them become what you would like. Your children come into this life with their own karmic seeds and tendencies. When you have a child, you have no idea what you are getting. You have the responsibility to give your children love and life skills, but you cannot control what happens to them.

Then there are job problems. You need a job to provide for your family. Your spouse wants you to work more, so the family has more money, or she wants you to work less, so you are at home more. You strive for financial security, but who do you know who feels completely financially secure?

The analogy of *parents slain by their own cherished children* is poignant. It refers to the disappointment we experience when our great expectations fall flat. We believe that material possessions, family, success at work, and physical comforts will bring us happiness, yet even when we have them, something in our hearts is still not peaceful. Fulfillment eludes us.

The remedy to this is to *renounce worldly life.* This could mean renouncing mundane life and taking monastic ordination, which is often called "leaving the householder life and entering the homeless life." Or it could mean that your mind—no matter if you are a lay practitioner or a monastic—relinquishes the attachments of a householder to family, money, possessions, job, house, and so forth and turns toward nirvana. Instead of focusing on the happiness of this life or even a good rebirth in cyclic existence, you aspire for liberation or full awakening. Sometimes we may think we have given up attachment, when a small event shows us we have not. For example, many of us may say, "I'm not attached to my shoes." But if we go outside and our shoes are gone, we discover we are actually attached to them! We're angry that they're gone and want them back.

Taking the five lay precepts or monastic precepts provides structure and discipline that sets parameters on how far we can go in acting out our attachment. It puts us face-to-face with our craving, because we may want to do something, but previously we reflected on the situation and voluntarily took a precept saying we will not act or speak in a certain manner. Our precepts are like a burglar alarm saying, "The thief of attachment or anger is trying to steal your joy and your virtue!" We then apply the Dharma antidote to subdue that affliction, so it doesn't lead us into misery.

7 Seize the Enemy

IDENTIFYING SELF-GRASPING IGNORANCE
AND THE SELF-CENTERED ATTITUDE

48

Since these are the facts, I have seized the enemy.
I've caught the thief who steals and deceives with stealth.
Aha! It is indeed self-grasping, without doubt,
The charlatan who deceives me, disguised as myself.

HAVING MEDITATED ON the previous verses and seen that every unfortunate or painful situation we've experienced is the result of our own misguided actions motivated by afflictions and rooted in ignorance, we are now clear who the enemy is that continuously harms us. This *thief who steals* our happiness and virtue while all the time harming us is none other than self-grasping. This ignorance is not content with persons and phenomena existing dependently, but projects a false mode of existence onto them, grasping them as having their own nature, existing from their own side, under their own power, independent of everything else. It is indeed a *charlatan who deceives* us for it makes us believe that what doesn't exist—inherent existence—does exist, and blindly we follow its deception.

Recognizing self-grasping and its henchman, self-centeredness, as the causes of all our misery is not easy. They are like high government officials who duplicitously work for the enemy. They do a lot of harm and go totally unnoticed. We think they are on our side, while all the time they are working against us. Similarly, since beginningless time, self-grasping and self-centeredness have deceived and cheated us, pretending to be our friends while actually harming us. But now we have come to our senses and exposed them for the culprits they are.

These two are so insidious because they are *disguised as myself.* That is, we think that they are us and fear that if we give them up, we will be no one. However, by examining the situation with wisdom, we will see that counteracting these culprits will not destroy either our existence or our happiness. In fact, our lives will be more peaceful and beneficial for self and others.

Due to the kindness of the Buddha and our spiritual mentors, we have seen the truth. For countless lifetimes, we have been wandering in cyclic existence, following whatever impulsive thought came into our mind, unable to discern wholesome from unwholesome thoughts and actions. It is only because we have met a spiritual mentor who has kindly opened our eyes to the Buddha's teachings that we have been able to correctly identify the source of all our pain and misery.

While many people have been kind to us in our lives—our parents, teachers, friends, and health-care professionals—none of them have been able to lead us out of cyclic existence. The kindness shown to us by our spiritual mentors and the Three Jewels is peerless, for they lead us on the way to actual joy and freedom. Seeing this, our hearts fill with gratitude. For this reason we sometimes see our own teachers pause and wipe their eyes while teaching: they are remembering the kindness of their teachers and the Three Jewels.

49
Now, O Yamantaka, raise the weapon of action and
Spin the wheel three times fiercely above your head.
Your legs—the two truths—spread apart and eyes of method and
    wisdom wide open,
With the fangs of the four powers bared, strike the enemy!

Dharmarakshita was a practitioner of Yamantaka, a fierce-looking meditational deity whose name means "Destroyer of the Lord of Death."

Yama has three meanings. The outer yama is death, which stops our life. The inner yama is the afflictions, which make us take rebirth in cyclic existence without choice. The secret yama is the latencies of ignorance and the subtle dualistic perception through which things still appear to be inherently existent although they are not. Yamantaka destroys all three, enabling us to attain buddhahood.

Yamantaka has a provisional aspect and a definitive aspect. The definitive aspect is the wisdom of nondual bliss and emptiness—the realization possessed by all the buddhas and arya tantric yogis. This wisdom manifests in the form of a fierce deity, who is the provisional aspect, in order to communicate with us.

How does Yamantaka communicate with us? One way is through the symbolism of his body. *Your legs—the two truths—spread apart* refers to conventional and ultimate truths. Conventional truths are all objects we see around us, while ultimate truth is their actual mode of existence. Conventional truths appear to exist inherently, but in fact they are dependent arisings, and their actual mode of existence is empty of inherent existence. A person, who arises dependent on other factors, is a conventional truth; that person's lack of inherent existence is an ultimate truth. Both of these are inseparably there on the basis of the person. If the person did not exist, the emptiness of that person would not exist. If the emptiness of the person did not exist, the person could not exist. When we understand this, we know that the emptiness of true existence is here, right now. The ultimate truth is not somewhere far away. It is the very nature of everything that exists. It is not created by someone else, nor is it something we can know with our senses. It is directly known only to a mental consciousness that is the union of the serenity of deep concentration and the insight that arises through discriminating wisdom.

Yamantaka's *eyes of method and wisdom wide open* represent the method aspect of the path, which includes renunciation, compassion, bodhicitta, and all the practices, such as generosity, that accumulate merit. The wisdom aspect is the wisdom directly and nonconceptually realizing emptiness.

To gain such exalted realizations, we first need to purify our mind. This is accomplished *with the fangs of the four powers bared.* These four opponent powers, explained above, are regret for our destructive actions, taking refuge in the Three Jewels and generating bodhicitta to restore our relationship with those we harmed, making a determination not to do that action in the future, and engaging in some remedial action. By cultivating all of these qualities symbolized by Yamantaka's body, we will attain his enlightened state.

Raise the weapon of action refers to the four actions of pacifying negativities, increasing merit, influencing others to guide them on the correct path, and forcefully destroying hindrances. We request Yamantaka to employ whichever of these methods will be most effective to lead us on the path. *Spin the wheel three times fiercely above your head* indicates our aspiration to realize (1) conventional bodhicitta, the aspiration to attain full awakening in order to benefit all sentient beings; (2) ultimate bodhicitta, the wisdom directly realizing emptiness, and (3) the union of the two, which occurs at buddhahood.

50

The king of spells who confounds the enemy's mind:
Summon this precept-breaker who betrays self and others—
This savage called the self-grasping demon—
Who, while brandishing the weapon of karma,
Runs uncontrollably in the jungle of cyclic existence.

Somebody may appear compassionate but cheat us, whereas someone who regards us with kindness corrects our faults. Nevertheless, we ignorantly regard the latter as an enemy. In this case, Yamantaka is wrathful, yet he benefits us, whereas the lord of death smiles and butchers our life. Instead of fearing these fierce-looking deities, we should see them as our friends.

Here we are calling out to both the provisional and definitive forms of Yamantaka and expressing our wish to do away with our self-preoccupation and self-grasping that make us transgress our precepts and and sabotage the happiness of ourselves and others. We want to stop the demon of self-grasping that makes us create the polluted karma that binds us to cyclic existence. This enemy who chases us from the lowest hell realm to the peak of cyclic existence, *brandishing the weapon of karma,* is self-grasping ignorance, manifesting as Yama, the lord of death. Yamantaka—the union of method and wisdom that we seek to actualize in our minds—is the destroyer of the three yamas.

51

Summon him, summon him, wrathful Yamantaka!
Strike him, strike him; pierce the heart of this enemy, the self!
Dance and trample on the head of this betrayer, false conception!
Mortally strike at the heart of this butcher and enemy, the self!

Here, the repetition of *summon him, summon him* and *strike him, strike him* indicates the two bodhicittas. Conventional bodhicitta counteracts self-preoccupation, and ultimate bodhicitta demolishes the ignorance grasping inherent existence.

The enemy, the self does not refer to the conventional self, which exists by merely being designated in dependence upon the five aggregates. It refers to self-grasping and self-centeredness, which are the heart of the enemy.

I love the line *dance and trample on the head of this betrayer, false conception!* Picture the betrayer, false conception (our self-grasping, confused thoughts, wrong conceptions, attachment, anger, and other afflictions), manifesting in the form of the lord of death, and Yamantaka (the essence of bodhicitta and profound wisdom) joyfully dancing and trampling on his head! Another translation of this phrase is *roar and thunder,* which gives us the image of Yamantaka furiously roaring and thundering at our internal enemies. Nothing can stand up and show its head in the face of the wisdom that destroys all false conceptions.

Then we call out to our wisdom and bodhicitta manifesting as Yamantaka, to *mortally strike at the heart of this butcher and enemy, the self!* We're saying, "Enough of cyclic existence! Enough selfishness!" We want the genuine freedom that comes with knowing reality and having compassion for all sentient beings.

52

Hum! Hum! O great meditation deity! Display your
miraculous powers!
Dza! Dza! Bind this enemy tightly.
Phat! Phat! Release us from all bondage.
Shik! Shik! Cut the knot of grasping.

Here, too, the repetition of the syllables symbolizes conventional and ultimate bodhicitta. *Hum* is the "seed syllable" representing Yamantaka's wisdom mind, the subtlest clear-light mind that realizes emptiness directly. Here we invoke Yamantaka's perfect wisdom to *display his miraculous powers*—the four actions mentioned above.

Dza! Dza! means to bind or to tie, in this case the enemies of self-centeredness and self-grasping, so they can never escape from wisdom and bodhicitta. *Phat! Phat!* means to destroy the bondage of our self-grasping and self-preoccupation. We want freedom—not the freedom to follow our afflictions that we have in worldly life, but the true freedom that comes from a mind saturated with wisdom and compassion. *Shik! Shik!* Let's cut out the nonsense of our wrong conceptions and self-centeredness once and for all!

53

Appear before me, O Yamantaka, my meditation deity!
Tear it! Tear it! Rip it to shreds this very instant—
The sack of karma and the five poisonous afflictions
That mire me in karma's samsaric mud.

We again call out to *Yamantaka, our meditation deity,* who not only is the manifestation of the wisdom and bodhicitta of all the buddhas, but also symbolizes our future bodhicitta and wisdom. We request him to demolish our polluted karma and the *five poisonous afflictions,* which are hindrances to generating concentration: attachment to sense objects, malice, dullness and drowsiness, remorse and restlessness, and doubt. In a tantric context, the five afflictions are attachment, anger, ignorance, jealousy, and arrogance or miserliness. Under the influence of these afflictions we gather a huge *sack of {destructive} karma.* Even when we create virtuous karma, it is still polluted by grasping at inherent existence.

We may have noble aspirations, but we face so many hindrances. Why? Our destructive karma ripens, manifesting as any of the difficulties—true duhkha, the first noble truth—mentioned in the above verses. The five hindrances—included in the second noble truth of true origins—interfere with our ability to cultivate serenity and single-pointed concentration. Even though we want to purify our karma and counteract our afflictions, they themselves make this difficult. Here we ask Yamantaka, representing the last two noble truths—true cessations and the true paths—to tear these to shreds.

8   Dance and Trample

OVERCOMING THE INTERNAL ENEMIES

54

Even though it leads me to misery in the three lower realms,
I do not learn to fear it but rush toward its source.
Dance and trample on the head of this betrayer, false conception!
Mortally strike at the heart of this butcher and enemy, the self!

BEGINNING WITH THIS verse and going through verse 89, Dharmarakshita points out the contradictory and distorted ways of thinking and behaving that we fall prey to under the influence of self-grasping and self-centeredness. Each verse then concludes with the refrain of the last two lines. I find these verses especially powerful because they show that although we want happiness, under the influence of afflictions and self-preoccupation we create the causes for the opposite. Clearly illustrating beyond a doubt how these two sabotage our welfare, these verses activate us to change. Note the heartfelt calling out to Yamantaka for guidance and inspiration in the last two lines.

It is good to pause at this point to understand the evolution of all the situations described in the upcoming section of *The Wheel of Sharp Weapons*. All of our poor behavior and the difficulties we face due to it occur because we are in cyclic existence (samsara). Cyclic existence is not a place, so freeing ourselves from it doesn't involve moving to another universe. Cyclic existence is the body and mind that we live with twenty-four hours a day, seven days a week, this body and mind that we took under the influence of ignorance, afflictions, and karma. The reason we try to practice the Dharma in every moment is that we are in the unsatisfactory state of cyclic existence every moment. We can get a day off from work, but we cannot get a day off from cyclic existence. As long as cyclic existence is present, Dharma practice has to be present as well. Otherwise our situation will degenerate further, for the Dharma is what holds us back or protects us from suffering and unsatisfactory circumstances.

We need to relate the notion of cyclic existence to our lives. When we experience physical pain—which all of us dislike—it is not that physical pain is something unusual that should not be happening. Physical pain occurs because we took a body that is susceptible to illness and injury. Similarly, when we are mentally unhappy, it is not an aberrant situation. Mental unhappiness occurs because we have minds that are under the influence of ignorance, afflictions, and karma. Karma—our actions—originate in our mental afflictions, and these, in turn, are rooted in the fundamental ignorance that misapprehends how we and all phenomena exist. Believing everything exists inherently, under its own power, and as a self-enclosed entity that does not depend on any other factors, we assume that we are an independent being living in an objectively existent external world. From the perspective of this erroneous view, our task in life is to navigate our way through this world in such a way that we can get as much happiness as possible and protect ourselves from anything that endangers our well-being.

However, when we begin to scratch the surface and investigate this worldview, we see that it is created on a false basis. There is a body and a mind, but there is no findable person or self either in the body and mind or separate from them. Rather, in dependence upon the combination of the body and mind, the person, I, is imputed. We use "I" as a convention, so we can say, "I'm walking," instead of, "This temporarily conjoined body and mind is walking down the street." We exist by being merely conceived and designated "I," even though we mistakenly believe that there is a real, findable, independent person here.

This mistaken notion of an independent "I" is the source of our cyclic existence and all the problems we experience in it. We create so many identities that have to do with this "I": "I am this gender, race, nationality, socioeconomic class, religion, political party, education level, age, health, sexual orientation, and ethnicity." Of course, not everybody knows our identity or treats us in the way we believe we should be treated. We get upset: "Who do you think you are, acting like that to me?"

People in each culture have different ideas about manners and how people are to be treated. All these are created by the mind. When someone's behavior contradicts our society's idea of good manners, we are offended. Interpersonally, we have different ideas of how to deal with conflict. We want to talk about it; the other person believes it's better to leave certain things unsaid. We like to scream; the other person does not. Thus, in addition to the original disagreement, we now have the compounded problem of not agreeing on how to communicate with each other.

Here we see one concept building on another one, which is constructed on another one, and so on. Instead of seeing that things such as identities, manners, and good communication styles depend on conceptions our mind invented, we think they are completely true. Our conceptions of who we are, how others should treat us, who we should be, and what others think we should be imprison us. Yet they are all simply fabricated by our minds!

Based on these imputations and projections—the chief of which is grasping the I as inherently existent—we become attached to whatever gives us pleasure and angry at whatever interferes with it. To protect and pamper this I, we engage in many actions that harm others and thus ourselves as well: we steal to get what we want, talk behind the back of anyone who threatens our happiness, speak harshly to those we don't like or disagree with, and lie to conceal our misdeeds or to trick others into giving us what we want. At the time of death, depending on which of these karmas ripen, we are then attracted to different life-forms, and rebirth occurs once again.

Each time we read the refrain of each verse, we should remember this. Then, saying *Dance and trample on the head of this betrayer, false conception! Mortally strike at the heart of this butcher and enemy, the self!* will move our hearts and strengthen our determination to attain true freedom.

Returning to this specific verse, Dharmarakshita points out that under the influence of self-centeredness and self-grasping, we kill, steal, and lie. We hurt others by using our sexuality in unwise and unkind ways, talk behind others' backs, and are difficult to get along with because we always want to have our way. Although our deepest wish is for happiness, these behaviors *lead us to misery in the three lower realms.* Blind to the evolution of our difficulties, instead of cutting this chain of events, we *rush toward its source* by complaining, blaming, and becoming more self-centered.

One of the prisoners I correspond with became aware of this process operating in himself. He has a pattern of being so attached to his body, possessions, and reputation that he would become terrified whenever any of these were threatened. The fear made him angry, irrational, and violent, which led to the actions that landed him in prison on a murder charge. Discovering how these afflictions have caused him suffering made him aware of their danger, and he developed a "wise fear" of them. Now, he told me, he is "afraid" of breaking his precepts because he knows how easily his mind can be overwhelmed by distorted thoughts and emotions. As much as possible, he stays away from situations of confrontation where his mind could get pushed into this irrational mode that triggers violent behavior. In addition, he meditates on patience and fortitude.

I admire his ability to shift from self-centered fear for his own well-being to wise fear of his angry, violent behavior and the destructive karmic seeds it leaves on his mind. He is much more aware of his thoughts and behavior now and practices restraining them. To do this, I recommended that in his meditation practice, he look back on situations where his mind became irrational and violent and observe the specific and habitual way of interpreting such situations that triggered these emotions. Then, he should look in the book *Working with Anger* and practice at least one of the ways the Buddha taught to interpret those kinds of situations so that anger doesn't arise. I also suggested he contemplate antidotes to attachment as well, because anger arises when our attachment can't get what it wants. When we can let go of attachment, anger won't arise.

The last two lines call out to Yamantaka and reaffirm our determination to destroy self-grasping and self-centeredness. The *heart* is self-grasping ignorance; the *butcher* is self-centered thought. Together, they make us revolve in cyclic existence repeatedly and prevent us from actualizing our spiritual potential and attaining full awakening.

55

Though my wish for happiness is great, I do not gather its causes;
Though I have little endurance for pain, I am rife with the dark
*   craving of greed.*
Dance and trample on the head of this betrayer, false conception!
Mortally strike at the heart of this butcher and enemy, the self!

Each sentient being wants happiness. The first thought we have when we wake up, the thought we carry with us all day and even while we sleep, is, "How can I be happy?" However, do we create merit— constructive actions undertaken with a wholesome motivation—which is the cause for happiness? Although we often speak as if we believe in karma and its effects, we do not always act as if we do. Rather, we put our effort into arranging people and situations so that they'll make us happy. Similarly, we put great energy into avoiding what we dislike. In the process of doing this, we often don't stop to reflect on our motivation or to evaluate how our actions affect the people and environment around us. Thinking the causes for happiness are external to ourselves, we ignore the role our minds play in creating our experiences.

One way to create merit is by abstaining from the ten destructive pathways of actions. Taking and keeping precepts helps us to do this. Whenever we are not actively breaking a precept, we are automatically creating merit by keeping it. Merit is also created by doing the opposite of the ten destructive pathways of action and by practicing the six perfections—generosity, ethical conduct, fortitude, joyous effort, meditative stability, and wisdom.

While we want happiness, we often create the causes for pain. We are *rife with the dark craving of greed*—wanting this, craving that, never being satisfied with anything—yet we *have little endurance for pain*. We have no ability to endure any discomfort at all, including the "unpleasantness" of restraining our craving and greed. Our slogan is "I want what I want when I want it!" We expect the universe to comply, and our sense of entitlement prevents us from realizing that we need to create the karmic causes. For example, generosity is the cause of wealth. Ethical conduct is the cause of good rebirths. Subduing our anger and generating fortitude are the causes of an attractive appearance. But in our ignorance, we neglect to create these karmic causes and instead try to get the most and best for ourselves or our loved ones, ignoring the effects of our actions on those around us and dumping our anger and frustration on whomever happens to be around.

Not only do we lack endurance for pain, we don't like even the smallest discomfort or inconvenience. Wake up early to meditate? Offer the best food to the Three Jewels? Endure painful knees while meditating? Travel to go hear teachings? Donate to temples, monasteries, Dharma centers, or social-welfare organizations? That infringes on what the self-centered mind wants. However, we are willing to endure hardship to make money, to be with the people we like, and to climb the ladder of status and success. For worldly purposes we don't mind getting up early, working later, going without sleep, skipping meals, having tight shoulders, or missing social events.

All of us have a kind heart; we like to be generous, and we care about how our actions affect others. However, self-grasping and self-centeredness prevent us from acting according to these values. To express our determination to stop these culprits, we request Yamantaka for energy and inspiration: *Dance and trample on the head of this betrayer, false conception! Mortally strike at the heart of this butcher and enemy, the self!*

56

Though I want immediate results, my efforts to achieve them are feeble.
Though I pursue many tasks, I never complete a single one.
Dance and trample on the head of this betrayer, false conception!
Mortally strike at the heart of this butcher and enemy, the self!

We have high expectations of *immediate results,* both in our Dharma practice and our careers, but our *efforts to achieve them are feeble,* and we prefer to lounge around, procrastinate, or wait for someone else to do the work. We study a little and expect to understand all of the Buddha's teachings quickly. We hope that by doing a one-week retreat, we'll emerge with visions of deities or experiences of bliss and oneness. We want a raise and a more important position at our job but don't want to work hard. We expect good things to come our way without having to make much effort to earn them.

We *pursue many tasks,* volunteering to do this or that but don't *complete a single one.* We rush to get involved with interesting sounding projects without examining if we have the skills and time to carry them through to completion. Sometimes we accept the responsibility for a task but get bored part way through and stop, without informing the people who are expecting us to do the task. We don't ask for help, but wait for another person to finish it for us. Or we shrug our shoulders and expect someone else to bail us of our predicament.

In our Dharma practice, we start to study one topic but switch to another after a few weeks. Many Dharma books sit on our bookshelves half read. We begin this practice, but when it isn't producing any glitter in our meditation, we change to another. We promise our spiritual mentors to do certain tasks, take a lot of their time asking for copious advice, but back out shortly thereafter, having done hardly anything.

These verses are a good tool for self-examination. As uncomfortable as it may be for us to see in ourselves the behaviors and attitudes described here, we ask ourselves, "What is the mechanism that makes this happen?" It is definitely self-grasping ignorance and self-centered thought. Then we do more in-depth research: "How is my self-centered thought manifesting in this way? What's the pattern here, and how does it play out in other aspects of my life?" Wanting to change our bad habits, we investigate: "The next time I start to get into this pattern, how can I catch it when it's still small? How else could I think so that I don't continuously repeat the same foolish behavior?" Then we come up with a plan that we put into effect whenever we notice a specific unproductive emotion or behavior.

57

Though I am eager to make new friends, my loyalty and friendships are short-lived.

Though I aspire for resources, I seek them through theft and extortion.
Dance and trample on the head of this betrayer, false conception!
Mortally strike at the heart of this butcher and enemy, the self!

Although we want new friends who are exciting, interesting, and fun to be with, do we make the effort to cultivate sound, enduring friendships? Do we get to know people well before forming committed relationships with them? Or do we impetuously make commitments that we renege on later? When people show kindness to us or benefit us, do we feel a sense of loyalty toward them and wish to repay their kindness? Or do we take their kindness for granted?

Initially most people seem exciting because we do not know them. However, getting to know people on a deeper level, accepting their faults, and letting go of our unrealistic expectations of them is more difficult. It is also more rewarding. Learning to forgive others, encourage their talents, and yet avoid unhealthy dependency is challenging, but these friendships will last a long time and weather many circumstances.

Some people form one relationship after another with different spiritual mentors, ignoring the Dharma instructions of the previous one. Other people check out the qualities of spiritual mentors carefully before forming teacher-student relationships, and carefully put the teachings into practice. Even if these people do not live near their spiritual mentors, they still feel close to them and will continue to practice daily and to assist their spiritual mentors. More stable in their Dharma practice, these people progress steadily on the path.

It is helpful to ask ourselves: What are qualities that I look for in people that I want as friends? How can I be a good friend to others? Being loyal to friends is important, but that loyalty must be healthy. For example, thinking, "I'll stick up for my friends no matter what," is not necessarily a wise attitude. If our friend makes a mistake, lying to cover it up doesn't benefit our friend. The prisoners I work with tell me that the code of conduct in prison is that you stick by your homeys whether they are right or wrong. This mentality breeds gangs with a skewed sense of loyalty.

Though I aspire for resources, I seek them through theft and extortion. We eagerly consume others' gifts and are happy to accept their hospitality and freeload off them. If we cannot get the things that we want in a legitimate way, we make friends with people who get them for us in circuitous ways. Motivated by greed, we look for get-rich-quick schemes or manipulate others, all the while pretending to be their friend. Having lost our personal integrity and consideration for others, we plough ahead thinking only of our own success.

At the end of the day, we have to live with ourselves. How do we feel about ourselves when our egotistical, selfish mind has deceived others or used them for our own benefit? We don't feel good; our self-respect plunges. The way to feel good about ourselves is to treat others with respect and fairness. Seeing this, we request Yamantaka to roar and thunder *on the head of this betrayer, false conception.*

58
Though skilled at flattery and innuendo, my discontent runs deep.
Though assiduously amassing wealth, I am chained by miserliness.
Dance and trample on the head of this betrayer, false conception!
Mortally strike at the heart of this butcher and enemy, the self!

One factor in the noble eightfold path, the path leading to nirvana, is right livelihood. For lay practitioners this means earning our living in a way that does not harm others. This excludes, for example, making or selling weapons, poisons, pornography, and intoxicants, as well as overcharging or lying to customers and clients, cooking the books, and so forth.

Traditionally, monastics do not work for pay and rely on offerings given to them. *Flattery and innuendo* refer to the five wrong livelihoods, inappropriate ways in which monastics receive their requisites—food, clothing, shelter, and medicine. Lay practitioners may also engage in these five.

We *flatter* people with the motivation that they will like us and will give us something. Rather than speaking in a straightforward way, we *hint,* "The socks you gave me last year were so warm, but now they have holes in them, and winter is coming." We *give a small gift to get a bigger one,* making the other person feel obliged to give us something in return. With *coercion* we put people in positions where they cannot say no. "Everybody else has offered a hundred dollars to the Dharma center. How much do you wish to donate?" Acting with hypocrisy, we pretend to be a great Dharma practitioner—a true renunciate with deep compassion—so that people will give us offerings. But when the benefactors are not around, we get up late, neglect our daily practice, and watch movies all day.

Despite our conniving, our *discontent runs deep.* No matter what we talk people into doing for us, it's never enough. We complain, "I practice and work so hard, but I can't get this and that." This mind always hungers for things and accuses others of interfering with our getting what we want.

On the other hand, we *assiduously amass wealth,* and while we're happy to show off our possessions, we don't want to share them. Fearing not having what we need if we give things away, our mind remains *chained by miserliness* in a state of anxiety no matter how much we have. Financial security is a state of mind, not an amount of money in the bank. Due to our stinginess, we continuously feel poor, although we may have much more than others in the world.

When I lived in India, an old Tibetan nun and her sister invited me to their earthen-floor hut. The walls were made of rocks, and the roof was cut-up tins. They made tea on a kerosene stove and shared some of their *kaptse*—Tibetan fried bread. Although they were dirt poor, they were generous and content. When I returned from India, I stayed with two friends who lived in a two-bedroom apartment with a full kitchen, TV, and lots of furniture. Driving in their car on the way to a nice restaurant, they told me how poor they were. Poverty is indeed a mental state.

59

Though rarely rendering help to others, I remain most boastful.
Though unwilling to take risks, I am bloated with ambition.
Dance and trample on the head of this betrayer, false conception!
Mortally strike at the heart of this butcher and enemy, the self!

Blowing our trumpet loudly and proclaiming our benevolence and generosity, we promise a lot but deliver little. After contributing a little effort to a group project, we claim all the credit for ourselves. Arrogance and conceit make us immune to the feelings of others as we pride ourselves on our great knowledge and reputation, even though we've done little of substance.

Being able to evaluate ourselves accurately and fairly is a skill that needs to be developed. While avoiding bragging and boasting, we also don't need to hide our skills or deprecate ourselves. We can discuss our good qualities and accomplishments when necessary without embellishing them and then use our talents and abilities to benefit others.

When we help someone, rather than being puffed up with pride, it's good to reflect, "I'm practicing the bodhisattva path and have taken the bodhisattva vow, so I'm only doing what I promised to do. I'm grateful for the opportunity to do this." In that way, we avoid arrogance and at the same time rejoice in our virtue.

Some people are *bloated with ambition* yet do nothing to actualize their aims. *Unwilling to take risks,* they give up before they've even tried. Other people aren't necessarily ambitious but are full of new and exciting ideas. They take a few steps to implement these ideas and then forget about them because they either get distracted or discouraged. In both cases there was a lot of talk and no action. Others begin to lose faith in these people, but they remain convinced that their next new idea will be a great success.

Some people misinterpret the Buddha's teachings and think that all goals and plans are bad because we're supposed to remain in the present moment without thinking about the future. Wanting to "go with the flow," they don't initiate anything and wait for things to happen. This is not the meaning of 'being in the present moment," an expression meant to steer us away from getting lost in fantasies of attachment or anger about the past and future. However, this doesn't mean we should never think about the past or the future. We have to look at our past and see how it has conditioned us, so we can change the conditioning and purify past mistakes. We can think of the future and direct our energies and aspirations in a positive direction.

Someone once asked me if Buddhist practitioners have ambition. I said, "Yes, we want to be free from cyclic existence. We want to attain full awakening for the benefit of other beings." Of course, the selfishness and ruthlessness that are sometimes associated with worldly ambition don't help us in actualizing our Dharma aims, but wisdom and joyous effort do.

How do we *mortally strike at the heart of this butcher and enemy*, self-grasping and self-centeredness? Realizing emptiness and generating bodhicitta are our "virtuous weapons of mass destruction" that we drop on this inner enemy.

60

*Though I have many teachers, my capacity to observe precepts
   remains weak;
Though I have many students, my patience and wish to help are scant.
Dance and trample on the head of this betrayer, false conception!
Mortally strike at the heart of this butcher and enemy, the self!*

This verse deals with our relationships with our spiritual mentors and spiritual students. Although our teachers teach us well with wisdom, skillful means, and compassion, we don't make much effort to practice their advice. We are happy to take the five precepts, monastic ordination, bodhisattva ethical restrains, and tantric commitments, but we don't keep them very well. Transgressing them often, we go back to our teachers and renew them, and then break them again.

We're not expected to keep our precepts, pledges, and commitments perfectly—if we were able to do this, we wouldn't need to take them. However, it is important to learn what constitutes a transgression and then act within those limits. After all, we assumed these precepts voluntarily; no one forced us to take them. Our precepts and commitments are the root of our future progress on the path. Only on the foundation of pure ethical conduct will we be able to gain higher realizations.

Some spiritual mentors are very charismatic and *have many students* even though they lack knowledge and lack a broad understanding of the Dharma. Others may have knowledge, but their motivation for teaching is stained with the eight worldly concerns: they seek a good reputation, offerings, fame, and a group of dedicated students to surround them and sing their praises. However, their *patience and wish to help are scant.*

Dharma teachers need great patience and fortitude because students' minds are unruly and they make lots of mistakes. Students also call you at all hours, wanting your attention; they interrupt you when you are meditating, come to you sobbing, and repeatedly ask you a question that you've answered many times before. They project their authority issues on you, complain that you don't give them enough personal attention, or say that you are pushing them too hard. Without a stable Dharma practice that has continued for years, it is easy to get fed up and angry with students, which damages everyone involved. The student-teacher relationship is special, and there are commitments on both sides. Being in the role of a spiritual mentor requires great fortitude and a sincere wish to help others.

Many people tell me they want to be Dharma teachers. While it is wonderful to have the aspiration to share the Dharma with others, this aspiration must be accompanied by knowledge, compassion, and especially humility. First and foremost, we are Dharma students. Our prime duty and responsibility is to learn and practice the Dharma. If we don't do that, how can we even think of teaching others?

We are Dharma students from now until we attain full awakening. Thinking of ourselves as Dharma teachers can be dangerous. That is a role we play only temporarily. His Holiness the Dalai Lama says that he sees himself not as a Dharma teacher, but as an older brother sharing what he knows with others. If His Holiness doesn't say, "I am a spiritual mentor," it seems rather strange that those of us who have only 1 percent of his qualities—if that much—would say we are.

If we share the Dharma with others, it is crucial to remain under the guidance of our own teachers and to maintain a strong relationship with them. Our spiritual mentors will correct and instruct us, and we relate to them with humility. People who teach the Dharma but are not under the guidance of their teacher or do not have a close relationship with a teacher can easily go astray. Guiding others is a great responsibility. Misleading others on the path creates great destructive karma for the teacher and damages the students' faith in the Three Jewels, making it difficult for them to meet the Dharma again for many lifetimes. Therefore it's essential to be modest and cautious when we are in the role of teaching the Dharma.

Whether in our relationships with our teachers, students, or others, as Dharma practitioners we must always cultivate a sense of humility and genuine care for others. We should try not to be the powerful person who controls everything. Nor should we arrogantly think that we're as competent and realized as our own spiritual mentors.

61

Though eager to make promises, I remain weak in actual help.
Though my fame may be great, when I am probed, even gods and ghosts are appalled.
Dance and trample on the head of this betrayer, false conception!
Mortally strike at the heart of this butcher and enemy, the self!

The first line reiterates some of the previous points, putting us face-to-face with our tendency to *make promises* but not come through with what we said we would do. This behavior makes it difficult for others to trust us, because our words and actions aren't harmonious. Our *fame may be great,* but *even gods and ghosts are appalled* because we don't follow the advice we give others. Neglecting to practice what we preach, we make ourselves into hypocrites, which is repugnant even to gods and ghosts.

His Holiness the Dalai Lama always warns *tulkus* (those who have been recognized as an incarnation of a previous great master), "Don't coast along depending on your title and the reputation of your past life. Practice earnestly so you deserve the position you have been given." In other words, if you have a title, see it as an honor to live up to, not as an entitlement for free favors.

People in positions of power or authority have great responsibility to set a good example for everyone else. Effective leaders lead by example. Their lives correspond with the instructions they give others, and that inspires others to become the best people they can be. That doesn't mean leaders must be perfect or infallible. They err, as does everyone else, but when they do, they admit it and make amends. Our world is longing for true leaders who are exemplars of clear thinking and compassion. That is why people such as Nelson Mandela, Archbishop Desmond Tutu, Mother Teresa, His Holiness the Dalai Lama, and Dharma Master Cheng Yen are highly revered. But when leaders betray the trust of the people they are supposed to be serving, it breeds only disappointment and cynicism in the public. This, in turn, causes ethical conduct to decline in society in general, a condition that creates more suffering for everyone. The actions of one person can have extraordinary good effects or devastating bad ones. It is our choice.

Dharmarakshita does not pull any punches or let us off the hook. As parents, neighbors, clergy, businesspeople, politicians—whatever roles we play—let us realize the effects of our actions on others and restrain self-centered, inappropriate, or harmful behavior. Let us rise up to our human potential, so our good qualities will shine and bring benefit to all.

62
Though I am weak in learning, my penchant for empty words is great.
Though slight in scriptural knowledge, I meddle in all kinds of topics.
Dance and trample on the head of this betrayer, false conception!
Mortally strike at the heart of this butcher and enemy, the self!

Some of us have only studied the sutras and great commentaries a little, or maybe not at all, but we love to talk about the Dharma, especially when we can be the "chai shop guru." In Asia, a few Westerners who have attended a meditation course sit in the tea shops and preach to other Western travelers who haven't attended a course. They are *weak in learning,* but having heard terminology such as "clear-light mind," "union of bliss and emptiness," "the subject and object becomes one taste," they talk about these advanced and subtle concepts as if they were experts. Their *penchant for empty words is great.*

Similarly, some people are *slight in scriptural knowledge* either because they don't make the effort to study or they jump from one topic to another, from one book to another, and so don't learn anything in depth. They ask, "What is the difference between *dzogchen* or *mahamudra?*" when they haven't yet understood what taking refuge in the Three Jewels entails. This is sad; these people mean well, but their arrogance is making them waste their own and others' time.

Some newcomers say, "Why do I need to study? It's just a lot of words and intellectual concepts. I want to experience the nature of mind." They cite the story about the great yogi Milarepa scolding some learned scholars, telling them to stop studying and debating so much and to do more meditation. However, Milarepa was not telling them all their knowledge was useless. Speaking to a group of people who had spent years learning the sutras and treatises, he was saying that having intellectual knowledge is not the same as having deep experience and realization of the meaning. In other words, it would benefit them to do more meditation on what they have learned.

It is important to study the sutras and commentaries; otherwise, we don't understand how to meditate. If learning isn't important, why did the Buddha spend forty-five years teaching the Dharma?

Other people misunderstand the teachings and then practice incorrectly. This is a disadvantage of *meddling in all kinds of topics.* For example, some Buddhist meditation masters say, "Stop the flow of thoughts," and people mistakenly think they should sit there with a blank mind. They may develop the ability to concentrate on nothing, but what good does that do? Cows don't think much, but they aren't enlightened! The meaning of "stop your thoughts" is to stop the distracting thoughts that wander to past pleasures and failures and daydream about future desires. Stop the worry, anxiety, and attachment that ruminate about worldly concerns. On the basis of a calm mind, cultivate concentration and wisdom understanding reality.

63

Though I have many friends and servants, none have dedication.
Though I may have many leaders, I have no guardian I can rely on.
Dance and trample on the head of this betrayer, false conception!
Mortally strike at the heart of this butcher and enemy, the self!

This verse speaks about who we can rely on when we need help. We may have many friends (people we view as equals) or many employees, students, followers, servants, or children (people we see as juniors). But when we need help, none of these people step forward. We may also have parents, teachers, a boss, employer, or leaders—people who are in high positions who we believe should help us—but here, too, they don't protect us.

When this happens, we usually either get angry at the people we expect to aid us and blame them for being so unreliable and selfish, or we think others have unfairly abandoned us and feel sorry for ourselves. But when we look deeper, what is the karmic reason we are bereft of help when in need? To answer this, we must ask ourselves, "Do I step up when others need help, or do I make excuses why I can't be there for them?"

We have many opportunities to reach out and help others daily—passing the ketchup, making a cup of tea for a colleague, picking up a friend's child from school, doing an errand for an elderly neighbor, helping someone stranded on the highway to change a tire. These are small things that are easy to do, but when our self-preoccupied mind is in control, we feel too important, stressed, or busy to help. When we can't bring ourselves to overcome our self-centeredness regarding such small things, it's unreasonable to think that others will help us when we are in great need. Once again, we find the culprit is our self-centered thought that is quite happy to take from others, but not happy to give.

64

Though my status may be high, my good qualities remain less than a ghost's.
Though I may be a great teacher, my afflictions remain worse than a demon's.
Dance and trample on the head of this betrayer, false conception!
Mortally strike at the heart of this butcher and enemy, the self!

We may be well-respected because we have a high rank or title, but lack the qualities someone of that status should have. This may be because we advanced through the ranks through manipulation, deception, or by relying on family connections, friends, or wealth. Unfortunately, there are people in our society today who hold respectable positions as bankers, politicians, priests, or doctors whose ethical conduct is *worse than a ghost's*. Having an inflated sense of themselves, they misuse their authority or harm others, yet believe no one will find out, and if they do, their stature will protect them from those accusations.

We may be *a great teacher* because we studied hard and are charismatic, but our *afflictions remain worse than a demon's* because we have not put what we have learned into practice. The scriptures contain descriptions of the qualities students should look for in prospective Dharma teachers, and none of these mention charisma. Nevertheless, some people are enchanted by others' charm, good looks, witty stories, and seeming compassion. They spoil that person by doting on him, praising him, and building a high seat for him to sit on. Here, the students' actions contribute to the person's degeneration: the students yearn to adore a perfect idol and elevate an unqualified person to a position he is not equipped for. Jetsun Milarepa said that in this time of degeneration, people who are sincere practitioners are ignored, while people who are hypocrites or charlatans are exalted and become famous.

In other cases, people elevate themselves. This is evident in countries where Buddhism is still comparatively new and students don't know what qualities to look for in spiritual mentors. His Holiness the Dalai Lama comments that some people are unknown in the Tibetan community, but in the West they adopt great titles. Alternatively, some people have studied the Dharma only a little and claim to have realizations. In this way, unqualified people come to be regarded as great teachers.

People in the position of being called a "Dharma teacher" should be scrupulous in terms of ethical conduct and must not allow students to make them into idols or treat them as if they were royalty. All of us should study and practice diligently and avoid accepting positions of prestige when we lack the corresponding qualities.

Some people ask, "Why doesn't anybody say they have realizations? Why doesn't anyone show us miraculous powers? That way we would know they are genuine practitioners." First, having miraculous powers is not necessarily a sign that somebody is spiritually realized. Someone may have some type of clairvoyant powers due to karma. Other people, including non-Buddhist meditators, may have attained samadhi, but still lack wisdom and bodhicitta. Just having miraculous powers through karma or samadhi does not mean that someone will never be reborn in the lower realms or is free from cyclic existence. If someone proudly lets it be known that he or she has realizations, look out for your wallet!

Secondly, if people displayed magical powers, most people would be so captivated that they would worship those people instead of listening to their teachings and practicing. They would mistakenly think that the purpose of Dharma practice is to gain magical powers and would seek these, instead of cultivating the spiritual realizations that liberate them from cyclic existence.

His Holiness the Dalai Lama is an excellent example of a genuine Dharma practitioner. Although many people ask him if he is really Chenrezig, the buddha of compassion, he always replies, "I'm a simple Buddhist monk, nothing more. I work hard at my practice." He says, "I get a little bit of feeling for emptiness once in a while, but bodhicitta is much more difficult." You can tell through His Holiness's behavior the kind of practitioner he is—he keeps his precepts and commitments well. He is not greedy, angry, or jealous and greets everyone with friendliness. His compassion and wisdom are evident when you hear him teach.

65

Though my views may be lofty, my deeds are worse than a dog's.
Though my good qualities may be numerous, their basis is lost to
the winds.
Dance and trample on the head of this betrayer, false conception!
Mortally strike at the heart of this butcher and enemy, the self!

We may be well versed on the positions of the various Buddhist philosophical tenet systems and, of these, assert the *lofty* views of the highest system, Prasangika Madhyamaka, and yet our daily life behavior is *worse than a dog's.* While we may intellectually be able to identify the object of negation in the meditation on emptiness and know the arguments that refute it, we may not be able to identify that false sense of I in our own experience. As a result, self-grasping ignorance continues to run the show. Similarly we may know all the terminology and concepts concerning dzogchen, mahamudra, the nondifferentiation of of samsara and nirvana, and the wisdom of bliss and emptiness, and even be able to teach them, but because we haven't integrated even the basic Buddhist concepts into our lives, we continue to lie, use our sexuality unwisely and unkindly, and be condescending toward others. Our *good qualities*—here meaning knowledge of how to do rituals, lead chanting, make *tormas,* and recite many scriptures from memory—*may be numerous,* but their basis, ethical conduct and treating others with kindness and respect, *is lost to the winds.*

This occurs because our false conceptions—especially grasping inherent existence—and our self-centered conceptions are leading us astray. Perhaps we were lazy and were content with intellectual knowledge but neglected to apply the correct view to our own false sense of self and negate it. Alternatively, lacking the correct view of emptiness, we may have resorted to reciting high-sounding phrases—such as "Since everything is empty, there is no good and no bad"—and used them as reasons to behave recklessly. While in meditative equipoise on emptiness conventional things such as good and bad do not appear, on the conventional level in our daily life, they exist and function.

Virtuous deeds bring happiness, and nonvirtuous ones bring suffering. This is true no matter how profound one's spiritual realizations are. People who have the correct view of emptiness respect the functioning of the law of karma and its effects even more because they understand that the emptiness of inherent existence and dependent arising—as exemplified by the law of karma and its effects—come to the same point. In other words, the absence of inherent or independent existence does not mean total nonexistence. On the conventional level, things still exist and function dependent on each other. The realization of emptiness doesn't negate the fact that sprouts grow from seeds and happiness comes from wholesome actions. Understanding this, yogis take great care with their physical, verbal, and mental actions.

Lama Atisha, one of the Indian scholar-practitioners who brought Buddhism to Tibet in the eleventh century, is an excellent example of this. Whenever he had the smallest infraction of a tantric precept—which the rest of us break like rainfall—he would immediately confess it. Apparently, while traveling, if he had a negative thought, he would immediately stop, take a stupa (a Buddhist monument) out from his luggage, repent, and do prostrations to purify.

When doing meditation retreat, Kyabje Zopa Rinpoche seldom takes breaks. I heard that one time his attendant saw him out walking. Surprised, he asked Rinpoche what happened, and Rinpoche responded, "This is just a short break. I had a negative thought, so I'm going to start the retreat all over." This is a genuine practitioner.

While highly realized tantric yogis may behave in unconventional ways, their motivation is always compassionate, never self-seeking or confused. For these yogis who have realized the lack of inherent existence, sipping orange juice, imbibing alcohol, and drinking urine are the same. Those claiming high realizations as a reason for their unusual behavior should take a "taste test" and show the rest of us that they can do this!

Many of us take tantric empowerments even though we have not yet accomplished the prerequisites of stable renunciation, heartfelt bodhicitta, and at least an inferential realization of emptiness. Therefore, the emphasis of our practice must remain on cultivating these three principal aspects of the path. We do our best to keep our tantric precepts and commitments that our tantric master gave at the time of the empowerment. In this way we plant seeds in our mindstream so that when we become more qualified practitioners, we will meet and be able to practice tantra. However, now we should meditate principally on the stages of the path to awakening (*lamrim*) and thought training (*lojong*) in order to build the proper foundation for tantric practice.

Realizing emptiness is a gradual process. Initially we have the wrong view, believing that everything exists inherently, from its own side. After hearing teachings on emptiness, we generate doubt, thinking maybe things exist inherently and maybe they don't. With more study and reflection, we then progress to have a correct assumption, believing that phenomena don't exist inherently, but without completely ascertaining the reason for this. We continue to study and contemplate until we have a correct inferential understanding of emptiness, when the impact of things lacking inherent existence really hits us. This realization is incontrovertible, even though it is still conceptual. By continuing to contemplate and meditate, we gain a direct, nonconceptual realization of the emptiness of inherent existence. However, we must still familiarize ourselves with the direct perception of emptiness over time so that it can gradually eradicate every defilement on our mindstream, including the appearance of inherent existence that still occurs when we aren't in meditative equipoise on emptiness. Finally, when all stains are purified and all good qualities brought to fruition, we arrive at the state of full awakening, buddhahood.

Every unusual experience we experience in meditation is not indicative of realizing emptiness or bodhicitta. If we think, "It felt like my body dissolved. That must be a realization of emptiness. Now I won't get angry anymore!" we'll be sorely disappointed. It's best to think, "That was a strong experience. I need to check with my teacher and make sure it was a correct experience." If your teacher validates that you are on the right track, feel encouraged and invigorated, increase your faith, and continue to practice. It's best to discuss such experiences only with your spiritual mentors and perhaps very close Dharma friends. Talking about them widely dilutes their force and could serve to increase arrogance, thus creating more obstacles in your practice. In addition, don't cling to the experience and try to recreate it; that makes meditation more difficult.

Vajrayana (tantric practice) is done on the basis of the teachings in Theravada and general Mahayana. In the West, people often talk about Theravada, Mahayana, and Vajrayana as if they were three different types of Buddhism, unrelated to each other. That is incorrect. Vajrayana is a branch of Mahayana, not a separate tradition. Mahayana itself is practiced on the basis of Theravada practices—the four truths of the aryas, the noble eightfold path, and three higher trainings—but instead of seeking to become an *arhat,* Mahayana practitioners have the motivation to become a buddha in order to benefit all sentient beings.

9 — Integrity and Responsibility

66

I harbor all my self-centered desires deep within
And blame others for all my disputes for no reason.
Dance and trample on the head of this betrayer, false conception!
Mortally strike at the heart of this butcher and enemy, the self!

ALTHOUGH WE CREATE an air of confidence and the appearance of being successful and in control, we *harbor all our self-centered desires deep within.* Our attachment and anger are well nourished and protected beneath the veneer of being calm and knowledgeable. We may have difficulty with desire but don't want to admit it in front of others, especially when we want to make a good impression on them. Sometimes it's even difficult to admit to ourselves—"Every moment of my life, my focus is on what benefits me"—even though it's the truth.

Similarly, we blame others for our problems. Whenever there is a dispute, we insist on being right, even when we know we aren't. We must win every argument, and our ideas must prevail in every discussion. We push until the other person is tired of arguing and capitulates, and then pride ourselves on being smart and convincing them of our rightness. We are so intent on being right or on winning that we'll even sacrifice the well-being of those we care about, leaving them feeling humiliated and resentful. Unhappy, they aren't gracious or loving toward us afterward. Puzzled at their change of heart, we don't see that we're the one who dug the trench we're sitting in. In this verse Dharmarakshita urges us not only to be more honest with ourselves, but to put effort into cleaning up the mess self-centered thought makes inside our mind.

While we tell newcomers to the Dharma that our mind is the creator of our experiences, we strongly maintain that our personal enemies exist objectively. But just a little examination reveals the opposite: When people don't do what *I* want them to do, they are mean, ignorant, and worthy of scorn. On the other hand, when they do what *I* want them to do, they are wise, kind, and talented. We create friends and enemies by judging how people relate to *me*, the center of the universe!

Sometimes we project our faults onto others and then blame them for being so selfish. Other times, we get angry with them and accuse them of misdeeds as a way to release our inner tension. The other person often does not understand why we are angry, and we don't bother to explain. We just expect them to apologize and ask our forgiveness.

At the time we die, do we want to be thinking about this or that dispute? As we're taking our last breaths, will it matter who was right? We'll have long forgotten the argument, and winning it will be meaningless to us at the time of death. But the destructive karma we created through attachment and anger will remain on our minds. It will influence how we die and what our future rebirth will be. It obscures our mind, impeding us from realizing the nature of reality. Seeing this, while we're healthy and can still practice, let's call on the mind of wisdom and compassion manifesting as Yamantaka to *dance and trample on the head of this betrayer, false conception! Mortally strike at the heart of this butcher and enemy, the self!*

67
Though clad in saffron robes, I seek protection from ghosts.
Though I have taken precepts, my conduct is that of a demon.
Dance and trample on the head of this betrayer, false conception!
Mortally strike at the heart of this butcher and enemy, the self!

Those *clad in saffron robes* are the monastics—the fully ordained ones (*bhiksu, bhiksuni*), trainees (*siksamana*), and novices (*sramanera, sramanerika*). Having taken refuge in the Buddha, Dharma, and Sangha, we devote our lives to Dharma study and practice. However, instead of relying on these Three Jewels, we *seek protection from ghosts.* The buddhas are completely free from all defilements and have developed all good qualities limitlessly. Their sole purpose is to lead us out of duhkha and to full awakening, and they have the wisdom, compassion, and power to do this. The Dharma is twofold: the realizations of the path—especially the wisdom directly realizing emptiness—and the true cessations they bring about. The sangha consists of those who have realized emptiness directly. The Three Jewels are definitely reliable guides, so ignoring their guidance and following the advice of spirits and ghosts, who are stuck in cyclic existence just like us, is counterproductive and foolish.

When the Buddha and our spiritual mentors caution us about engaging in harmful actions because they lead to sickness and other suffering results, we nod our head but don't take the advice seriously. Similarly, when the Buddha advises us to do purification practices to stop the ripening of karma, we say, "Yeah, yeah," and promptly forget. But when a fortune-teller tells us that we'll get sick this year and we better do some strong purification, we jump up and are eager to follow those instructions. This is because our refuge in the Three Jewels is not sincere, and we value the advice of spirits and fortune-tellers more than the advice of the omniscient ones.

Along the same line, although we *have taken precepts*—the five lay precepts or one of the monastic ordinations—we don't take these commitments seriously and act opposite to them, making our *conduct like that of a demon.* For example, we take a precept not to take intoxicants, but when we are with family or old friends who are drinking, we rationalize, "If I don't drink, they'll think I'm puritanical and will think badly of Buddhism. They'll feel so much more relaxed if I drink. So I'll drink with compassion for them, so they won't think badly about Buddhism."

It's important to remember that we take precepts and commitments voluntarily. No one forces us to do so. Also, we take them because we have thought carefully about our behavior and about the law of karma and its effects and understood with wisdom and clarity that we want to avoid certain actions because they bring suffering to ourselves and others. To then ignore our own wisdom and compromise our word by acting inappropriately is self-sabotaging.

Many of the prisoners I work with tell me that when they were young, they got carried away with attachment or anger and never considered the effects of their actions. They only thought about what felt good in that moment. Being in prison has made them reflect on the circumstances that led up to their crime, and they have realized they have to change; otherwise, their resentment, greed, or jealousy will continue to ruin their lives now and in the future. Seeing those drawbacks of following their afflictions, they develop a strong determination to cultivate compassion and to not follow every impulse that arises in their minds.

68

Though the {Buddhist} deities bestow happiness on me, I propitiate malevolent spirits.
Though the Dharma guides me, I deceive the Three Jewels.
Dance and trample on the head of this betrayer, false conception!
Mortally strike at the heart of this butcher and enemy, the self!

The *Buddhist deities* are buddhas and bodhisattvas such as Chenrezig, Tara, Manjushri, Yamantaka, and so on. Although they are a reliable refuge that will not lead us astray, we turn our backs on them, and instead of meditating on them, we *propitiate malevolent spirits.* Although *the Dharma guides* us and all happiness comes from implementing the Dharma teachings in our lives, we *deceive the Three Jewels* by ignoring their advice, not revealing our negativities, and lying to our spiritual mentors. Although we may appear clever, we are only deceiving ourselves. Self-grasping and self-centeredness are making us cut our lifeline to happiness and peace.

Propitiating malevolent spirits could mean following the eight worldly concerns: trying to make a quick buck, cheating on our partner, feeding our addiction to video games and texting, and spending our time creating alternate personalities in online games. It could also mean taking refuge in evil spirits and making offerings to them in order to attain our worldly aims.

Instead of having the short-term view that seeks only my happiness now and giving in to these harmful habits, we need to cultivate a long-term view seeking the peace and joy of full awakening for all living beings. This happiness goes beyond sensual pleasures and is derived through purifying our minds and accessing our buddha-nature.

Given that the Three Jewels are our real refuge, you might wonder why the Central Tibetan Administration, the Tibetan government-in-exile, seeks the advice of the Nechung oracle. In the Tibetan view, the universe is populated not only by human beings and animals, but also by spirits, demons, and celestial beings who play an active role in influencing human affairs. In this regard, Nechung plays a unique role in Tibetan culture and has a long history. When Buddhism first arrived in Tibet, there were many hindrances from spirits. The Tibetans requested Padmasambhava, a great Indian yogi, to come to Tibet to subdue these demons. Padmasambhava not only subdued the spirits, but made them promise to protect the Dharma. One group of five spirits or deities, collectively known as "Nechung," made a promise to support the Dharma in Tibet and protect practitioners. As time went on, Nechung became a protector of the Tibetan government and of His Holiness the Dalai Lama. The Tibetan government and some monasteries consult Nechung on important worldly issues, and Nechung gives them practical advice. They do not take refuge in Nechung to the exclusion of the Three Jewels.

In all these verses, Dharmarakshita publicly exposes our faults. He does this not to pick on us, embarrass us, or make us defensive and miserable. He does this so we can become convinced of the defects of ignorance and self-centeredness and work to eliminate them from our mindstream. His is a kind of "tough love," a form of compassion used to help us change.

69

Though always living in solitude, I am swept away by distractions.
Though receiving sublime Dharma scriptures, I cherish divination
*   and shamanism.*
Dance and trample on the head of this betrayer, false conception!
Mortally strike at the heart of this butcher and enemy, the self!

We may *live in solitude*—here meaning either in a monastery or in a retreat situation—a place which is ideal for study and practice, but we get distracted by other activities. We are *swept away by distractions* and run around keeping ourselves extremely busy. For instance, we may spend a lot of time creating the perfect situation for meditation, building a retreat cabin with everything we could ever need. But then we get distracted by getting involved in the affairs of our friends and relatives and never enter retreat.

For this reason, people whose self-discipline is weak are encouraged to do group retreat, where there is a shared daily schedule and common discipline that everybody follows. The support of the group helps us stay on course. Everyone relies on everyone else to be there for all the meditation sessions, and each of us makes sure we attend for the sake of the others. If someone is missing, the group will check and see what's happening, giving aid if the person is ill or offering support if he or she is having a hard time. Building community in this way is very helpful to us on an emotional level, as well as an aid to our practice.

Although we hear teachings from *sublime Dharma scriptures* in a direct lineage from the Buddha, instead of cherishing this rare fortune, we spend our time and energy on *divination and shamanism*. Divinations and shamanistic practices were in Tibet before Buddhism came, and they remain popular. While some people find them helpful, and doing these practices doesn't interfere with their refuge in the Three Jewels, other people get very distracted by them to the extent that their refuge in the Buddha, Dharma, and Sangha is adversely affected.

Most divinations, horoscopes, and pujas to stop spirit interferences have been influenced by Buddhist beliefs and Buddhist culture. Many lay people request monastics to do these services; while they bring income to the monasteries, they can become a distraction to serious study and practice. In one country where I've gone several times to teach basic Buddhist topics, people tell me that among the Tibetan practitioners who visit there I'm the only one who does not do a lot of rituals. All the others do elaborate pujas and empowerments, complete with bells, drums, trumpets, deep chanting, big hats, and blessed water. The lay people who make large donations when they request these rituals feel that they are receiving a huge blessing. It seems that the more elaborate the ritual and the less they understand what is happening in it, the greater the blessing they feel they receive.

The Western version of getting distracted by divination and shamanism is becoming fascinated with New Age philosophies, crystals, astrology, tarot cards, and opening our third eye. Alternatively, some people become mesmerized by playing the stock market or trading currencies. We may talk about Dharma, future lives, liberation, and full awakening, but we live according to what will immediately benefit our present lives. Actually looking at our own minds and changing them is much more arduous than going to a psychic or tarot reader or following the latest fad that will supposedly cure our dissatisfaction. Staying focused on the path to awakening takes great effort and concentration. If attaining buddhahood were easy, all of us surely would have become enlightened by now. Therefore, let's develop faith based on reasoning and through wisdom remain focused on the path.

70

Forsaking ethical discipline, the path to liberation, I cling to my household.
Casting my happiness into the river, I chase after misery.
Dance and trample on the head of this betrayer, false conception!
Mortally strike at the heart of this butcher and enemy, the self!

For a lay practitioner, *clinging to your household* refers to being overly attached to your possessions, family, social status, and so on in a way that makes you *forsake ethical discipline* and get involved in unwholesome actions. For example, due to being attached to family and friends and wanting to enjoy certain experiences with them, people may act in ways opposite to precepts or engage in the ten unwholesome paths of action in order to obtain what will make their family happy.

There is great benefit to taking and keeping precepts, be they the five lay precepts or monastic precepts. When we take precepts, we establish a strong intention of how we want to behave, and when we act that way, living in accord with our precepts, we create great merit or constructive karma that will bear good results. Each moment we are not breaking a precept, we are accumulating the good karma of intentionally abandoning certain actions. For example, two people are having a conversation, and one has the precept not to kill while the other does not. Neither one of them is killing at the moment, but the person with the precept creates the good karma of abandoning killing, while the person who hasn't taken that precept does not. Furthermore, keeping precepts interferes with the karmic tendency to do the same destructive actions repeatedly.

The five lay precepts and monastic precepts regulate physical and verbal actions, so keeping them helps us become more mindful and aware of what we say and do. Mindfulness remembers our precepts and how we want to act and speak; introspective awareness monitors our body and speech to make sure we are doing that. This, in turn, makes us more mindful and aware of what we are thinking and feeling, because our mind must form an intention before we speak or act. This mindfulness and introspective awareness developed by living in ethical conduct help us develop the mindfulness and introspective awareness that are crucial to cultivating concentration. Stable concentration improves our meditation and enables our wisdom to grow to the point where it can penetrate the nature of reality. Thus our practice of the three higher trainings—the path leading to liberation from cyclic existence—proceeds well.

Monastics have many more precepts, so they are able to create more good karma and purify their negativities more strongly. Monastic life also removes a lot of distractions and provides external circumstances that are conducive for Dharma practice. Without a spouse and children to support, monastics don't need to work a job, worry about mortgage payments, or be concerned about their children's education and behavior.

When somebody disrobes because they want to have an intimate emotional and sexual relationship, children, wealth, and a comfortable life, it is said that, *casting their happiness into the river, they chase after misery.* Why does Dharmarakshita see a lay life as one of misery? People get married expecting to remain happily married, but for many people that is not what happens. Couples quarrel; they break up; they get hurt and hurt others. Even for those who have good relationships, inevitably one of them dies. Loved ones cannot stay together forever.

People also believe that children will bring them happiness. When the children are infants, parents are sleep deprived because they must get up in the middle of the night to feed them. Toddlers demand, "I want this! I want that!" When they become teenagers, they prefer video games to talking to their parents. They want the car keys but don't want to be told what time to be home.

You have to work hard to get money, but it goes quickly, and credit card debt follows. During the day, you face problems at work. You want to practice Dharma, but your day is full of activities, and when you get home in the evening, you're exhausted.

This verse also comments on situations where monastics live and act like laypeople. Some Western monastics do not have money or a place to live because there are very few monasteries in Western countries, so they must go to work to cover their rent and food. This situation is stressful for someone who ordained with the wish to delve deeply into the Dharma. In Asia, where monastics have monasteries and good circumstances to practice, sometimes their minds seek desirable objects, and they prefer to go to the city and do business. Instead of staying in a monastery, they choose to live on their own, and more often than not, their ethical conduct declines. Confusion, anger, and attachment proliferate in their minds as they create more and more causes for misery. Dharmarakshita warns us against the temptation to do this.

71
Forsaking the gateway to liberation, I wander in wilderness.
Though obtaining a precious human life, I seek the hell realms.
Dance and trample on the head of this betrayer, false conception!
Mortally strike at the heart of this butcher and enemy, the self!

This verse is similar to the previous one. *Wilderness* refers to places that lack Dharma teachers, teachings, and a supportive Dharma community. We may have a good situation for dharma practice at the moment, but attachment pops into our mind, and we begin seeking fun or adventure, relinquishing conducive circumstances to purify our mind, accumulate merit, and plant the seeds of the realization of the stages of the path to awakening in our minds. Perhaps we are bored and want some excitement; perhaps we feel our practice isn't getting anywhere, and we'd like to do something thrilling. Maybe we have doubt about the practice and path. In any case, we choose the excitement of cyclic existence over going through the difficulties of subduing our afflictions in order to attain the peace of liberation. Of course, we don't describe it that way to ourselves. We use other words so that our bad choices appear to be wise.

Whoever we were in previous lives accumulated a huge amount of merit that resulted in our *obtaining a precious human life,* but getting distracted we use our lives to create the causes that ripen in hellish rebirths. Our worldly affairs keep us so busy that we lack time to do purification practice, check our motivation, or even making offerings to the Three Jewels. Although we still hold the wish to get back to our Dharma practice, we get immersed in office politics, make deductions on our income tax that aren't quite legal, and flirt with others' spouses.

The meditation on precious human life comes at the beginning of the stages of the path so that we will appreciate our opportunity and use it wisely. Understanding the meaning of being trapped in cyclic existence boosts our meditation on precious human life, for we understand how difficult it is to have our present conducive circumstances, and we see that it is all too easy to let this life go by without making an effort to progress on the path. However, after we have done the meditation on precious human life a lot, we come to treasure the opportunities our present life offers and don't want to waste our time on the eight worldly concerns. Instead, we want to dedicate our lives to purifying and transforming our minds, cultivating the heart of loving compassion, and investigating the ultimate nature of reality. By resetting our life's priorities in this way and following through, we will have a good rebirth that can act as the basis for continuing to practice the Dharma. By creating the causes for a series of fortunate rebirths, we will be able to generate bodhicitta and the wisdom realizing emptiness and eventually attain full awakening.

Some people become very self-critical after they recognize their tendencies to spend time immersed in the eight worldly concerns. Other people criticize people whom they deem "insincere in the spiritual path." Judging ourselves or others simply creates more negativity. The path isn't about being better than others. The Buddha certainly didn't teach the Dharma so that we would use it to make ourselves feel inadequate or to scorn others. Instead, let's cultivate compassion for ourselves and others, and criticize the self-centered thought that deprives us of the opportunity for awakening. Noticing our own mistakes, we regret them but do not feel guilty or get stuck in self-loathing. Instead, we make a strong determination to set wise priorities in the future and to live according to our values.

72

Putting aside spiritual developments, I pursue the profits of trade.
Leaving my teacher's classroom behind, I roam through towns
  and places.
Dance and trample on the head of this betrayer, false conception!
Mortally strike at the heart of this butcher and enemy, the self!

Imagine somebody who has the opportunity to study the Dharma with excellent spiritual mentors and to do meditation retreats but would much rather engage in business and make money. It takes so much constructive karma to meet a fully qualified Mahayana and Vajrayana spiritual mentor. This person has met such a mentor but doesn't take advantage of this rare opportunity because he is enticed by the prospect of worldly wealth and the pleasure, status, and power it brings. He cheats, lies, and backbites to get money, and then, drowning in conceit, he becomes miserly and doesn't share it. He doesn't realize that worldly wealth is transient; we aren't sure to have it our entire life, and even if we do, at the time of death we'll definitely have to separate from it. Everything we worked so hard to obtain stays here while our mindstream continues on to the next life, taking with it the imprints of the actions we did to procure and protect this wealth.

Leaving our teacher, we travel the world, looking for riches, adventure, or love. When I ordained in 1977 at age twenty-six, I regarded with envy the young Himalayan and Tibetan boys who were monks. While I had spent my first twenty-four years creating destructive karma almost nonstop, they had met the Dharma as children, ordained, and were able to memorize texts, attend religious ceremonies, and listen to teachings. Ten years later, these young boys had become teenagers and young adults. Enamored with the glitter of consumer products, many of them had disrobed in order to sell sweaters in Mumbai. "How could they do this?" I wondered. They had so many good conditions that I lacked—they spoke Tibetan and could read the Dharma texts; they could talk directly to the respected teachers; they didn't have visa problems; and they had a monastery to live in. How could they give up the Dharma in order to get the consumer items that I had given up to go live in India and Nepal? Why would they jump at the opportunity to wash dishes in a New York restaurant, leaving their spiritual mentors and Dharma opportunities to do so? It has to do with previously created karma, as well as their present way of thinking. Dharmarakshita points out that the false conception of an inherently existent self and self-centered thought are the chief culprits.

73
Forsaking my own livelihood, I rob others of their resources.
Squandering my own inherited wealth, I plunder from others.
Dance and trample on the head of this betrayer, false conception!
Mortally strike at the heart of this butcher and enemy, the self!

Instead of working and being responsible for maintaining ourselves, we *forsake our own livelihood* and live by deceiving and conning others. *Robbing others of their resources* does not necessarily mean we break into someone's home and rob them at gunpoint. It can also mean we cunningly manipulate people to give us things. On top of that, we hoard what we have and leech from others, asking for more.

Alternatively, our relatives or friends sacrificed and worked hard to earn a living. With love and wanting us to be secure, they bequeathed us their wealth when they died. But unappreciative and reckless, we squander the inheritance so that at the end we live by *plundering from others.* One prisoner I corresponded with told me he spent seventy-three thousand dollars of an inheritance in a year while he was incarcerated, frittering it away on snacks at the commissary and buying illegal drugs inside the prison. I am blunt with inmates and censured him for not respecting the love his family had for him. It is important to use an inheritance wisely and to create merit by making offerings to the Three Jewels and donations to charities. We then dedicate this merit for the deceased person and pray for him or her to have a fortunate rebirth, to meet the Dharma, and to have all the conducive conditions to practice it.

Robbing others of their resources and *plundering from others* also includes depriving the sangha of offerings. For example, when somebody wants to make an offering to the monastic community, you say, "They won't use it. Give it to me instead." We monastics create a transgression if a benefactor has the intention to give an offering for a particular purpose and we use it for another, or if the benefactor makes the offering to the community and we either take it for ourselves or give it to our friend.

We have to be very careful with things offered to and owned by the sangha, as it is difficult to purify stealing from the monastic community. This applies to monastics as well as lay people. The person keeping the accounts for a monastery must be meticulous and above board about income and expenditures. Caring for Sangha property or finances is a big responsibility, because these people are striving for awakening. If we misuse their property, we interfere with their ability to progress on the path and thus impede all other sentient beings from receiving the benefit of their subduing their minds and enriching their excellent qualities.

74

Alas, though my endurance for meditation is poor, I have sharp clairvoyance.
Though I have not even reached the edge of the path, my legs are needlessly fast.
Dance and trample on the head of this betrayer, false conception!
Mortally strike at the heart of this butcher and enemy, the self!

It's rather absurd to think that when our *endurance for meditation is poor,* we will *have sharp clairvoyance,* because unless it is a case of having supernormal powers due to past karma, such abilities depend on single-pointed concentration. Nevertheless, some people arrogantly claim such abilities, and others mistakenly believe they have powers they do not have. The *vinaya*—the texts on monastic discipline—contains specific instructions in this regard. Even if someone has supernormal powers, that person is not permitted to announce this to others. If someone does not have such powers, yet deceptively claims to, he or she transgresses a root precept and no longer is a monastic.

On the Buddhist path, clairvoyance and other special powers are considered secondary attainments. They are not the purpose of the path. Single-pointed concentration is instrumental in cultivating the core of the path—bodhicitta and wisdom—for without the ability to focus consistently on the object of meditation, these realizations will be unstable. Bodhisattvas cultivate psychic powers in order to be able to benefit others more effectively. For example, knowing who they have close karmic connections with due to previous lives' interactions enables bodhisattvas to lead those individuals with greater ease.

Similarly, *although we have not even reached the edge of the {bodhisattva} path*—which is feeling spontaneous bodhicitta when encountering any sentient being—it is ludicrous to think we have attained the supernormal power of *fast legs* that allows someone to travel quickly through the sky. Even if we attained such supernormal powers by cultivating concentration, without great compassion, there is the risk that we would misuse such powers for egotistical means, harming ourselves or others in the process. This verse makes fun of people who do not have the right priorities on the spiritual path and put on airs of having supernormal powers.

75
*When someone gives me useful advice, I view them with hostility
 as a foe.
When someone fools me with treachery, I repay the heartless one
 with kindness.*

Dance and trample on the head of this betrayer, false conception!
Mortally strike at the heart of this butcher and enemy, the self!

There is a Tibetan saying that words given with care and concern are never pleasant. To prevent us from going down the wrong road, friends give us *useful advice* because they can see things about us or the situation that we are blind to. How do we respond? Seeing them *as a foe,* we get defensive and defiantly tell them to mind their own business.

For example, someone has a substance abuse problem. Relatives tell him, "Your substance use is interfering with your family and your job. You want to be happy, and this problem is making you lose everything that is important to you, including your self-esteem. Will you consider going to treatment?" But the person cannot hear it. He says, "I'm not an addict! I use it recreationally just like everybody else. You do it too! Get off my back!"

This happens among Dharma practitioners as well. A Dharma friend tries to give us useful advice—for example, reminding us to keep the precepts—and we become hostile, glare at him or her, and turn our back. For this reason, some monastic precepts stress the importance of listening to admonition. When the community confronts us with our own corrupt behavior, we are penalized if we respond by accusing the community of having partiality, hatred, fear, and ignorance.

On the other hand, somebody may try to use us or get something out of us, and because he or she flatters us and is kind to us, we allow ourselves to be deceived. Later, when we wake up to this conniving, we blame the person for taking advantage of us, when it is actually our attachment to praise and reputation that made us suckers. As long as someone treats us nicely and boosts our ego, we will disregard her unethical actions and deceitful behavior toward others. This is foolishness on our part. Again, the responsibility lies with our self-centeredness that makes us so gullible.

You may doubt: "You're blaming yourself when it's that person who is being manipulative." That person may be deceitful and lie to me, but I cannot control another's intention nor their actions. However, I am responsible for my part. As a child, I may have been innocent and trusted someone who was not trustworthy—that is a different case—but now I'm an adult, and it is clearly my attachment to praise and affection that is making me bite the hook. If I were wiser, I would not look to other people to make me feel good about myself. Instead, I would establish a valid sense of self-confidence, believing in my buddha nature. Then I would not be susceptible to others' machinations. I'm not blaming myself for my naïveté, but am taking responsibility for overcoming it.

When we first begin to learn the Dharma, our practice may be a combination of Dharma practice and worldly practice. However, over time it becomes easier to identify our self-centered worldly aims and consciously cultivate a better motivation for all we do. This shift in attitude involves being open to receiving useful advice and not being taken in by another's duplicity.

76

When people treat me as their family, I reveal their secrets to their foes.
When people befriend me with affection, I betray their trust with no
    pangs of conscience.
Dance and trample on the head of this betrayer, false conception!
Mortally strike at the heart of this butcher and enemy, the self!

All of us seek close relationships with people who understand us and whom we can trust. To have such relationships, it is important to honor the confidences people share with us. When others *treat us as their family* and confide in us, we are privileged because they trust us. Perhaps they shared with us something that is difficult for them to say—they felt ashamed of past behavior—or revealed events they do not feel comfortable letting others know. Without any sensitivity to their feelings, we turn around and tell others about their personal life. Word gets around and puts them in a difficult position. Worse still, stories quickly get distorted, so our "small embellishments" of a good story get exaggerated until the story going round is not only embarrassing but also inaccurate. If word reaches their foes, the people who trust us could be severely harmed. Such behavior on our part is disrespectful and unappreciative.

When others *befriend us with affection,* we have the responsibility to repay their kindness. Lacking gratitude, self-preoccupation makes us use them for our own benefit. Betraying others' trust not only sparks their anger, and sometimes fear, but also it also makes it more difficult for them to trust others later on. When word gets out that we revealed others' confidential matters or used them for our own gain, others lose respect and trust in us as well. This will continue into future lives, making it difficult for us to trust others and difficult for them to trust us. Trust is an essential ingredient in fulfilling relationships, which our behavior will deprive us of.

In a reversal of the situation, when somebody tells me something about another person's confidential business, unless it is an extraordinary situation that calls for this information to be revealed, I know that I should not trust that person. Why not? He is likely to blab what I say in confidence. Similarly, if I see someone mistreat someone else, I stay clear of that person, knowing that if I become friendly with her, there's a high likelihood that she will treat me the same way.

There are certain situations where it is necessary to reveal something said in confidence, for example, if you know somebody has committed or is about to commit a crime. In many places, clergy, teachers, or therapists are required by law to reveal this information. It may also happen that someone who is confused or in great pain tells us something in confidence. Because the person is too confused to seek help at that moment, we may have to contact people who can help him or her. In this case, we are acting with compassion for the benefit of our friend.

Sometimes, people in a company, Dharma center, or family are so afraid of exposing secrets or of engaging in divisive speech that nobody will discuss problems. Meanwhile, the situation worsens, endangering others' well-being. The cover-up of sexual abuse in the Catholic church is an example of this. In such situations, with a motivation of kindness for everyone involved—victim and perpetrator alike—we need to make information public in a skillful manner.

77

My ill temper is intense, my paranoia coarser than everyone's.
Hard to befriend, I constantly provoke others' negative traits.
Dance and trample on the head of this betrayer, false conception!
Mortally strike at the heart of this butcher and enemy, the self!

The Tibetan word that is translated as "paranoia" in the first line is *namtok*. We encountered this word previously: it means preconception or superstitious thought that makes up stories. Here, our mind is fabricating the story, "These people are gossiping behind my back," or "They're plotting to do something against me." We become unnecessarily suspicious, anxious, and fearful. Sometimes the suffering caused by anxiety and fear is greater than the suffering of the situation actually occurring.

It has happened to all of us that others are talking, and when we walk into the room, they go silent. Our superstitious thought thinks, "They're talking about me." We don't clarify our assumption because we are sure our interpretation is right. Becoming ill-tempered, we accuse others of having negative thoughts, saying untrue words, or doing harmful actions they have not done. Whatever they say to clarify the issue, we refuse to listen, making ourselves and them miserable. Rather than worry about people gossiping about us, we should be more aware of our gossiping about them.

Another effect of our preconceptions may be our becoming so skeptical and full of doubt that we are paralyzed and cannot act. "Is this happening? Or is that happening? Should I do this or that?" Our *namtok* proliferates, like rabbits in the summer. People feel like they have to walk on eggshells around us, because whatever they say or do, we take it the wrong way. Eventually, people shy away from talking to us because we misinterpret almost everything they say and accuse them of motivations that they do not have.

Our preconceptions stimulate jealousy as well, prompting us to compete with others and overcome them because we're afraid they will control us. Paranoia, doubt, and jealousy make us form cliques with a few people who agree with us, and together we make others the enemy. Whether it is in a family, political party, socially engaged group, Dharma community, office, or sports team, whenever somebody starts creating factions out of paranoia, it becomes unpleasant for everyone involved. People get worked up, making much ado about nothing.

Hard to befriend, we constantly provoke others' negative traits and are a trial to be around. Somebody is friendly, but we're so irritable and constantly in a bad mood that we won't give him or her the time of day. Careless about what we say or do, we treat others like our servants, provoking their anger. Looking out only for what benefits ourselves, we annoy others or make comments that set people against each other. We may ask someone to lie on our behalf, ridicule someone about a sensitive issue, or take someone with a substance abuse problem who is trying to stop to a party where people are drinking and drugging.

Other times, we are fussy and want everything done in the most comfortable way for *me*. "Does meditation have to be at five thirty? I want it at five thirty-five." We always want to be the exception: We need a different bed than everyone else has; otherwise, we can't sleep. The food at the restaurant is cooked too well, so we scold the waiter and send it back. The room is too hot or cold for us, but rather than adjust how much clothing we wear, we insist on the temperature being changed no matter what others want.

Once, at the end of a retreat in Mexico, the participants performed a hilarious skit about a typical meditation session. One person opened the window, and a minute later, another person closed it. A minute after that, someone opened it halfway. One person turned the pages of a book, so another person told him to be quiet, and then a third person made noise looking for paper to write notes telling both of them to be more considerate.

Of course at suitable times, we can voice our needs and preferences, but we should not be so inflexible that we insist that everything must be our way. If it is more convenient for others to do something another way, those of us aspiring to be bodhisattvas and buddhas should adapt. After all, who ever heard of a self-centered bodhisattva?

Our complaining, lying, gossip, and irresponsibility make us *hard to befriend*, even though we want friends. Lacking introspective awareness of our own behavior, we don't understand why others get irritated with us or avoid us. When we ask our family for the umpteenth time for money, even though we spent what they gave us before on frivolous things, we are dumbfounded when they blow up. Our mindless behavior triggers *others' negative traits,* which they don't like any more than we do.

When people voice ideas that we disagree with, instead of feeling threatened, we can give them space to say what they need to say. Sometimes when I hear an idea I disagree with, I panic: "I've got to stop that idea now; if not, we'll go down the wrong path, and everything will be a mess!" However, if we give somebody the space to speak, especially in a group discussion, others may voice their doubts, and that person may come to see that the idea is not feasible. Sometimes, people just need to be heard, and then they drop their opinion. We don't need to immediately and aggressively shoot down every idea we disagree with.

We need to be able to discern when *namtok* arises. Familiarizing ourselves with what self-centeredness and compassion feel like in our mind and body is helpful. To do this, we practice being aware of the "tone" of our mind or the "flavor" or "texture" of various thoughts. We pay attention to our body. Is there a part of our body that tightens or relaxes slightly when a particular emotion manifests in our mind? Cultivating this sensitivity gives us much information about ourselves, and that, in turn, enables us to regulate our thoughts, emotions, and actions.

78

When people ask for favors, I ignore them yet covertly cause them harm.
When someone respects my wishes, I don't concur but seek disputes
* from afar.*
Dance and trample on the head of this betrayer, false conception!
Mortally strike at the heart of this butcher and enemy, the self!

Sometimes, people ask us for help, and we blatantly pretend that we did not hear them, or we use our stash of excuses. The current universal excuse is, "I'm too busy." Of course, we always have time to do the things that we like, but when somebody asks us for a hand and we don't feel like helping, we are definitely too busy. Not only do we ignore people's requests, we also turn around and *cause them harm.* Obnoxious and mean, when people ask for help, we instead cheat them, steal their things, and ruin their relationships.

Even when somebody is nice to us and *respects our wishes,* we are still dissatisfied and stir up conflict. Someone tries to make amends after an argument, but we keep hammering in that we are right and he or she is wrong. Some people thrive on conflict—they feel uncomfortable when a group is harmonious. Perhaps their family life was chaotic when they were children, so whenever they join a group, their automatic tendency is to *seek disputes.* Discord feels more natural to them, but of course others don't like that.

When others ask for advice, they are sincerely trying to gain clarity. Turning on them at that time is unkind. Likewise, if someone is new to a group and relies on us, we should not humiliate or embarrass him or her in front of others, but make the person feel welcome. What does our self-centered thought think it will get out of making others feel bad? Certainly welcoming others and helping them to feel comfortable in a new environment creates the happiness and goodwill that all of us seek.

10   Pain in the Neck

OVERCOMING ATTACHMENT TO PRAISE AND REPUTATION

79
I dislike advice and am always difficult to be with.
I am easily offended, and my grudges are always strong.
Dance and trample on the head of this betrayer, false conception!
Mortally strike at the heart of this butcher and enemy, the self!

WE DON'T LIKE to hear others' *advice and are always difficult to be with.* Any suggestions given to us with compassion are seen as threats to our autonomy or intelligence. Anyone in a position of responsibility is seen as trying to control us. Our authority issues blind us to kindness and lead us to reject the instructions and encouragement we need. We want our independence without the "burden" of being considerate of others.

Our egotism is so strong that small events are interpreted in terms of "I," "me," "my," and "mine." Someone makes an offhand remark, and believing he or she is attacking us, we respond with fury. Our arrogance is so pronounced that we readily misinterpret most innocuous comments as someone denigrating us. Taking everything anyone says personally, we are *easily offended* even though the other person had no intention of insulting us. Our *grudges are always strong,* and we vow to retaliate. And then we wonder why people don't like to be around us!

Easily hurt, we pout and sulk, believing others don't appreciate us. Someone says with affection, "You look sad today. Is something wrong?" We grimace and say, "No, everything is fine," and turn our back on him or her. When problems arise in relationships, rather than work them out, we immediately leave the place, never giving ourselves the chance to learn how to communicate over sensitive issues. It's either my way or the highway.

We don't have to make things into either-or situations: either I push and get my way, or I capitulate and do it someone else's way out of fear that the person won't like me. Instead of dominating others, we can voice our preference without being attached to the outcome. If the group decides to adopt another person's plan, we can go along with the decision because we genuinely care about them, not because we fear their rejection and crave their approval.

Seeing our self-centered thought's antics, it's helpful to learn to laugh at ourselves and not take ourselves so seriously. A sense of humor is crucial for Dharma practice. What our afflictive mind comes up with is funny, isn't it?

80

I crave for high status and regard sublime beings as foes.
Because my lust is strong, I eagerly pursue the young.
Dance and trample on the head of this betrayer, false conception!
Mortally strike at the heart of this butcher and enemy, the self!

Here, Dharmarakshita reveals more of the games that our wrong conception plays. We *crave for high status* and want to be recognized as special in a variety of areas. We want to be rich, good-looking, athletic, artistic, competent, compassionate, intelligent, wise, creative, and the best Dharma student. Plus we want others to know that we excel at our profession and are someone to be respected (and maybe even feared).

Seeking high status, we see others as competitors who may be better than us and want to destroy them, or at least their reputation, lest they become more famous or highly regarded than we are. If we crave to be renowned as a spiritual person with deep insights and abilities, we see *sublime beings as foes* to discredit. Our self-centeredness wants to denigrate others' virtue, realizations, and good qualities because, in doing so, we believe that others will then view us as supreme.

To strengthen our Dharma practice, the attitude to cultivate regarding holy beings—bodhisattvas, our spiritual mentors, and highly realized practitioners—is to rejoice and appreciate their excellent qualities. Humble and receptive in their presence, we want to serve them and learn from them. Quite the opposite here, we see them as enemies and competitors. We become envious of them over disciples and offerings, and instead of seeing them as compassionate guides, we see them as threats to our status.

Such an attitude is poisonous. Acting disrespectfully toward sublime beings, we create destructive karma. Arrogance prevents us from learning from them. Who, then, will we learn from if we disregard wise beings? How will we ever gain Dharma realizations if we're more concerned with reputation and offerings than with wisdom and compassion? With this state of mind, even if the Buddha appeared before us, we would see him as a menace, not someone to take refuge in.

Instead, we should develop the mind that rejoices in others' virtue, good karma, talents, and knowledge. We can rejoice when they have the opportunity to study, do retreat, or run a charity. "Isn't it wonderful that somebody knows more than me? If I were the epitome of Dharma knowledge, the Dharma would be lost in this world because I don't know all the eighty-four thousand teachings of the Buddha. I'm delighted that there are others who are better than I am and who can guide me, because I need support and good role models!" Having this perspective, our mind is open and receptive.

It takes a great deal of strength to work with our arrogance and transform our minds by thinking like this. Our self-centered thought resists it, but as we continue training our minds on a daily basis, changing our attitudes becomes easier.

When we move into the role of being a senior Dharma student or even a teacher, our self-centered thought may proclaim, "I'm not a student anymore. *I'm* a teacher." For this reason, it is essential that we understand that until we attain full awakening we are students. Once in a while, we are in the role of teaching others, but that is a privilege and responsibility, not something to get puffed up about.

Geshe Sopa embodies this beautifully. Every year when his students offer him a long-life puja, one of the students reads a heartfelt praise he wrote about Geshe's qualities as a spiritual mentor. Each year, at the end of the puja, Geshe says, "From the students' viewpoint, it is beneficial for your practice to have respect and regard for your teacher, because that helps your practice. But from my side, it's like an old dog pretending it's a lion." This is a *geshe lharampa*—a teacher of some of the great geshes alive today, who debated with His Holiness the Dalai Lama when he took his geshe exams before fleeing Tibet—who looks at himself this way! That is precisely why he is a great teacher. The rest of us think, "Everybody, notice me! Aren't I wonderful!" although our good qualities are weak. We look so foolish and pathetic tooting our own horn when there is nothing to proclaim.

In addition, our *lust is strong,* and we *eagerly pursue the young.* Although our mind should be focused on benefiting sentient beings and contemplating the emptiness of true existence, it single-pointedly looks for attractive, young sexual partners, eager and trusting Dharma students whom we can deceive and manipulate to fulfill our sexual craving. It's really rather disgusting to see someone with such inverted priorities.

Since we have human bodies and minds under the control of ignorance, we have lust. Sexual thoughts arise, but we do not have to buy into them and dote on them. Sexual conquests are not the purpose of our life. If sex were the ultimate happiness, doing it once should satisfy us forever. We have the responsibility to restrain ourselves from harming anyone due to unwise or unkind sexual behavior. Monastics have a precept of celibacy. If a monastic does not want to keep that precept or is unable to, it's fine to return one's ordination and be a lay practitioner.

To help free us from lust, the Buddha and Shantideva taught the meditations on the ugliness of the body. To counteract the mind that proliferates with sexual fantasies, look closely at the body of the person you are attracted to. Peel away the skin and see the muscles and tissues; then closely examine the bones, spleen, intestines, stomach, and brain. They are disgusting, hardly something we would want to embrace and kiss. If we want to embrace the body, which is just a sack filled with those organs, Shantideva tells us it's cleaner to hug a pillow!

81

Because of fickleness, I cast afar my past friendships.
Infatuated with novelty, I talk animatedly to everyone. .
Dance and trample on the head of this betrayer, false conception!
Mortally strike at the heart of this butcher and enemy, the self!

Cultivating friendships with people who have good values and holding those friendships over a long time is very rewarding. Because these people live ethically and show kindness to others, they inspire us to do the same. Furthermore, because we have known each other for a long time, they can give us helpful feedback. When we make mistakes, they can pull us back; and they will support us when we feel shaky.

Of course when we speak of long-term friendships, it does not mean being friends with just anybody. Before we started practicing the Dharma, we may have gone drinking and drugging, watched porn, or gotten involved in shady business deals with our old friends. As we start practicing the Dharma, our values and activities change, so it is natural to seek new friendships with people who are going in the same direction spiritually that we are. This is not a case of *casting afar past friendships;* it is the process of attuning our friendships to our aspirations and interests.

Casting afar past friendships refers to ignoring good friends because we have self-centered motives and are looking to become close to people who are rich or well-connected and can help us fulfill these base motives. Fickle, we befriend one person after another based on what they can do for us and leave behind anyone who ceases to enhance our reputation, power, and wealth. When we meet someone new, we are *infatuated with novelty* and *talk animatedly,* displaying a great personality to attract others. When people bite the hook, we then use them to make us feel good, and when we tire of them and they no longer serve our purposes, we drop them. This inflicts great pain on others, because they may have developed affection for us, thinking we were one way, while we turned out not to be the image we presented.

One aspect of being *infatuated with novelty* and *talking animatedly to everyone* is trying to impress people with our grandiose ways. We name-drop, pretend to be kind and lovable, buy someone gifts, and make many empty promises. We mislead people to make ourselves look good and appear important. When they see through our act, they will lose faith in us and warn others about us. Therefore, for our own and others' benefit, we should make sure we do not present a false image to others and instead are honest in our relationships and cherish good friends.

Besides creating the causes for lower rebirths, such behavior creates karma to have difficulty in forming and maintaining friendships in future lives when we are born human. At that time, we will be the person who gets used and trampled on. Not wanting to experience that situation ourselves, let's stop causing others to experience it, and be sincere and honest in how we present ourselves to others. This includes acknowledging and talking about our faults and not neglecting old and trusted friends because we have met others who are more tantalizing.

82

Having no clairvoyance, I resort to lies and deception.
Having no compassion, I betray others' trust and cause their
*   hearts pain.*
Dance and trample on the head of this betrayer, false conception!
Mortally strike at the heart of this butcher and enemy, the self!

Like the last verse, this one points out our poor character habits when it comes to relating to others. *Having no clairvoyance,* we pretend to have supernormal powers in order to receive offerings and respect. This happens especially in Asia, where people go to monastics to ask for divinations and make offerings in return. In the West, it may take the form of dropping hints that we are a tulku who hasn't yet been identified or that we've had special meditative experiences. Sometimes this is self-deception, where the person genuinely believes he or she is more spiritually advanced than is the case. Other times, people resort to lies and deception. Projecting an image of having clairvoyant power, someone may receive many offerings and a grand reputation, but in the process hurt others and make a mess of their lives.

Once, the monastics at the abbey were invited to have a table at a New Age fair. On either side of us were psychics. People flocked to the psychics, ignoring us. They would sit, gazing with devotion and interest at the psychics, who then told them this and that about their lives and gave them advice. While the Buddha is the infallible guide who can lead us to lasting happiness, people were much more interested in the psychics, who discussed *their* life, *their* wealth, *their* love life.

Beyond pretending to have clairvoyance, this verse could refer to any type of false advertising, including presenting ourselves falsely as having abilities we do not have. Usually when I mention this, people respond, "But that's what we do at a job interview. If you don't embellish yourself, nobody will hire you!"

If I were hiring people, I would look for those who could also talk about their weaknesses. I am suspicious of people who consistently claim to know everything: such a person will be difficult to work with because he or she will be too proud to ask for help. Someone who says, "These are my talents, and these are the things I don't know much about but am willing to learn," is more honest and will be a better employee. When people are so eager to be hired that they embellish their qualities and abilities, they are likely to wind up with a job that they do not like or that they lack the qualities to do well.

We may lack *compassion, betray others' trust, and cause their hearts pain* in a variety of ways. We lead people on, make them think well of us, and then destroy that trust due to our self-centered ways. Some people have a string of painful, broken relationships behind them due to their lack of consideration for others. We need to take care and be honest and sincere when developing relationships, be they professional, friendly, or Dharma relationships.

If we are in the position of guiding others spiritually, it is especially important to be compassionate and trustworthy. There have been so many accounts of religious leaders who have been either intentionally deceitful or unaware of their problems and have broken trust by abusing children, leading young women on, or exploiting people with wealth. On the side of the teacher, honesty and integrity are important. From the side of the student, knowing the qualities to look for in good spiritual mentors and not getting entranced by glitter are important. We need spiritual mentors who are wise, learned, compassionate, patient, and straightforward in their interactions with people. We do not want to have teachers who superficially are charismatic but are blind to their faults or have an inflated sense of self. Because it is our job to select those whom we want to be our spiritual mentors, we need to go slowly and be smart. Of course, if we wish to have a spiritual mentor with those qualities, we should also cultivate them ourselves and not try to impress our teachers with our wealth, cleverness, connections, or power. Realizing we are bound in the suffering cycle of samsara, we should approach spiritual mentors with receptivity, respect, and interest in the Dharma.

83

Though my learning is feeble, I guess wildly about everything.
Since my scriptural knowledge is scant, I engender wrong views
*   about everything.*
Dance and trample on the head of this betrayer, false conception!
Mortally strike at the heart of this butcher and enemy, the self!

If we have not studied extensively and our *learning is feeble,* when somebody asks us a question, we respond with a wild guess. We make up answers, change the subject, or make the person asking the question look foolish to avoid saying the three truthful words, "I don't know." Making up answers in the context of the Dharma is very damaging to others, because we mislead them. What people learn during their initial contact with the Dharma has a strong influence on the future of their spiritual journey. If they learn something incorrect at the beginning, they struggle with it for a long time afterward, often doubting the knowledge of a later teacher who gives them correct information.

When we don't know something, there is nothing wrong with saying so. I recall during a panel discussion in front of a huge audience with experts in a field, His Holiness the Dalai Lama said, "I don't know," when asked a question. The room fell silent. Here was the chief expert who said he didn't know, and people were shocked. In my eyes, that was an illustration of His Holiness's integrity. He cared more about others than about faking it to protect his reputation.

Taking the time to be aware of what we know and do not know is important. A saying goes, "When you know what you do not know, you are starting to become wise." If we teach people who already know something and we say something incorrect, they will wisely question us about it. However, if we are giving a talk to new people, they will take it as the truth, which can start them down a wrong path.

Due to our lack of *scriptural knowledge,* we are full of wrong views that we then put into practice. For example, some people dabble in tantra and then tell others, "You don't need to keep the *pratimoksha* or bodhisattva precepts because tantra goes beyond rules and restrictions." In fact, realized tantric practitioners are very careful with ethical conduct and keep their precepts impeccably. Other people say, "Vajrayana is not built on the foundation of the teachings in the Pali and Mahayana scriptures. It is a different kind of Buddhism all together." This, too, is incorrect. In fact, to enter tantra, we must first train well in the teachings on the four truths of the aryas and the bodhisattva path, and have some experience of the renunciation of cyclic existence, bodhicitta, and wisdom realizing emptiness. Without these, trying to practice Vajrayana is at best make believe and at worst dangerous.

Studying the sutras, treatises, and commentaries gives us broad knowledge. We learn what to practice and what to abandon on the path. We get a broad view of what the path to awakening entails and guidance on how to practice in a gradual way that will bring results. With that broad understanding and worldview, we know where different teachings fit in when we hear them and do not get confused.

Some people just study and do not practice, while some say study is useless and advocate only meditation. In fact, both are necessary. Without study, we don't know what or how to practice correctly. Without practice, our knowledge remains only at the intellectual level and cannot effect a deep change in us. Buddhism is not about practicing one meditation technique until we attain nirvana. Our minds are complex and have many facets, so we need many types of meditation to deal with them. To learn how to do those meditations and to be able to measure our success in them, study is essential. We have to understand exactly what our situation in cyclic existence is and what causes it. We need to know the qualities to cultivate and those to counteract in ourselves and to understand exactly what the purpose and end result of our practice is. Meditating without studying is like driving a car without having a map or knowing how to read road signs.

What makes us *guess wildly* and *engender wrong views*? It is our self-centered thought that has been too lazy to study and our self-grasping ignorance that does not want to take the teachings to heart. Once again, we can see that these two are behind all our difficulties and bad habits. The antidote is to combine study and practice, doing both in a complementary way. We need to be patient with ourselves in this process; it will take time. But as long as we are going in the right direction, we can be satisfied with our efforts, rejoice at others' success, and continue to grow in knowledge and understanding, as well as in wisdom and compassion.

84

Habituated to attachment and anger, I insult all those who oppose me.
Habituated to envy, I slander and denigrate others.
Dance and trample on the head of this betrayer, false conception!
Mortally strike at the heart of this butcher and enemy, the self!

Habituated to attachment to possessions, status, views, and people, we become angry and *insult all those who oppose* us or interfere with our getting what we want. People differ in their objects of attachment: some are more attached to their comfort and material possessions; others to their status, image, and reputation. Another group is more attached to appreciation and love, while others are attached to being right. They turn discussions into conflicts that they must win at all costs. Whenever any of these attachments are thwarted, anger erupts and we want to harm whomever or whatever gets in our way.

Attachment to our teacher, lineage, and religion makes us sectarian, and we put others down. Although such attachment and the divisive behavior it stimulates is contrary to the Buddha's teachings, we revel in our ignorance. A skillful teacher, the Buddha knew that sentient beings have different dispositions, inclinations, and tendencies and that religion was not a one-size-fits-all affair. People need teachings suitable for their own way of thinking and their own capability. Thus he taught in such a way that a vast diversity of beings could find teachings and a way to practice suitable for them. This diversity is a reason to respect the Buddha, not to put others down and proclaim that our way is the best and only one.

From the Buddhist viewpoint, it is good that there is a variety of religions in the world. Each one helps its followers to live more ethically and to be kinder and more generous to others, and for this reason all of them should be respected. We can debate the philosophical underpinnings of different religions with an attitude seeking the truth, not with an intention to triumph over others.

It's natural that when we study and gain a deep understanding of our religion, we come to have great respect and gratitude for its founder, our teachers, and the tenets of the religion itself. Such faith, trust, and loyalty are virtuous and important for our practice. They differ from attachment in important ways in that they make our mind joyous, not restless and competitive. In addition, we don't expect everyone to see things our way, and we have no need to compete with other religions for members, wealth, or status. We respect others' beliefs, although we may not follow them ourselves. In short, religious harmony does not depend on either converting everyone to one religion or saying all religions say the same thing. Rather, the key is to rejoice that each person has found a belief system that makes sense to him or her and that will help him or her to be kinder.

Within Buddhism, many different views exist, even between wise teachers and their devoted students. For example, Atisha had incredible respect for his guru, Serlingpa, so much so that when Atisha merely said his teacher's name, his eyes filled with tears of gratitude. Nevertheless, Atisha held the Madhyamaka view of emptiness, while Serlingpa held the Cittamatra view. If such esteemed teacher and student can have differing ideas on such an important topic as the nature of reality and yet still have profound respect and gratitude for each other, surely our differences of opinions with our teachers regarding politics, the role of women, and the benefit of butter tea are trivial. To rely on our teachers in a beneficial way, we don't have to accept their opinions on such topics. To teach us the two truths, our teachers don't need to agree with our culturally conditioned views. There are many situations where students have deep devotion, respect, and honor for their teachers but disagree with them on certain fundamental principles in the Dharma. That does not make them doubt everything their teacher has ever taught them or their teacher's value.

In addition to being plagued by attachment and anger, we are *habituated to envy.* Unable to rejoice in others' good fortune, virtue, opportunities, knowledge, or success, we *slander and denigrate them.* For example, one professor at a university may be envious of another who got tenure or who is more popular with students. One factory worker may envy another one who gets a promotion. In a family, one sibling may be jealous of another who receives more attention or kudos from their parents. Envious of others who we believe look, speak, or behave better than we do, or who are richer, more knowledgeable, or more loved than we are, we seek to bring them down by *slandering and denigrating them.* This is a good example of creating problems where there were none.

Just knowing these verses intellectually isn't sufficient. We need to apply them to our daily lives. In this way our actions becomes genuine Dharma because it involves transforming our minds from an unwholesome to a wholesome state. By so clearly pointing out our faults, these teachings encourage us to exercise introspective awareness, to notice these disturbing emotions and actions. Then, instead of justifying or rationalizing them, we can apply their antidotes and be free of them.

85
Failing to study, I have forsaken the vast {scholarly} disciplines.
Failing to rely on teachers, I defame the scriptures.
Dance and trample on the head of this betrayer, false conception!
Mortally strike at the heart of this butcher and enemy, the self!

Failure to study can take many forms. We may think that study is unnecessary or that we have done enough of it and understand everything we have heard. If we do study, we may not follow a proper procedure. Instead of going through a text or a topic from beginning to end, we read a little bit here and there, jump around, and do not learn anything well. As a result, it becomes difficult to gain any understanding when we meditate, because we do not understand well the topics of meditation or the methods of meditation.

One example of *forsaking the vast scholarly disciplines* is not understanding how the various teachings the Buddha gave fit together to form a seamless noncontradictory whole. For example, not understanding that the *pratimoksha,* bodhisattva, and tantric ethical codes fit together and help people counteract defilements at different levels of the path, we criticize them as contradictory. Or, not understanding why in some scriptures the Buddha said there was a foundation consciousness while in others he refuted this, we disparage the scriptures when in fact we are ignorant.

Failure to rely on teachers may occur through arrogance, believing that we can piece together a path to awakening. We take a little from Buddhism, a little from Christianity, some Kabbalah and Sufism and mix them together to form our own spiritual soup. Or, not trusting others' wisdom or skill, we think we don't need a teacher and are capable of guiding ourselves to awakening, even though we don't know any of the signposts along the path and aren't aware of possible pitfalls and detours.

At the beginning of the path, it is easy to be humble and see how our teacher knows more than we do. After a while, however, we may become arrogant, thinking that we have studied sufficiently. After all, we are a good orator, and other people are impressed by our words. In fact, we know a lot of words and concepts, but our understanding is pitifully lacking.

This arrogance creates obstacles in our spiritual progress. While the awakening activity of the buddhas is always present, we need to make ourselves receptive to it. We do that by relying on a qualified spiritual master, who acts as the vehicle conveying the Buddha's awakening influence to us. For example, the sun shining on a piece of paper does not start a fire, but if we have a magnifying glass and focus the sunbeams, it will kindle a fire. The sun is like the Buddha's enlightening activity, and our teacher is like the magnifying glass that focuses it and enables the fire of wisdom to ignite in us. Our spiritual mentors make the teachings real for us, explaining complex concepts so that they become useful tools we can use to purify our minds. In addition, our spiritual mentors show us a living example of sincere practitioners. By observing their behavior, we will see the difference that Dharma practice makes in life. Their reactions to daily life events are noticeably different from those of ordinary beings.

Furthermore, our spiritual mentors correct our behavior when it is happening, perhaps commenting, "You seem a bit out of sorts today," or "Did you really mean what you said to that person?" Books cannot do that, and in that sense reading a book may be more comfortable for our ego. We pick up a book when we feel like it and put it down when we are tired. They do not talk to us and say, "Be careful; you're being bossy!"

Failure to rely on our spiritual mentors may result in our becoming narrow-minded. When the Dharma teachings strike at our self-centered thought, we may become hostile to Dharma. We may also become lazy, receiving the teachings as intellectual information, without contemplating: What does this mean? How do I practice it? What is the result of meditating on this correctly? *Failing to rely on our teachers,* we may also develop contempt for our teachers and, by extension, contempt for the lineage. This can lead us to lose faith in the Dharma or even to stop practicing. This is why properly relying on our spiritual mentors is so important.

86

Instead of teaching the discourses, I expound lies of my own invention.
Failing to cultivate pure perception, I utter insults and threats.
Dance and trample on the head of this betrayer, false conception!
Mortally strike at the heart of this butcher and enemy, the self!

Instead of teaching what we have learned, contemplated, discussed, meditated on, and understood of the Buddha's teachings, we make up our own tenet system and path to awakening and teach that. Some people who give erroneous teachings may have a good motivation and believe that what they teach is correct. Due to their own blindness, they do not recognize that they have misinterpreted the Buddha's meaning. Other people consciously change the teachings, believing that the traditional explanations are wrong or limited. They disparage the explanations of the great sages not because they have refuted them using reasoning but simply because they don't like them. They prefer to teach a path that pleases their ego. This "path" is supposedly quicker and easier, and thus gullible people find it more attractive. Pretty soon, the person teaching this "path" becomes rich and famous.

When I first encountered Buddhism, I was impressed that all the teachers I went to said pretty much the same thing. There were no contradictions in what they taught, and they referred to passages in the sutras, treatises, and commentaries to support their teachings. Before that, the teachings of the "spiritual" people I had gone to contradicted each other. I didn't know who to believe, which was very confusing. The fact that Buddhist teachers were consistent in their basic message and that people had practiced these teachings for centuries and attained realizations enabled me to have confidence in what I was learning. Testing the teachings out for myself and examining with reasoning increased my trust.

Some people who claim to have realizations may be lying, but some actually think they are realized beings. This is because they have not studied and do not understand the meditative signposts of the stages of realization. In addition, they have not checked with teachers who can properly assess their progress. They may think, "This must be a realization of emptiness," when it is simply an unusual experience. Or they feel a lot of energy in their body and think, "This must be the blissful wisdom." It is actually sexual energy—people just misunderstand.

In tantric practice, we practice *cultivating pure perception*—seeing the environment as a pure land, those around us as deities, and our spiritual mentor and ourselves as deities. However, *failing to cultivate pure perception, we utter insults and threats* because we have allowed our superstitious thoughts and preconceptions to run wild. Without meditating on emptiness, we imagine ourselves to be deities, and then motivated by arrogance, we believe that all those who disagree with us are threats to the pure Dharma and must be stopped.

In tantra, pure perception is cultivated to help us overcome afflictions. While it usually entails seeing ourselves and everything around us as pure, another way to apply it is to practice looking at situations with wisdom and compassion, as a deity would. In this case, we see the person who disturbs us as a sentient being who simply wants to be happy. Instead of regarding someone else as hopeless, we contemplate their buddha-nature. Rather than follow our self-grasping ignorance, we practice seeing ourselves and others as empty of inherent existence, as a deity would.

But instead of imagining his mind to be pure like the deity's mind, someone who misunderstands pure perception believes that the deity's mind is like his mind and believes his afflictions are wisdom. He then may use threats to manipulate others. "If you don't do this, the Dharma protector will strike you down! If you don't do exactly what I say, you are breaking *samaya*—your sacred commitments—and will go to hell!" Unfortunately, these things have happened in recent years, so it is important for us to check potential teachers well, and it is equally important to be careful that we don't misinterpret the Dharma and damage others by such behavior.

87

Refusing to condemn deeds that are contrary to Dharma,
I level various criticisms against all well-spoken words.
Dance and trample on the head of this betrayer, false conception!
Mortally strike at the heart of this butcher and enemy, the self!

Rather than *condemn* and abandon nonvirtuous *deeds that are contrary to Dharma,* we rejoice in them with perverse satisfaction. Instead of valuing excellent teachings, we *level various criticisms against well-spoken words*—that is, against the Buddha's teachings. Even in the Buddhist community, some people criticize the vinaya, the teachings on monastic discipline, saying, "These rules are useless. They just say, 'You can't do this; you can't do that!' They must be for people who aren't very mindful of their behavior." Sometimes they say, "People become monastics because they have problems with intimate relationships and repress their sexuality. Celibacy is counterintuitive!" These people forget that the Buddha himself was a monastic and lived according to the vinaya. Do they really believe that the Buddha practiced incorrectly and that they know better than our Teacher?

Perhaps people level such criticisms because they themselves would find celibacy difficult or because they do not understand that monastic life eliminates obstacles to Dharma practice. Someone who has studied the bodhisattva and tantric ethical codes and taken them to heart knows that it is inappropriate to criticize monastic precepts or to ridicule those who keep them.

If criticizing the teachings is one extreme, immediately believing everything we hear and suppressing all questioning and examination is another. Debating, questioning, and discussing the teachings are encouraged, for they help us understand the Dharma correctly. However, our motivation for questioning should be to get at the truth, not to put down the teachings or show how adept we are at convincing others that our wrong views are right. When our minds are cynical, skeptical, or sarcastic, it is a sign that afflictions are polluting our inquiry. At that time, it is helpful to pause and ask ourselves, "It's clear my buttons are getting pushed. What are those buttons? How can I see the situation more clearly and not be robotically reactive?"

In brief, this verse is about misplaced rejoicing: we rejoice at destructive actions and brush off Dharma teachings. If we notice ourselves doing this, we should stop and ask ourselves, "I'm acting opposite to the teachings that I esteem. What is the issue that is actually troubling me?" Using introspective awareness to identify our fears, we can then ask ourselves, "Is that fear realistic? The Buddha gave teachings in order to liberate me, not to make me afraid or to control me. I must be misconstruing the teachings. What do they actually mean?" By doing this, we will be able to dispel whatever affliction or wrong view is tormenting us. This is real Dharma practice.

88

Failing to regard objects of disgrace as a source of shame,
Perversely I hold what are objects of honor as a source of shame.

Dance and trample on the head of this betrayer, false conception!
Mortally strike at the heart of this butcher and enemy, the self!

Both this and the next verse are about people who denigrate whole-some actions but think destructive behavior is just fine. For instance, instead of seeing killing as an *object of disgrace,* we develop theories on why it is permissible or even necessary. "Society is entitled to kill a murderer to deter others from killing. Capital punishment is not kill-ing; it is justice."

Similarly, we make up many reasons to justify unwise or unkind sex-ual behavior. "I didn't rape her; she asked for it by dressing in that way." "Although I am HIV positive, I did nothing wrong by having unpro-tected sex. It was the other person's responsibility to take precautions."

Holding what are objects of honor as a source of shame, we are embarrassed about practicing the Dharma and engaging in wholesome actions. When we return to work after a weeklong meditation retreat and our colleagues say, "What! You spent your vacation sitting on a cushion looking at your navel? Go get a life and have some fun!" instead of feel-ing inner satisfaction regarding our spiritual practice, we are embar-rassed and make excuses, "I went because my friend wanted me to go."

When we have thought a great deal about the values and principles we want to use to guide our lives, we are confident and do not feel insecure if others question them. If others do not agree with our val-ues, that is fine. We do not need to apologize for our values or agree with theirs. If those people are interested in open-minded discussion, we can explain our priorities, and if they are able to see our reasoning, good. If not, that is OK; we are confident in our beliefs and can tolerate differences.

Even when we have made a decision we believe corresponds to the Dharma, doubts and attachment may still arise. In such cases, repeat-edly walk yourself through the ethical reasoning behind making that decision, so that your mind will become familiar with it and reaffirm it. Doing this is true Dharma practice because we are really working with our minds.

Both fortitude and joyous effort are important in our spiritual practice. Sometimes we encounter negative attitudes that resemble these two wholesome ones. For example, telling ourselves we "should" or "shouldn't" do something resembles effort in that we try to get ourselves to act constructively. But the mind is resistant and unclear, so that our effort lacks the joy that takes delight in virtuous action. To have joyous effort, the heaviness of "should" needs to be abandoned. This can be done by remembering our precious human life, its great purpose, and the rarity of obtaining it. This eliminates the sense of unwilling obligation and creates joy in our mind, so we are eager to do what is meaningful.

Fortitude enables us to remain balanced when our mind fabricates grandiose expectations of quickly attaining buddhahood and is impatient to see results. We need to accept our present level and our present abilities and abandon unrealistic expectations, and at the same time know that we can grow and improve in the future. Knowing that change comes slowly, fortitude and joyous effort give us the strength to persevere without discouragement.

89
Failing to pursue any suitable deeds,
I perform instead all that is despicable.
Dance and trample on the head of this betrayer, false conception!
Mortally strike at the heart of this butcher and enemy, the self!

When our mind is scattered, we do not focus on what is important in life and fail to do *any suitable deeds*. We may have many ideas about the Dharma treatises we will study and retreats we will do, but we do not act on any of these ideas. Distracted with daydreams, we follow whatever impetuous thought comes into our mind. Thinking we are "acting spontaneously" and are "unencumbered by inhibitions," we are, in fact, giving attachment, anger, resentment, and jealousy free rein. The result of this is getting involved in *all that is despicable*—drinking and drugging, gambling, looking at porn, roaming the streets, stirring up trouble, and encouraging others to do these as well. Exhausted after our escapades, we have no energy or interest in working to benefit others. In short, we simply waste our time actively creating the causes for our own misery.

Rather than allowing the enemies of self-grasping and self-centeredness to ruin our lives, we identify and counteract them. Contemplating karma and its effects is a good antidote to this, as is thinking about our precious human life, impermanence, and death. This will motivate us to take refuge in the Three Jewels for spiritual guidance to help us change our bad habits. While it may initially be difficult to subdue our unruly mind, remembering that our long-term happiness is a worthwhile goal will give us the inner strength to undergo hardship in order to accomplish what is valuable.

Hearing the word "hardship" may make us hesitant and fearful. However, we are used to undergoing hardship for the sake of self-centered aims: we go to school for years, listening to lectures and taking exams. We go into financial debt to get an education because that can help us to make money. Once we start working, we quickly get out of bed in the morning, so we can get to work on time, willing to undergo the hardship of being short on sleep or of not eating breakfast some days. We do this in order to earn money, eagerly planning what we will spend our paycheck on. However, when the alarm rings to get out of bed for meditation, it is just too difficult to get up. We have no time to review the notes from Dharma class but have lots of time to surf the Internet and send text messages. While saving money to cover transportation to a meditation retreat is undue hardship, we happily spend it on all sorts of things we don't need.

We have the ability to undergo hardship—it is just that our mind is only willing to do it if there is a samsaric perk. Here is where we need to reorient our values and priorities, contemplating what is meaningful and valuable in life. When our priorities are clear, activities we previously considered difficult now become easy. Recalling the fleeting nature of samsaric pleasures, we no longer make them our priority and instead cultivate a sense of contentment. While contentment does not lead to the giddy happiness of sense pleasure, it does bring more mental stability and inner satisfaction. We make our priority generating merit, deeper concentration, love, compassion, and wisdom.

11

Safe at Last

TAKING REFUGE IN THE THREE JEWELS
AND CULTIVATING STRONG RESOLVE

V ERSE 90 BEGINS a new section in our text. In the previous section, we repeatedly contemplated the disadvantages of self-centeredness and self-grasping, always coming to the same conclusion: *Dance and trample on the head of this betrayer, false conception! Mortally strike at the heart of this butcher and enemy, the self!* To counteract them, we now appeal to wisdom and bodhicitta manifesting in the form of Yamantaka.

90
Powerful one, possessor of the sugata's dharmakaya,
Destroyer of the demon of the self-grasping view,
O wielder of a club, the weapon of the wisdom of selflessness,
Turn it above your head three times without hesitation.

We now take refuge in Yamantaka, the wrathful deity that is the embodiment of blissful wisdom and compassion. His ferocity is directed not at sentient beings but at the self-centered thought and self-grasping ignorance that are the real enemies. This is signified by his *wielding a club* that represents the *wisdom of selflessness*—the Buddha's wisdom that directly realizes the emptiness of inherent existence of all persons and phenomena and is supported by bodhicitta.

Yamantaka is a fully awakened buddha, a *sugata,* or "one gone to bliss." A buddha is called "one gone to bliss" because he or she has eliminated the two obscurations—the afflictive obscurations that prevent liberation and the cognitive obscurations that prevent omniscience.

Free from these two obscurations and the suffering and hindrances they bring about, buddhas have gone beyond samsara to the blissful state of nonabiding nirvana.

A buddha has four *kayas,* or "bodies," that are sometimes consolidated into two. Here "body" means a collection of qualities. The two bodies of a buddha are the truth body (*dharmakaya*), which pertains to a buddha's mind, and the form body, which relates to the perceptible form that a buddha takes in order to benefit sentient beings. The dharmakaya can be further subdivided into (1) the nature dharmakaya, which is the emptiness of inherent existence of a buddha's mind and its cessation of duhkha, and (2) the wisdom dharmakaya, the omniscient mind of a buddha. Yamantaka is a *possessor of the sugata's dharmakaya.*

There are two types of form body: (1) the enjoyment body, a mental body that is the manifestation a buddha takes in the pure lands when teaching arya bodhisattvas, and (2) the emanation body, such as the historical Shakyamuni Buddha and other physical manifestations of a buddha that we can directly encounter in our world. *The powerful one* refers to Yamantaka's form body.

When someone attains awakening, all four bodies are attained simultaneously. They are the same nature, but we speak of them differently in order to point out their different qualities. A buddha appears in various forms because we cannot communicate with an omniscient mind directly. When you have the opportunity, study the great treatises and commentaries to learn more about these four bodies. They will open the door to a deeper understanding of the buddhas' qualities and how buddhas benefit sentient beings.

A buddha's omniscient mind is the perfect abandonments and the perfect realizations. The perfect abandonments are the abandonment of all afflictive obscurations (ignorance, afflictions, and the karma that causes rebirth in cyclic existence) and of all cognitive obscurations (subtle stains on the mind and the dualistic appearance they bring about). The perfect realizations are the full development of all excellent qualities. These qualities include impartial love, compassion, and the six perfections. The potential to develop these wonderful qualities exist in our mind right now. The teachings often speak of what to abandon and what to practice. These lead respectively to the perfect abandonments and perfect realizations.

Yamantaka destroys the *self-grasping view*, the root of our cyclic existence. The term "self" has different meanings depending on the context. When referring to "ourselves" (for instance, being kind to ourselves), or when we talk about the conventional self that walks, talks, creates karma, and experiences its results, "self" means the person, the I that exists by being merely designated in dependence on the aggregates. According to the perspective of the Prasangika Madhyamaka, in the term *self-grasping*, "self" means inherent existence, the object of negation that is refuted in the meditation on emptiness. The *self-grasping view* is the mind that grasps persons and phenomena as existing inherently. The absence of a self—the absence of inherent existence—is selflessness.

Within that self-grasping view, there are the self-grasping of persons and the self-grasping of phenomena. The self-grasping of persons grasps or apprehends persons—any being in any of the six realms—as existing under their own power, independent of all other factors. Within the self-grasping of persons, we speak of the "view of a personal identity" (sometimes translated as the "view of the perishing aggregates"). This view grasps at our own I as inherently existent; it does not grasp other persons as inherently existent. The self-grasping of phenomena grasps all other phenomena—especially the aggregates that are the basis of designation of the person—as having their own independent essence.

The Heart Sutra says "looking at the emptiness of inherent existence of the five aggregates also." The emptiness of inherent existence of the five aggregates is the selflessness of phenomena, and the wisdom realizing this destroys the self-grasping of phenomena. The word "also" refers to the emptiness of inherent existence of the person. Just as the five aggregates are empty, the person that is designated in dependence upon them is also empty. If the basis of designation lacks inherent existence, the designated object—in this case, the I—that depends on it is also empty of inherent existence.

Yamantaka and other meditational deities (Tib. *yidam*) are not inherently existent. Like all other phenomena, they are empty of inherent existence and arise dependent on other factors, for example the collection of merit and collection of wisdom that are its principal causes. They exist by being conceived and designated in dependence on the basis of nondual bliss and emptiness that manifest as a form body.

Yamantaka is an embodiment of the Three Jewels of refuge. True paths and true cessations are the actual Dharma Jewel because when actualized in our mindstream, they prevent all duhkha and destroy all defilements. True paths are wisdom consciousnesses that eradicate the two obscurations, and true cessations are the eradication of a portion of the obscurations in such a way that it can never return. True cessations are also the purified aspect of the emptiness of a mind that is free from some portion of obscurations. Through actualizing the Dharma refuge, we become the sangha refuge, and when all our obscurations have been eliminated, we become the Buddha refuge.

Nondual means "not two." Its meaning differs according to the context, and here it refers to the nonduality of subject and object. That is, the subject (the blissful wisdom realizing emptiness) and the object (the emptiness that it is realizing) are not experienced as separate. Usually when we cognize objects, there is the perception that there is the consciousness on one side and the object being perceived on the other. But in this case, since the wisdom is directly perceiving its own ultimate nature—the lack of inherent existence—there is no such feeling of subject and object being cut off and distinct from each other. Of all the consciousnesses we sentient beings have, only an arya's meditative equipoise on emptiness—the wisdom directly realizing emptiness—is nondual. To all other consciousnesses, the subject and object appear different.

Nondual wisdom is the definitive deity, while the form this wisdom appears in is the provisional or interpretable deity. Without this understanding, we may think of various buddha figures as independent beings out there, like the theistic notion of a God. Or we may regard nondual wisdom as an inherently existent cosmic energy out of which everything manifests. However, the Buddha refuted the existence of any independent or inherently existent being or phenomenon. For this reason, it is important to remember that the basis of designation of a deity is the nondual wisdom of bliss and emptiness appearing in a particular form. This wisdom realizes the absence of inherent existence of all phenomena, so it itself cannot be inherently existent.

Yamantaka *wields a club, the weapon of the wisdom of selflessness* that destroys the enemy of self-grasping. The skull at the top of this bone club reminds us of impermanence and death, which, in turn, motivate us to make use of our precious human life to practice the Dharma while we have the chance. We request Yamantaka to *turn it above his head three times without hesitation.* The first turn indicates the destruction of the afflictive obscurations. The second turn represents the destruction of the self-centered attitude that prevents us from entering the Mahayana path and confines us in the self-complacent peace of our own liberation even after we have eradicated the afflictive obscurations. The third turn represents the destruction of our polluted aggregates, the body and mind that arose under the influence of ignorance or the latencies of ignorance.

The three turns of Yamanataka's club also represent actualizing the realizations of the path of highest yoga tantra: the clear light, illusory body, and their union. To actualize the clear light, one must be able to realize emptiness with the extremely subtle mind that arises when all of the energy winds have dissolved into the heart chakra. The illusory body is the manifestation of those energy winds in the form of a deity. This deity body is not made of flesh and bones. The union of the clear light and illusory body is the inseparability of the body and mind of a buddha. A buddha is able to perceive both ultimate and conventional truths directly and simultaneously without any error. Except for a buddha, no other being can do this, even the arya bodhisattvas.

Beginning with verse 90, we entreat Yamantaka and express clear aspirations regarding how we want to live life now that we are completely certain that self-grasping and self-centeredness are our real enemies. Although the subsequent verses are addressed to Yamantaka, we are also appealing to our own internal wisdom that will increase and one day become the Buddha's wisdom.

91

With your great ferocity, obliterate this enemy!
With your great wisdom, dismantle this false conception!
With your great compassion, protect me from my karma!
Help destroy this self once and for all!

While the ultimate *false conception* or false grasping is grasping at inherent existence, there are other distorted conceptions that are also important to obliterate. These are the four distorted conceptions: (1) holding that which is impermanent as permanent, (2) holding that which is unclean as clean and beautiful, (3) holding that which is unsatisfactory by nature as pleasurable, and (4) holding that which lacks a self as having a self. Making inroads to counteract these is a prerequisite for realizing the ultimate nature of all phenomena, their emptiness of inherent existence.

The first distortion sees impermanent things—things that are unceasingly changing in each moment—as permanent and static. We think of ourselves and the world around us as stable: we are the same person as we were yesterday, the place where we live is the same, and so forth. Yet, in fact, everything is in constant flux. On the coarse level, things end. A building falls down; a person dies; people are separated. Even though we intellectually know this, we are still shocked when a person we love dies or when a relationship we value ends. Deep down, we expected these to last forever and are upset when they cease. Coarse impermanence occurs due to subtle impermanence, the fact that nothing endures as it is in the next moment. It is not that we are young and then suddenly become old. Rather, from the very moment we are conceived, we are aging and approaching death. From the moment a relationship begins, it is changing and approaching its end. It is impossible for two people to always remain together. One person or the other will die, or the two may grow apart.

Change is our very nature; it is the very fabric of our lives. The ignorance that blinds us from seeing and accepting this is the source of suffering. It makes us reject the reality of unwanted change. Due to ignorance, we hate aging and rail against death, as if rejecting them could prevent them from happening. On the other hand, when we accept impermanence in both its coarse and subtle forms, our minds become more flexible; we are able to adapt much easier to change because we already have accepted that the present will not last.

The second distortion views unclean things—specifically our body and the bodies of others—as clean and attractive. If we imagine looking under the skin of our body or the body of someone we are sexually attracted to, what we see is not clean and attractive. Some people faint or scream when they see the inside of the body. Something unclean comes out of each orifice of our body. Food looks good on a plate, but after we chew and swallow it, it looks disgusting.

Contemplating this is a good antidote to clinging to our body: what is the use of clinging to this bag of dirty substances? It also remedies sexual fantasies because instead of imagining another person's body as attractive, we see it for what it actually is.

Although our body is unclean and not something desirable that is worth being attached to, we should not hate it. Our body is the basis of our precious human life, and we take care of it and use it to practice the Dharma.

The third distortion views things that are unsatisfactory in nature as pleasurable and the source of happiness. Anything that arises under the influence of afflictions and karma is said to be polluted and thus unsatisfactory and unable to provide us with lasting joy and peace. We previously discussed the three types of duhkha, or unsatisfactory circumstances. (See verse 3.) While all beings recognize the duhkha of pain as unsatisfactory, it is more difficult to accept that worldly happiness—the duhkha of change—is unsatisfactory because we do experience some happiness. However, this happiness does not last, and in the end we are disillusioned, dissatisfied, or in pain. That is because what the world calls "happiness" is, in fact, a small suffering that will only grow bigger as we pursue the object that is its source. Eating feels great when we're hungry, but that, in itself, does not guarantee happiness. If it did, the more we ate, the happier we would be, which is not the case!

Freeing ourselves from this distortion enables us to generate renunciation and the determination to be free from cyclic existence.

Renouncing unsatisfactory circumstances, we set our sights on liberation and awakening, true happiness and peace.

Eliminating this distortion also helps us to accept the situations we encounter. Instead of expecting everything to be nice and happy, we realize that things do not always go the way we want them to. Accepting this, we stop getting so angry and cease our attempts to control every situation and the people in it.

Furthermore, we stop being so attached to external things as the source of happiness, because we understand that they do not have the ability to bring us lasting satisfaction. This actually allows us to enjoy things more, because we release unrealistic expectations. At the same time, our intention to gain spiritual realizations grows, because we realize the Dharma will lead us to an actual state of happiness. This helps us to reorder our priorities and focus our energy on what is important in life.

The fourth distortion is seeing things that do not have a self as having a self. On a superficial level, this refers to believing in a permanent, unitary soul or self that does not depend on causes and conditions. A subtler self that we grasp is a self-sufficient, substantially existent person, and the subtlest self we mistakenly hold as existing is the inherent existence of both persons and phenomena. The latter is the fundamental ignorance that is the root of samsara: seeing everything as existing out there, objectively, independent from causes and conditions, from parts, and from concept and designation.

These four distortions work in tandem to make us confused and unhappy, but we are so used to seeing things in these four distorted ways that we don't even realize we are doing this, let alone realize that they are the source of misery. Understanding how out of touch with reality our mind is indicates that our understanding and wisdom are growing. We can see these four distortions even if only for an instant: "I'm holding things that are in constant flux as stable and predictable. I consider things that are unclean as clean and desirable. I'm holding things that are unsatisfactory by nature and cannot possibly bring me lasting joy as the source of bliss and fulfillment. I believe that I and everything in this universe exist with an independent essence, even though that is not the case. I've got to take the medicine of the Dharma to heal the distortions in my mind." With this recognition, we appeal to Yamantaka to help us *dismantle this enemy of false conception* by applying *great wisdom, to protect us from* experiencing the suffering of our destructive *karma* by *his great compassion,* and to *help destroy* this self-grasping and self-centered attitude *once and for all.*

How does Yamantaka do this? He dismantles our false conceptions by teaching us the Dharma, specifically the Prasangika Madhymaka view. By learning, contemplating, and meditating on these teachings, our false conceptions are dismantled and our own wisdom grows. To protect us from our destructive karma, he teaches us the four opponent powers to purify it. (See verse 26.) The ultimate way to purify negativities is to meditate on the emptiness of inherent existence of these negativities and of ourselves as the agent who created them. In this way, we come to see that all these exist like illusions; they exist nominally, not inherently.

Help destroy this self once and for all does not mean that we seek self-annihilation and the destruction of the conventionally existent self. Here *self* refers to self-centered thought and self-grasping ignorance. With great compassion and bodhicitta, we destroy self-centeredness; with wisdom of the ultimate nature, we destroy self-grasping and all other obscurations. What remains is the conventional I who has abandoned all false conceptions and who possesses all the excellent qualities of a fully enlightened buddha.

The most difficult point in the meditation on the selflessness of the person is to get a sense of the object of negation—the self or I that we believe exists but does not. To do this the great masters recommend remembering an occasion when we were falsely accused and then, with one part of our mind, examining how the I appears to exist. That is the I whose existence we want to refute. Another way to help us get a sense of the object of negation is to contemplate dependent arising, thinking, "I exist because the causes and conditions for me existed." We are a caused phenomenon; we don't exist on our own. When we contemplate this for a while and then compare the "softer" sense of I to our usual feeling of being a "solid," objectively existent person that is a self-enclosed entity and wants to control everything—we see there is a huge gap between these. Our gut feeling is, "I am truly real and independent!" We don't think of ourselves as existing only because the causes for us exist. This "concrete" I that appears to exist independently is the object of negation.

There are certain times and circumstances when we can more easily observe the appearance of an inherently existent I. For example, when I lived in a Chinese monastery, we washed our clothes by hand and were supposed to use the brush in a certain way. Once I was washing my clothes, and another nun came and corrected me, showing me the "right" way to move the brush. A strong sense of I arose in my mind: "*I* know how to wash clothes; don't tell *me* what to do!" Right at the moment that happens is the time to pause and observe how the person, the I, appears to exist. There seems to be a real I there, whose identity as an adult who knows how to do a simple action such as wash clothes is being threatened. The inherently existent I appears more clearly when we feel threatened and respond defensively.

Then examine whether it is possible for the I to exist in the way it appears. If it did, we should be able to find the I, the person, either within the body and mind that are its basis of designation or separate from them. Am I my body? My mind? The collection of body and mind? Something independent of the body and mind?

If we get in the habit of doing this, then getting upset becomes very interesting. When we are stirred up, instead of whole-heartedly jumping in and defending ourselves and aggressively blaming the other person, part of our mind reflects, "Now I have the chance to look at the object of negation. Here's the chance to check if I exist in the way I appear to."

92
Whatever sufferings that exist for the beings in cyclic existence,
Pile them all decisively upon this self-grasping.
Wherever the poisons of five afflictions are found,
Heap them all decisively upon that which shares the same nature.

This verse focuses on the taking part of the taking-and-giving meditation. Thinking of all the various unsatisfactory and outright painful experiences that sentient beings undergo, with compassion that wants others to be free from them, we take them on and *pile them on the self-grasping* ignorance that is the fundamental cause of our own duhkha.

The *five afflictions* are ignorance, anger, attachment, jealousy, and arrogance. When these five afflictions are manifest in our minds, they make us miserable. When we act under their influence, our actions destroy others' happiness, as well as our own, leaving seeds of destructive karma on our mindstream.

Sometimes we understand viscerally the reason these afflictions are called "poisons." For example, we may be in a situation where people's afflictions are out of control: people are arguing viciously or greedily looking out to get more for themselves without any sense of integrity, fairness, or consideration for others. In the midst of this, we feel physically ill. It's as if the emotions poisoned the people's minds as well as the environment, resulting in our feeling mentally and emotionally depleted and physically nauseated. At this time, it's helpful to think, "Similarly, when I lack mindfulness and introspective awareness and my afflictions are out of control, they poison my mind and the environment and make others feel ill."

As a remedy to this, this verse advises us to fearlessly take the five afflictions of ourselves and others as well as the contaminated energy of the environment and heap them on the lump of self-grasping at our heart, completely demolishing it. After you have done this, feel the calm in your heart and in the environment.

93
Through having thus recognized the root of all evil
Through critical reasoning and beyond any doubt,
If I continue to abet it and act in its defense,
Then destroy the very person, the grasper himself!

By the kindness of the Buddha and our spiritual mentors who teach the Dharma, and due to the kindness of the meditation deity

Yamantaka, who inspires our minds, we have at last identified the source of all problems. It is neither the apple in the Garden of Eden nor Satan, but our self-grasping ignorance and self-centered thought. Through our own *critical reasoning* and examination, we have concluded that self-grasping is *the root of all evil:* that is, the root of duhkha and its causes. Having the courage, as well as the intelligence, to examine our mental states and our experiences with others, we know *beyond a doubt* that our suffering is rooted in this fundamental misconception and wrong grasping in our minds.

Nevertheless, we have a deeply entrenched habit of attributing our misery to other people and external circumstances. If we ignorantly abet the self-grasping that is our enemy and *act in its defense,* then Yamantaka wake me up! Don't let me continue to sabotage myself. Help me to see that the true causes of my misery lie within my mind and to have the courage to overcome these disturbing emotions and the repugnant behavior that they produce.

In short, if our awareness of the disadvantages of self-centeredness and self-grasping is only intellectual, we *continue to {hide and} abet* the enemy within, and eventually this enemy is going to sabotage us. On the other hand, in a time of great pain or confusion, if we see the situation as Yamantaka waking us, then we will grow and make progress on the path.

Destroy the very person, the grasper himself does not mean that we want to self-destruct or harm ourselves. The *grasper himself* refers to the self-grasping ignorance that mistakenly holds the I to exist inherently. Through wisdom, we want to destroy self-grasping ignorance, which is the object negated by the path, and to realize that inherent existence, which is the object negated by reasoning, does not exist. However, the conventional I, the mere I that nominally exists, continues, and by practicing the path, this I will attain buddhahood.

12   Compassionate Action

BECOMING THE PERSON WE WANT TO BE

94
Now I will place all the blame onto one source,
And for all beings, I will contemplate their great kindness.
I will take into myself the undesirable qualities of others
And dedicate all my virtuous roots for the benefit of all beings.

NOW OUR MIND is clear, steady, and determined. We're not going to let self-grasping and self-centeredness continue to ruin our lives. Instead of blaming others for our problems, we're taking responsibility for our lives and accepting that our misery arises due to polluted actions we have created in the past. "I don't like the present situation and wish things were not like this. But I accept that I am abiding in samsara due to my own reckless, selfish actions. Some of these may have been created in past lives and I don't remember them, but even in this life I can see that many of my actions have been less than kind. In fact, they've been downright inconsiderate, disrespectful, and harmful. Since I don't like the results I'm experiencing right now, I must learn from this situation and stop creating the causes for such circumstances. If I can learn to release my anger, greed, vengeance, jealousy, and arrogance, and replace them with love, generosity, forgiveness, and empathy, then going through this pain will have been worthwhile. As one step in doing this, I'm going take on others' suffering with compassion and give them my happiness with love."

We then do the taking-and-giving meditation. *Placing all the blame onto one source*—our self-grasping and self-centeredness—we generate the courage to confront these enemies. *We take into ourselves the undesirable qualities of others* and the painful results of these qualities and give them to these enemies, obliterating them.

Dedicating all my virtuous roots for the benefit of all beings flows naturally from *contemplating their great kindness.* Frequent meditation on the kindness of others will transform our life and open us to see the goodness in others. Sometimes we believe that the world is a cold, uncaring place where we can't trust anyone. Other times we think we are a great gift to the world and entitled to have everything we want. Neither of those attitudes is true. In fact, we came into the world completely broke, with no money and no letters of recommendation. Once we got here, we cried, peed, and pooped. Yet others took care of us, and the proof is that we are still alive today. Without the kindness of others who protected us, we would have died of hunger, thirst, injury, or illness hundreds of times as helpless infants and unaware children.

Our parents or other caregivers cleaned up after us, taught us to talk, tied our shoelaces, and brushed our teeth. Without their efforts, we would lack all the essential life skills that we now take for granted. We were not born with the ability to communicate well—others had to decipher our baby talk and teach us to pronounce words correctly. They made sure we got an education, even though we may have wanted to play instead. If we had been able to do whatever we pleased as children, what a mess we would be in right now! When we look at the talents and knowledge we have as adults, we see that they came from the people who took an interest in us and taught us. Without their efforts and encouragement, where would we be now?

Everything we have and use was created by the efforts of other living beings. We drive on roads and live in houses that exist due to the hard work of people who built them. We have water due to the efforts of people who build water systems. Everything we use daily was made by other people, many of them in other countries that do not have the same comforts we do. We need to appreciate their efforts and labor and feel a sense of responsibility toward all these beings who have been so kind to us.

Sometimes we create an identity of being a victim of others' bad intentions. However, when we contemplate the kindness of others, we see the opposite: more often than not we have been recipients of a tremendous amount of kindness. Consider how hard our parents and others worked for us to have all the food we have eaten since we were babies. Think about the efforts of our teachers to educate and encourage us. Whether we grew up in developed or developing countries, our being alive depends on the kindness of others. If we spend some time reflecting on what others have done to help us, the victim identity evaporates. Reflecting on the kindness of others is not only spiritually sound, it is also psychologically healthy. On the spiritual level, contemplating the kindness of others enables us to generate love and compassion. On the psychological level, it helps us relinquish old, habitual self-images that prevent us from growing.

To practice mindfulness of others' kindness, look around and, with respect to each thing you see, think, "This came due to the kindness of others." When you pick up a pen, be aware that so many people's life energy was involved in designing, manufacturing, and transporting the pen. "My ability to use a simple object like a pen came due to the kindness of all these people, who are just like me, wanting happiness and not wanting pain. I don't even know them and can't thank them personally, yet I'm indebted to them." Look at the chair you're sitting on and other objects around you, and think the same thing. Then include in your awareness the walls and roof of the building, the flooring on which your feet rest, the lamp and the electricity that fuels it—behind each of these is the life energy and thus the kindness of many living beings. Let this reality sink into you.

From this reflection automatically a feeling of connection with others arises, as well as a strong wish to give to them in return. This wish for them to have happiness and its causes is love. Before we can give them happiness by sharing our possessions, body, and merits, we must remove their misery. The aspiration that they be free of suffering and its causes is compassion. At this point we're ready to do the taking-and-giving meditation. Take on their *undesirable qualities* that make them act in ways that harm others and bring unhappiness to themselves. Give them your *virtuous roots,* so that they develop beneficial and wholesome mental states that are the causes of joy.

The deeper our understanding of the four truths of the aryas, the more effective the taking-and-giving meditation will be. *Undesirable qualities*—such as ignorance, anger, and attachment—are the origin of duhkha (the second truth). Due to them, we experience duhkha—the duhkha of pain, of change, and of pervasive conditioning (the first truth). We want to free ourselves and others from these two truths. *Virtuous roots*—such as compassion, love, joy, equanimity, generosity, ethical conduct, fortitude, joyous effort, concentration, and wisdom—are the path that frees us from these (the fourth truth). The path brings about the cessation of duhkha and its origins. This cessation is nirvana, the state of peace (the third truth).

The taking-and-giving meditation is good to do when we aren't getting along with someone. When we experience difficulties with others, usually we do not consider that they are suffering. We focus only on the pain we experience after they say or do something. However, if we ask, "What is this person thinking and feeling that makes him speak and act in this way?" we realize that he is unhappy and believes that that behavior will dispel his misery and bring him happiness. This person is confused, just like we are when we act in inconsiderate, obnoxious, or harmful ways. At this point, it's helpful to consider, "What painful emotions are afflicting this person? What wrong conceptions are tormenting him?" Take on the suffering he experiences due to his afflictions and use it to smash your own resentment. Then without miserliness give this person your body, possessions, and merit and imagine him relaxing and gaining mental clarity and peace. An enemy who has a clear, peaceful mind is no longer an enemy, because when people are content and peaceful, their minds are free from the afflictions that motivate bad behavior.

Usually, we have difficulties with the people whom we spend the most time with, not strangers, as there is more opportunity for interaction and more expectations. When you are irascible due to the actions of a close friend or dear one, change your perspective and recall everything that person does that influences you positively. Instead of dwelling on the one action she does that bothers you, think of all she does that is a real gift to you.

By doing so, we see that those who seem to be difficult have also been kind. They might have one or more attributes that grate on us, but when we compare it to everything else they do, we see that we are interconnected and benefit each other. While we can stockpile all the petty things that happen each day in order to make the case about how rotten others are, how do we benefit from doing that? Allowing our minds to think like that will make us bitter and cynical. If we don't want to become like that, we have to steer our thoughts and emotions in more realistic and beneficial directions, because we are the primary one affected by our thoughts and emotions.

95
As I take on myself all the destructive deeds of others
Committed through their three doors throughout all three times,
Like a peacock that has colorful feathers because of poison,
May the afflictions transform into factors of awakening.

Here we come around to the theme at the beginning of the text: just as peacocks become more beautiful by consuming poisonous plants, we can progress on the path by transforming afflictions into factors of awakening. Actions *committed through their three doors* refers to the physical, verbal, and mental actions, and the *three times* are the past, present, and future. With compassion, we take on the *destructive deeds* of terrorists and governments that oppress people. We take on the negativity of people whose greed leads them to exploit others. We take on the jealousy and arrogance that lead to vendettas that traumatize ethnic and religious groups for generations.

Taking on all this negativity with compassion makes us fearless in the face of the world. Because we now have a way to dispel despair and still remain connected to the situation in a positive way, we no longer cower and turn our eyes away from what exists. No matter how awful a situation is, it becomes material to use in our taking-and-giving meditation. Instead of erecting smoke screens or burying our head in the ground, we have the courage to look at suffering and its causes with honesty, and transform them into something constructive by using them to demolish our self-centeredness and self-grasping and to inspire our cultivation of love, compassion, and wisdom.

This is the practice of bodhisattvas. Problems no longer provoke fear and hesitations in them. They do not shy away from doing what is difficult because they have deep refuge in the Three Jewels and confidence arising from their own experience that the Dharma methods work whenever they are sincerely practiced. Their lives are vivid and meaningful, and their minds joyful.

How sharply this contrasts with us ordinary beings, who desperately grasp at a false sense of self and focus on our own welfare. We are the kings and queens of moping. When people don't do what we want in one place, we move to another. When people in the new place again don't treat us as we like, we pick up and move again. Meanwhile, we never stop to consider how we treat others.

We are like Ping-Pong balls bouncing from one place to another; technology makes traveling quick and easy for us. In olden times, people had to stay where they were and work through difficulties, because there was no other place to go. If you wanted to go somewhere in old Tibet, you had to walk or to ride a yak for days and deal with bad weather and bandits. You had to think about what you were doing and take time to plan your journey. That prevented the dissatisfied mind from impulsively acting out. Instead of being like a flea-ridden dog who moves to the other side of the street to get away from the fleas but finds they come with him, people had to find a way to get along with others because going somewhere else was very difficult and dangerous.

Having said that, there are times when a break from our environment relaxes our mind and gives us the mental space to look at situations from new perspectives. While we may decide to return to the situation and work things out, we may also decide to leave it. But whatever the decision, it is made with wisdom and compassion, not out of fear and dissatisfaction.

96

As I offer my roots of virtue to sentient beings,
Like a crow that has consumed poison and is cured by
*   an antidote,*
May all sentient beings hold the lifeline of liberation
And swiftly attain the buddhahood of the one gone to bliss.

Dharmarakshita commences now with some verses of aspiration and dedication. As crow-like ordinary beings at risk of dying because we are immersed in the poison of our afflictions, we are cured by the antidote of practicing the taking-and-giving meditation. Thus now we are able to *offer all our roots of virtue to sentient beings* with the sincere wish that all of them—friends, enemies, and strangers—are able to *hold the lifeline of liberation.* We wish for them to develop the two bodhicittas: conventional bodhicitta, which is the aspiration to attain full awakening for the benefit of sentient beings, and ultimate bodhicitta, which is the wisdom realizing emptiness. Bodhicitta counteracts our self-centered thought, and wisdom realizing emptiness is the opponent that destroys ignorance. May all sentient beings aspire for liberation, create the causes for it, and be safe from the danger of falling into the lower realms. May those who have precious human lives not waste them seeking the happiness of only this life or striving only for upper rebirths or even personal peace. May they have the highest, most noble motivation of bodhicitta, and may they fulfill that aspiration by attaining all qualities of a fully awakened buddha.

97

Until all those who have been my parents and I have attained
{Full} awakening in the Akanistha realm,
May we all care for each other from our hearts,
Even as we wander through the six realms due to our karma.

"Akanistha" refers to a pure land where awakening is attained. One Akanistha is in the fourth material realm and is a place where nonreturners can attain nirvana. Another Akanistha is the pure land of Vajrayogini.

Seeing all sentient beings as having been our parents, we feel close to others. Contemplating the kindness of our parents or whoever took care of us when we were young heals any rifts or disturbing feelings we may have toward them, which enables us to see all others as loveable. This leads us to wish them to have the highest joy: full awakening.

In the animal world also, parents take care of their children. When I lived at Kopan Monastery in Nepal, there was a dog named Sasha. With two crippled legs, she could not walk and just dragged herself around. Maggots squirmed in a wound on her head. Then she had a litter of puppies, which was undoubtedly painful for her. Nevertheless, she loved her puppies. Sasha painfully scavenged for food so that she could nurse her puppies. She took care of them, no matter the hardship it caused her.

Seeing that other sentient beings have loved and cared for us just as Sasha cared for her puppies, we dedicate our merit so that all of us will *care for each other from our hearts, even as we wander through the six realms due to our karma.* In order to dedicate our merit in this way, we must expand our heart and be extremely tolerant and forgiving of others. When people act in ways that do not meet our standards, we remember that they are wandering in cyclic existence, just like us. Their minds are obscured by afflictions, so naturally they will do things we don't like. In addition, since our minds are obscured by afflictions, we're likely to misinterpret even the kind actions they do, projecting harm where there is none. Furthermore, others may have different priorities than we do, and we need to learn to accept this diversity. In samsara, everything is not going to go the way we want.

This does not mean we acquiesce and assent to whatever anyone does. Remaining calm, we can convey our feelings and needs to others and make suggestions about how to do things. For example, some people who lack structure in their life or who have difficulty in setting priorities properly need structure and instruction. Depending on the situation, we can set up a structure for them or help them set one up.

Similarly, we can teach them ways to evaluate various options and make wise decisions.

Sometimes we may have to act in ways that others do not like, but we do this with compassion. Similarly, sometimes they engage in actions that we don't like or disapprove of. Internally, we contemplate a wise and effective way to respond. We understand that these beings are wandering in the six realms; their minds are affected by ignorance, and they don't understand the functioning of karma and its effects. Sometimes our relationship with them is such that we can talk about destructive and constructive actions and how to abandon the former and cultivate the latter. Other times, it's wiser to remain silent because the other person will not be receptive to advice at this time. In this case, we do the taking-and-giving meditation to keep our hearts open toward them.

May we all care for each other from our hearts, helping one another because we're all in the same boat—samsara. His Holiness the Dalai Lama frequently speaks about ants and bees cooperating with each other for the common good. They have an instinctive sense that they depend on each other and act accordingly without complaining. The queen doesn't whine, "I can't move. All you workers bring me what I need, but actually I'd like my freedom to go outside the hive. And sometimes I'd just like to be left alone!" The workers don't complain, "We have to fly around going from one flower to another. We're so exhausted! The queen doesn't even say, 'Hello,' although we keep her alive." The male bees, who have short lives, don't moan, "You're just using me to make more bees. You don't really care about me as an individual! I quit!" Rather, they all help each other for the common good.

Some people believe that dog-eat-dog competition and coming out on top is the path to progress. In fact, that leads to destroying each other. No other species harms its members the way we human beings do. Conversely, when we cooperate, everyone prospers and our species and planet will continue.

Sometimes, Dharma practitioners have the notion, "All the great yogis of the past went to do retreat alone, independent of sentient beings. I want to be a great yogi living in a cave too." Of course, we prefer a nicely decorated hut that's well insulated, with running water and a comfy bed. Electricity and plumbing would be convenient too. Food should be delivered at least once a week—only the food we like, of course. Then we'll meditate on compassion and bodhicitta. Since we're such kind, caring people to start with, this shouldn't be too difficult. Then after a week, we complain, "The people who are supposed to help me during retreat are so stupid! They're disorganized; they bring the food late; they don't bring what I like. The cave is too cold, the bed is too soft, and birds chirping interfere with my concentration. How can I possibly meditate here?"

We don't realize that we're indulging our self-centeredness in the guise of meditating on compassion for other sentient beings. Although we're dependent on others, we don't appreciate what they do and instead grumble when our preferences aren't fulfilled. Furthermore, we blame them for making so much noise that we can't concentrate while meditating on compassion!

Think about it: there is no place we can ever go where we are not in relationship to other sentient beings. Given that, doesn't it make sense to care for each other from our hearts, especially all of us who are wandering through the six realms under the influence of afflictions and karma? We have to care for each other if any of us is going to stay alive, let alone attain full awakening. We depend on other sentient beings to help us with practical concerns. Creating the merit that will support a realization of emptiness is also done in relation to sentient beings. We can't practice generosity, ethical conduct, or fortitude without other sentient beings, and without these practices, there's no way to progress through the bodhisattva stages and attain buddhahood.

In addition, generating great compassion, which is preliminary to entering the bodhisattva path, depends on sentient beings. If we leave out one sentient being from the field of our compassion—one stink bug, one coyote, or one politician—we cannot become awakened. In order to become a fully awakened buddha, we need to have love, compassion, and bodhicitta for each and every single sentient being, excepting none.

Thus it makes sense to be kind to all these sentient beings. Let us cherish each other from now until we become awakened. Instead of competing and comparing ourselves with others, let us let us look out for and support each other for our mutual benefit and for the flourishing of the Dharma.

98

During that time, even for the sake of a single being,
May I immerse myself in the three unfortunate realms.
And, without compromising the conduct of a great bodhisattva,
May I relieve the sufferings of the unfortunate realms.

The next set of verses emphasizes benefiting beings in the unfortunate realms. Some people question the existence of multiple realms of existence; others accept the existence of other realms but feel uncomfortable with the thought of being born in them. Some people cite the existence of the hell realms as a reason they left Christianity. "I didn't like being told that we could be reborn in hell if we did certain actions or didn't believe particular doctrinal points. But now I come to Buddhism, and here they talk about the hell realm too. I don't know what to believe." Confused, one person said, "If I'm Christian, I'm afraid of going to the Buddhist hells, and if I'm Buddhist, I'm afraid of going to the Christian hells."

In Buddhism no state of rebirth is permanent, and our rebirth is neither a reward nor a punishment. It is simply a result of our actions. Considering that our present mental states correlate with possible rebirths may help to ease us into understanding the different realms of rebirth. Sometimes a person is so thoughtless, inconsiderate, and negligent in his actions that we say he acts worse than an animal. Wouldn't it make sense, then, that such actions and the mental states motivating them would propel the person to be reborn in an animal body? Similarly, a mind filled with anger colors everything we perceive to the extent that when we take rebirth, we may be reborn as a hell being whose life is immersed in rage, fear, and torment. Craving, greed, and attachment in this life taint the mind so much that our rebirth environment could be one of poverty and inability to satisfy our desires, even the most basic ones for food and drink. This is rebirth as a hungry ghost.

While these rebirth states are related to the mind, they are not just mental states. In the same way that our present rebirth does not feel like just a mental state, so too do rebirths in other forms feel real when we are born there. The other realms are as real or as unreal as our present life as a human being.

Upper rebirths exist, and beings born in many of them experience great pleasure or peace. Nevertheless, contemplating rebirth in the unfortunate realms is helpful for a variety of reasons. First, it motivates us to restrain from engaging in destructive actions, because we understand that our actions influence where and in what life-form we will be born. Second, it broadens our mind to see the diversity of life and therefore expands our compassion to include more beings. We begin to see that our problems are not the most important events in the universe, that many others have it a lot worse, and that we are actually extremely fortunate. That increases our courage to endure whatever difficulties we undergo when practicing the Dharma for the benefit of all sentient beings.

From our present perspective as an ordinary being at the initial level of the path, bodhisattvas' aspirations to immerse themselves in the three unfortunate realms to benefit even a single being there seems like an impossible aspiration. As our admiration for bodhisattvas deepens, our aspiration to become like them will too. At that time, our mind is more willing to aspire to help beings born in unfortunate realms by living among them. To overcome any fear we may have, we practice happily tolerating and transforming inconveniences in our daily life. When things that we did not plan or do not want to happen occur, we cultivate fortitude and acceptance. Then, we move on to generating fortitude in more difficult situations, such as illness, injury, aging, betrayal of trust, and untrue accusations of misconduct. Our fortitude and acceptance become genuine; they do not involve suppressing emotions or pretending that we are not adversely affected.

When, through practice and experience, we can bear the suffering that is the result of our own karma, we expand our mind and consider bearing suffering for the benefit of others. This is based on a deep understanding that everyone wants happiness and freedom from suffering as intensely as we do, and everyone deserves happiness as much as we do. We then contemplate others' suffering and with compassion wish them to be free of it. Reflecting on their kindness, we see sentient beings as loveable and with love want them to have happiness and its causes. We gradually train our minds to derive as much joy from doing things that benefit others as from activities that benefit ourselves.

At first, we are willing to undergo a little bit of suffering if we get some kind of perk in return. As we continue practicing, our motivation changes, and we focus more on the welfare of others, without caring whether we get something in return. Our perk is the joy that comes from being of service.

Gradually, our horizons and our capability expand even more. We become able to make seemingly outrageous aspirations to be born in unfortunate realms for the benefit of sentient beings. Training ourselves by making such aspirations strengthens our compassion. Just thinking like this shifts our usual way of thinking to a more compassionate one. Then, by virtue of familiarity with positive aspirations, when we encounter situations in our lives when we can actually benefit someone, we act without hesitation.

Although infinite buddhas exist, it is important for us to become a buddha. While we are in samsara, we develop karmic connections with particular beings. After attaining awakening, we have greater capability to exert positive influence on these beings than do other buddhas who do not have such a strong karmic connection with them.

Even in this life, we see that we have the ability to benefit particular people whom holy beings, such as His Holiness the Dalai Lama, cannot directly benefit. His Holiness doesn't live with our family or go to our workplace, but we do. Therefore, we have the opportunity to benefit the people we encounter daily in a way that some holy beings may not have, simply due to the karma we have this lifetime. Let's take this opportunity and do what we can to improve the lives of others. If we are concerned simply with our own pleasure and reputation, we lose so many opportunities to be of benefit. We may think they are small opportunities, but we never know the long-term impact a small action may have on an individual.

It's important to train our mind to take delight in benefiting others. That is, we don't expect a reward, approval, or even a thank you. Our reward is seeing others' situations or mental states improve even a little bit. Able to evaluate our actions accurately, we become impervious to praise and blame. Sometimes people go to a Dharma teaching and, for whatever reason, become angry and leave. My teachers don't mind. They don't tremble, thinking, "Did I do something wrong?" People pleasing and ego games are not in the repertoire of bodhisattvas. With clarity of purpose, they remain steadfast in doing what needs to be done and pray to be able to benefit those who are not presently receptive.

When we have great compassion for the beings born in the lower realms and find their suffering unbearable, we will be motivated to be reborn or to manifest there. Upon attaining the bodhisattva path of seeing, *without compromising the conduct of a great bodhisattva,* we will be able to *relieve the sufferings of the unfortunate realms.*

99
At that very instant, may the guardians of the hells
Relate to me as their spiritual teacher, and
May their weapons turn into a cascade of flowers;
Free of harms, may peace and happiness flourish.

Wouldn't it be wonderful, if at the very moment we are born in the hell realm, *the guardians of the hells relate to us as their spiritual teacher?* Seeing us, the guardians of hell query, "Who are you, and what are you doing here?" We reply, "I'm so-and-so bodhisattva. I saw that a lot of beings are suffering unspeakable horrors here, and I want to benefit them." Suddenly the guardians of the hell realms wake up and realize they never knew such a compassionate being could exist, and through their mind opening at that moment, they come to see us as their spiritual teacher.

Through the combination of their receptivity and our ability to teach them, *their weapons turn into a cascade of flowers;* all of their harmful intentions evaporate and they stop torturing others, and their anger and hatred transform into the *flowers* of love and compassion. The beings in the hell realm are now *free of harm,* and *peace and happiness flourish* in their minds, as well as in their environment. Without peaceful minds there is no possibility of having a peaceful environment.

We may think that this is a wishful fantasy, but imagining such events does affect our mind. While we may not be able to eliminate all the suffering in the hells, we can increase our mental strength—our fortitude and compassion—so that whenever there is the opportunity to reach out and help others, we don't hesitate due to fear, laziness, or anger. If we can't *imagine* stepping into an area of pain and violence, we'll never be able to *do* it. This is why as children we dress up and in our play pretend to have different careers. Being able to imagine being a teacher, an inventor, or a parent sets the stage and enables us to become one in the future.

To benefit beings in situations of extreme pain, such as the hell realms, first we must help them on a practical level by reducing or eliminating their physical pain. Someone in extreme physical or mental pain is too immersed in misery to listen to the Dharma. Thus a bodhisattva would first manifest as rain to extinguish the fires in the hot hells and as sunshine, heaters, and thermal blankets to help the beings in the cold hells. Mentally a bodhisattva would send love and compassion to all these beings to eliminate their anger, hatred, depression, and isolation. When beings are burning with anger or freezing in rejection, they cannot listen to the Dharma, so first we help meet their emotional needs so that their hearts can open to the Dharma.

This necessitates a lot of skill and courage on our part. When we are around people who are burning with rage or frozen with fear, we often feel frightened or uncomfortable and want to get away from them. We have to cultivate the mind that wishes to benefit those beings and the strength and fortitude not to abandon them.

I heard the account of a Dharma teacher who headed a monastery with many disciples. One particular disciple was extremely obnoxious, did not keep his precepts well, and was difficult to live with. Other disciples approached the master to request, "Please expel this person.

He is disturbing us. He is too thick skulled, and there is no use trying to teach him." The master replied, "You already have some openness to the Dharma and have heard a lot of teachings. You are able to practice. He lacks this fortune. Since he desperately needs the teachings the most, I want him to remain here."

In so saying, the master gave the disciples the teaching they needed the most at that moment.

> 100
> *May the beings of the lower realms, too, obtain clairvoyance and mantra,*
> *And may they attain human or celestial birth and generate bodhicitta.*
> *May they repay my kindness through spiritual practice,*
> *And may they take me as their teacher and rely upon me.*

Having eliminated others' physical misery as described in the previous verses, we wish that they have fortunate rebirths from now until they attain full awakening and quickly gain all Dharma realizations. Born in the human realm or as a desire realm god, beings have the possibility of attaining the Mahayana path of seeing—the direct realization of the emptiness of inherent existence that is informed by bodhicitta. If, with compassion and by means of mantra, they cultivate *clairvoyance* and other super-knowledges, they will have increased abilities to benefit others.

Sometimes, people ask why bodhisattvas are so happy even though they are aware of the suffering of others. How can they bear to see all that suffering? We ordinary beings can easily confuse compassion with personal distress. Whereas the focus of compassion is others, the focus of personal distress has shifted to ourselves: "*I* can't bear to see their suffering. Seeing so much suffering, I feel hopeless and a sense of despair overwhelms me." We need to recuperate from being in touch with or even knowing about so much misery.

Bodhisattvas, on the other hand, keep their focus on others and meet others' misery with a genuine wish for them to be free from suffering and its causes. In addition, bodhisattvas know that others' suffering can be eliminated because it is possible to eliminate its causes, especially its root cause, the ignorance grasping true existence. Because ignorance is an erroneous mental factor that misapprehends how people and phenomena actually exist, it can be overcome by the wisdom that correctly apprehends how people and phenomena exist. When the light of wisdom shines in the mind, the darkness of ignorance is dispelled. As we become more familiar with the wisdom realizing reality, ignorance gradually loses strength until it is forever eradicated.

Bodhisattvas know that each and every sentient being has buddha-nature—the ultimate nature of each sentient being's mind is pure and the defilements are adventitious. They know that each and every sentient being has the potential to generate the wisdom realizing the emptiness of true existence and thus to free themselves from the prison of cyclic existence. Although each being may take a long time to do this, knowing that it is possible brings bodhisattvas much joy and abolishes any trace of discouragement that may cross their minds at the prospect of working for the benefit of all sentient beings until cyclic existence ends.

Bodhisattvas do not aspire—*"May they repay my kindness through spiritual practice, and may they take me as their teacher and rely upon me"*—with an egotistical motivation. Rather, they think, "I have a relationship with these beings and want to benefit them. By the power of my caring for them, may a virtuous mind arise in them that wants to repay kindness. Through the power of my practicing on the path and gaining realizations, may I become a qualified teacher by my teaching, may others practice the Dharma and progress on the path." Such an aspiration is made with humility.

101

At this time, too, may all beings of the higher realms
Meditate thoroughly on selflessness, just like me,
And without conceptualizing the duality of existence and
*   pacification,*
May they enter the meditative absorption of their equality.

While abiding in the hell realms, suffering from extreme heat and cold, or the hungry ghost realm, experiencing extreme hunger and thirst, or the animal realm, overwhelmed by ignorance, it is difficult to receive teachings, let alone think of selflessness. Beings in the higher realms—human beings and celestial beings—have more conducive circumstances to learn and practice the path. Dharmarakshita now turns our thoughts to benefiting them, especially by teaching them the method (that is, compassion) and wisdom aspects of the path.

Celestial beings in the desire realm have difficulty settling the mind to meditate on selflessness because they are captivated by the abundant sense pleasures of the celestial realm. When we have so much pleasure, our renunciation of cyclic existence fades, and our motivation to escape from the cycle of uncontrolled rebirth goes into hibernation. The human realm is considered the most advantageous for Dharma practice because there is the requisite balance of suffering and happiness. We have enough happiness and respite from gross suffering to have the time and opportunity to consider our situation in cyclic existence, but enough misery to remind ourselves that cyclic existence is imbued with duhkha and we need to get out of it.

When we pray for the beings of the higher realms to *meditate thoroughly on selflessness, just like me,* this assumes that we are meditating on emptiness and not indulging ourselves while telling others to meditate! Bodhisattvas' aspirations are not opportunities for hypocrisy.

Selflessness has different meanings according to the various Buddhist traditions and philosophical tenet systems. To review, the word "selfless" has a different connotation than our usual meaning in English, where it refers to compassion. Here, in the Dharma, "selfless" refers to the lack of inherent existence. In this context, the word "self" refers to the object of negation in the meditation on emptiness—the inherent existence of persons and phenomena. Persons and phenomena are selfless in that they lack inherent, independent, or true existence. "Selflessness of persons" refers to the lack of true existence of the person. "Selflessness of phenomena" refers to the lack of true existence of all other phenomena.

Selflessness is the opposite of what is conceived and grasped by ignorance. Thus generating the wisdom realizing selflessness entails seeing that what is conceived and grasped by ignorance in fact does not exist at all. When we understand this, ignorance has no footing to stand on and is eradicated. Eradicating ignorance stops the afflictions that arise from it, which in turn halts the creation of the karma causing rebirth in cyclic existence. That, then, ceases rebirth in cyclic existence. Thus generating the wisdom realizing the emptiness of inherent existence is our lifeline to freedom and peace.

All phenomena, both those in cyclic existence and those in nirvana, are empty of inherent existence and exist dependent on other factors. Thus they have the same ultimate nature, emptiness. In saying *without conceptualizing the duality of existence and pacification, existence* refers to cyclic existence—true duhkha and its origins, ignorance, afflictions, and polluted karma. *Pacification* refers to nirvana, the state in which true duhkha and its origins have been forever overcome. There is no duality in their ultimate nature: both lack inherent existence. It is in this sense that they are equal. However, on the conventional level, samsara and nirvana are different: cyclic existence is unsatisfactory by nature while nirvana is peaceful and deathless.

In brief, the nonduality of samsara and nirvana does not mean that these are the same. Conventionally they differ, and a person in samsara is not in nirvana and vice-versa. However, both samsara and nirvana share the same ultimate mode of existence: the emptiness of inherent existence. Someone in meditative equipoise directly perceiving emptiness perceives the emptiness of both samsara and nirvana without any differentiation between them. This person has *entered the meditative absorption of their equality.* The fact that both are empty of inherent existence means that samsara can be overcome and nirvana actualized. If samsara and nirvana existed inherently, they would be self-enclosed entities, unrelated to everything else. In that case, ignorance could not be eliminated, and eradicating samsara and abiding in nirvana would be impossible.

While a meditator directly perceives emptiness, only emptiness appears to his or her mind. That person's mind perceives only the absence of inherent existence, the ultimate nature that characterizes all phenomena. There is also no sense of duality between the subject, the mind that is meditating, and the object, in this case emptiness. Conventionally existent phenomena, such as the difference between samsara and nirvana, do not appear at that time.

When aryas—those beings who have gained direct perception of emptiness—arise from their meditation, conventionalities appear to them, and they again falsely appear to inherently exist. This is the case for all aryas who are not buddhas. However, buddhas never arise from meditative equipoise on emptiness and continuously and simultaneously directly perceive both conventional phenomena and the emptiness that is their ultimate nature. This is due to their having eliminated both the afflictive obscurations and cognitive obscurations, unlike arhats who have abandoned only the former.

People who grasp samsara and nirvana as inherently existent think that samsara is inherently disgusting and have strong resistance to appearing in samsaric realms to benefit sentient beings. They see nirvana as inherently blissful and want to abide in this state of peace and have nothing to do with beings suffering in samsara. However, not seeing samsara and nirvana in this dualistic fashion, arya bodhisattvas and buddhas do not experience suffering when they manifest in samsaric realms to benefit sentient beings.

This discussion may initially seem complex, but as we study and reflect more, our understanding will grow. We start with learning the meaning of words such as "selflessness," "emptiness," and the "object of negation," and of concepts such as "ultimately phenomena are empty of inherent existence but conventionally they appear and exist." Without first learning the words and concepts, we risk the danger of inventing our own definitions and then becoming totally confused! When we spend time at the beginning patiently learning, discussing, and asking questions, gradually our understanding of difficult topics will increase, and one day we will directly realize the ultimate nature of reality.

13 — Growing Our Wisdom

EMPTINESS AND DEPENDENT ARISING

102

If I do this, the enemy will be vanquished!
If I do this, false conceptions will be vanquished!
I will meditate on the nonconceptual wisdom of selflessness.
So why would I not attain the causes and effects of the form body?

METHOD AND WISDOM are the two wings of the path that vanquish the two enemies of self-centered thought and self-grasping ignorance. As mentioned before, method refers to renunciation, bodhicitta, and all the practices we do to accumulate merit. Wisdom is the correct realization of emptiness that contributes to the collection of wisdom. These two collections—of merit and wisdom—lead to the kayas, or bodies, of a buddha. The method aspect of the path principally concerns our relationship with conventional truths—the people, things, and environments that we encounter on a daily basis, as well as all the conditioned path factors, such as generosity and so forth, that we develop in our practice. Through learning how to relate to these without clinging and with compassion, we create great merit through virtuous deeds. The collection of merit primarily leads to the form bodies of a buddha: the enjoyment body that a buddha manifests to teach the arya bodhisattvas in the pure lands and the emanation body that a buddha manifests to teach us ordinary beings. The wisdom aspect of the path principally concerns the realization of the ultimate truth—the emptiness of inherent existence that is the ultimate nature of all persons and phenomena. This wisdom eradicates self-grasping ignorance, which is the root of samsara. The collection of wisdom primarily results in a buddha's dharmakaya, or truth body, which is comprised of a buddha's omniscient mind and nonabiding nirvana.

BASIS	ASPECT OF THE PATH	PRINCIPAL ENEMY THAT IS VANQUISHED	WHAT IS PRACTICED	COLLECTION	RESULTANT BODY OF A BUDDHA
Conventional truths	Method	Self-centered attitude	Renunciation, compassion, bodhicitta, generosity, ethical conduct, fortitude, etc.	Merit	Form bodies: enjoyment body and emanation body
Ultimate truths	Wisdom	Self-grasping ignorance	Meditation on emptiness	Wisdom	Truth body

This gives us an idea of the correlation of basis, path, and result with respect to method and wisdom as they are cultivated in the bodhisattva vehicle. Just as a bird needs both wings to fly, both aspects of the path need to be fulfilled in order to attain both the truth body and the form bodies. Thus, our daily Dharma practice should include both method and wisdom to be successful. This makes sense because a buddha is a well-balanced individual who has developed all excellent aspects of him- or herself. Someone who generates bodhicitta but neglects cultivating wisdom can enter the bodhisattva path, but cannot advance to its higher levels. Likewise, someone who realizes emptiness directly but lacks bodhicitta will practice the hearer path and attain arhatship, but cannot attain full buddhahood. Through practicing the method aspect of the path, bodhisattvas strengthen their minds so that when they meditate on emptiness, their wisdom has the power to eradicate all grasping at inherent existence. By meditating on emptiness, they reduce their grasping, which reduces prejudice and other blockages to generating great love and great compassion equally for each and every sentient being.

By *meditating on the nonconceptual wisdom of selflessness* supported by bodhicitta, we unite method and wisdom. In the tantric vehicle, the union of method and wisdom is meditating on subtle emptiness with an extremely blissful mind. This bliss is not ordinary samsaric pleasure. Rather it arises from dissolving the wind energies into the central channel, making manifest the fundamental innate mind of clear light. That extremely subtle mind is then used to realize emptiness. Through meditating on this repeatedly, the meditator actualizes the resultant form body and truth body of a buddha.

In short, this verse explains that by practicing the causes (method and wisdom), the results (the two buddha bodies) will come about. Each of us has buddha-nature, the basic potential to attain buddhahood. Since dependent arising is infallible, if we practice the path properly, accumulating merit and wisdom, *why wouldn't we attain the causes and effects of the form body* and the truth body?

Understanding that buddhahood comes about through creating its concordant causes motivates us to remain focused on creating those causes without getting distracted by doubt, attachment, or self-preoccupation. If we put energy into creating these causes, the resultant state of a buddha will certainly come. We don't have to worry about this. If we focus too much on the result, we may become impatient, wanting to attain it immediately. This infects our mind with grasping, which becomes an obstacle to progressing on the path. However, if we are content to create the causes, the result will naturally arise. When we plant viable seeds of a beautiful flower, water it, apply fertilizer, and make sure it gets the right amount of light and heat, the flowers will grow. We don't waste energy digging up the seeds every day to see if they've sprouted yet, and we don't waste time fretting over when or if the seeds will sprout. Instead we relax and enjoy the process of creating the causes for the beautiful blossoms.

His Holiness the Dalai Lama says that one of the biggest problems for Westerners is that we expect to gain realizations quickly without having to exert much effort. Such an unrealistic expectation actually slows us down because when our mind doesn't change quickly, we become discouraged, thinking, "I've been practicing *one year,* and my mind is still filled with anger and attachment and jealousy. *When* am I going to be awakened?" When discouragement sets in, we stop practicing—that is, we stop creating the causes for awakening—so obviously the result won't come about.

It is important to have a long-term vision and have the strength of mind and the courage to work toward our final goal of full awakening for the benefit of all sentient beings. When we want samsaric pleasure, we sacrifice a lot and work hard to get it. We go to school for many years, studying late into the night, and take exams to get a degree. Then we get a job where we also work hard, even working overtime to earn the money needed to buy what we desire. We remain focused on our goal through all the ups and downs, the discomfort, the weariness, and setbacks until we finally obtain what we want. Seeing that we can work hard to obtain what we value, let's apply that same energy and perseverance to attain our spiritual aims, which will bring lasting happiness and joy to both ourselves and others.

103

Listen! All this is but dependent arising.
Dependent and empty, they are devoid of self-existence.
Like false apparitions, they change from one form into another.
Like a ring of fire {made by a rotating torch}, they are like mere
    illusions.

Listen! Dharmarakshita is going to tell us something important: *all this is but dependent arising.* In samsara or nirvana, nothing exists inherently. Even an initial understanding of this statement begins to tear our cyclic existence to shreds. At present all phenomena appear to us to exist inherently, and we assent to that appearance by grasping them to exist in that way. Inherent existence is synonymous with independent existence: in other words, phenomena existing without depending on any other factors whatsoever. Independent phenomena would be self-enclosed entities, existing under their own power, unrelated to causes and conditions, parts, the mind that conceives and designates them, and so forth. Independent and dependent are mutually exclusive: nothing can be both. Thus, if all phenomena are dependent arisings, it is impossible for them to exist independently or inherently. Thus everything we currently take for granted as existing "out there" as objective entities that are cut off and distant from the perceiving mind do not exist that way in the slightest.

What does *dependent arising* mean? There are different levels of dependence. All Buddhists accept conditioned phenomena—impermanent things that are produced due to their respective causes and conditions— as dependent on these causes and conditions. The Buddhist teaching on the twelve links of dependent arising embodies this principle and describes the process by which we enter cyclic existence and the way we can free ourselves from it by stopping the causal sequence of events that leads to rebirth in samsara.

Dependence on causes and conditions also means that everything we encounter around us—people, their bodies and minds, things in the environment, desirable and undesirable situations and events—all arise due to their own causes and conditions. A sheet of paper depends on trees, loggers, a paper mill, and so forth. We exist dependent on our parents, the continuity of our consciousness coming from previous lives, the previous karma we have created, and the food we have eaten. Nothing happens causelessly. Everything exists only because the causes and conditions for it existed and gave rise to it. Because functioning things are dependent on their causes and conditions, they are empty of inherent existence.

On a deeper level, all phenomena—both impermanent products and permanent phenomena, such as permanent space and nirvana—exist dependent on their parts. What we call "I" has parts—the five aggregates, the body and mind. Similarly, our body is made of many parts: it is not one partless, unified object. Our mind too is made of many moments of clarity and awareness.

Permanent phenomena are also dependent on their parts. For example, emptiness is permanent—it does not change from one moment to the next—but emptiness has different "parts": the emptiness of the table, the emptiness of the person, the emptiness of functioning things, the emptiness of permanent phenomena.

In addition, phenomena are mutually dependent: long and short, teachers and students, causes and effect, the three times (past, present, and future)—all depend on each other. A seed could not be considered a cause unless there is the possibility of it producing its effect, a sprout. Samsara and nirvana exist mutually dependent on each other. So do a reliable cognizer and a reliable object that is cognized. The emptiness of the table is dependent on the table, the conventional object that is empty. Without one, how could we have the other? Because all phenomena depend on their parts and depend on their relationship to other things around them, they do not exist independently or inherently.

Going even deeper, dependent arising means that all phenomena depend on the mind that conceives and designates them. An easy-to-understand example of this is a person becoming the president or prime minister of a country, which occurs only after the people of that nation agree to designate that term to him or her. There is nothing inherent in that person that makes him or her the president, their having the power and responsibility of the president occurs only when that group agrees to designate him or her as such on the basis of being elected by the population.

Similarly, all phenomena exist by being designated with a term in dependence on a basis of designation. Nothing exists independently, without being merely designated by the mind. A flower exists by our agreeing to refer to the collection of petals, stigma, stamens, and filament and so forth by the name "flower." In dependence on the association of a body and a mind, we designate "I" or "person." While we designate a collection of parts in a particular formation as being a certain object, there is nothing in that collection of parts that *is* the actual object. Because all phenomena depend on being conceived and designated in dependence on a basis of designation, they do not exist inherently, in and of themselves.

For example, when an engine, wheels, axle, hood, and so forth are arranged in a particular formation that can be used to transport people and goods, we call it a "car." That collection of parts is the basis of designation. However, when we look into that basis of designation, there is nothing that individually and in isolation can be identified as the car. And the car cannot be found somewhere separate from that collection of parts either. The car exists by being merely designated in dependence on that collection of parts. "Merely" eliminates the car having any existence that is independent of its being designated on that basis of designation.

Although we designate objects, it is as if we have forgotten that we gave them that name, and instead we believe they *are* that thing; we think the designated object is the basis of designation or can be found in that basis of designation. If we label a particular constellation of events "problem," we react to it as if it were a truly existent problem. We feel heavy, burdened, and even depressed. If we call the same events "opportunity," we relate to it in a totally different way, approaching it with eagerness and creativity. That combination of events, in fact, is in and of itself neither a problem nor an opportunity. It is empty of inherent existence.

Although we may intellectually agree that phenomena exist dependently in these ways, the way they appear to us is as if they had their own essence or nature. Our ordinary minds go along with that appearance and grasp them as existing in that way. This brings many problems, especially the deleterious arising of afflictions and the generation of polluted karma. The understanding of dependent arising is a most wonderful tool that can destroy the ignorance that grasps inherent existence, and thus dependent arising is termed the "monarch of reasonings."

In our view, things then become very solid, leading to many conflicts. For example, border disputes between two countries that may even devolve into wars are basically quarrels over which term to call a certain segment of dirt. Do we call this piece of dirt "India" or "Pakistan"? Criminal trials are deciding what term to designate someone: "innocent citizen" or "convicted criminal." According to the term we give someone or something, we create an image of who that person is and impute a wide array of prejudices and expectations. All of this is a product of the human mind; it does not exist inherently within a person or object.

Forgetting that we created these categories, we respond to what seems to us to be an objective reality with attachment, fear, aversion, and so on, as our mind proliferates with more and more projections dependent on the term we have designated. Realizing that countries, situations, and people are merely designated helps us to understand that they lack their own inherent nature. This gives us more mental space to clear away false projections and to relate to things in a more relaxed and realistic manner.

Many people become upset when others act in a way they consider rude. However, "polite" and "rude" are mere dependent arisings. For example, in Tibetan culture, blowing our nose the way we do in the West is considered rude; that behavior is labeled "rude." Covering our head and face and then blowing our nose is called "polite." In Western culture, if we put our jacket over our head and blow our nose, people would look at us strangely and consider our behavior rude. In fact, neither behavior is intrinsically polite or rude.

This doesn't mean that we should say, "Manners are empty of inherent meaning, so let's discard manners all together." That would lead to chaos. Wherever we live, we relate to people according to their culture. This creates harmony and well-being in the world. However, instead of automatically calling certain behavior "impolite" or "obnoxious," and thinking it is inherently so, we should consider that it is only labeled as such and depends on culture conditions.

It is helpful to apply this understanding to our afflictions as well. We often think of our psychological states as solid, saying, "I have suppressed anger," as if there were concrete, permanent, unchanging anger inside of us. However, anger, too, is a dependent arising. The seed of anger—that is, the potential to become angry in the future—exists in the mindstreams of us ordinary beings. When the seed gets activated by our interpretation of external events, we experience a series of mind moments that have similar qualities—based on the exaggeration of the negative aspects of a person, situation, or thing, we want to strike at it or flee from it. We designate "anger" in dependence on these similar mind moments. Anger is only what is merely designated in dependence on those moments of mind. It is nothing more. Understanding dependent arising in this way makes us more flexible.

Because things arise dependently, they are empty of inherent existence. Because they arise dependently, they exist: they arise dependent on causes and conditions, parts, and the mind that conceives and designates them. In this way dependent arising shows that emptiness and conventional existence are compatible. Dependency negates existing from its own side; dependency also establishes existence dependent on other factors.

Everything that exists, exists dependently. If it were not dependent, it would be independent and unrelated to any other phenomena. If it were unrelated to any other phenomena, it would be difficult to say it existed, because no mind or person would perceive it.

While phenomena are empty of inherent existence, they appear to be inherently existent to our minds that are polluted by ignorance. Thus they are *like false apparitions* in that they appear one way but exist in another. If things were inherently existent, they would be fixed and unable to change because they would be unrelated to causes and conditions. However, in fact *they change from one form into another.* They are like mere illusions in that they falsely appear to have their own objective essence although they do not. If we take a torch or a stick of incense and whirl it in a circle, *a ring of fire* appears to be there. However, no ring of fire exists; it is only an appearance.

Only when we analyze, do we discover that what appears to be there—a ring of fire—is not there. When we don't analyze, the ring of fire falsely appears. Similarly, when we don't analyze, people and phenomena appear to exist out there, as objective, independent entities. Only when we analyze, do we realize they are empty of existing in that way. When we don't analyze, however, people and phenomena appear and function. How do they exist? Dependently, falsely, conventionally, as mere appearances.

104

Like a plantain tree, life force has no inner core;
Like a bubble, life has no inner core;
Like a mist, it dissipates as one bends down {to look};
Like a mirage, it is beguiling from a distance;

Like a reflection in a mirror, it appears tangible and real.
Like fog, it appears stable and enduring.

A *plantain tree* resembles a banana tree; however, it is actually a bush, not a tree, and has a deceptive appearance. From the outside, it appears to have a solid trunk, which is in fact layers of leaves. For that reason, when the "trunk" is split open, it is hollow and has no core. Just as a plantain tree can easily break, our life force can also easily shatter. Externally, we appear to exist so solidly. We think of who we are at this moment as being a very real person who is impervious to death and who will live for a long time. We believe this false appearance to be true, when in fact, the life force that sustains us is fragile. We lack an unchanging *inner core* as well as an inherently existent nature.

A bubble looks so real, and then suddenly—pop!—it is gone. There is nothing substantial about it. Similarly our life lacks any truly existent, permanent core. While we may feel, "Here *I* am, real and in control," how much can we really control? Can we prevent ourselves from falling ill, aging, or dying? Can we sit down and make our mind concentrate? To what extent can we control our emotions? In fact, our life is under the influence of causes and conditions. It does not last forever and is without an essential, stable nature. It is here one moment and gone the next, just like a bubble. Although we feel we are so important, we can die at any moment, and the world and everyone in it will continue on without us. We feel we have every right to be angry at someone who is late for an appointment, yet a hundred years from now, no one will even know our name.

We want people to remember us, to write about us, to keep photos of us for future generations to see. Is this really important? Many of the most famous people on the planet have died and been reborn in unfortunate realms. While people may talk about them now—praising their talents or fame—that doesn't help in the least to stop their suffering if they have been born as hell beings, hungry ghosts, or animals. We want to secure our posterity and legacy, but after we die, these things do not benefit us in any way. Only our karma and mental habits come with us into future lives, and sadly we neglect cultivating virtuous traits and actions while we are alive. In short, what others think of us and our pride in our worldly attainments don't matter at the time of death. Only the karmic seeds of our actions do. These follow us into the next life, not our photographs, trophies, and reputation.

When we look at a valley shrouded in mist, the mist seems very real. However, when we walk into the mist and *bend down {to look at it}, it dissipates* and we don't see it. Similarly, when we look at conventional phenomena without analyzing their mode of existence, they appear to have a findable, real essence. Yet, when we analyze them, investigating, "What is that car really?" and search for the car within the collection of parts, we cannot locate a car. The appearance of a real car evaporates. We cannot identify what exactly the car is: it is not the engine, the tires, the axle, or any other individual part. It is not the collection of parts, but it cannot be found separate from its parts either. Only a car that exists by mere designation is there. No matter how much we search, we cannot find anything more than this that is a car.

Feeling great thirst while traveling through a desert, we see a *mirage*. We rush toward it, thinking that water is there, but find only sand. We are equally beguiled by the pleasures of cyclic existence, believing these seemingly desirable things to be truly existent and doing whatever necessary to obtain them. We are sorely disappointed when they disappear due to their impermanent nature or when they fail to fulfill our craving due to their being unsatisfactory by nature. We thought they had an abiding essence of happiness, but they do not.

A mirage appears to be water due to causes and conditions—the sand, the sun, the angle of the light, and so forth. Similarly, the enjoyments of cyclic existence appear and exist due to causes and conditions, but no enjoyments that exist from their own side or under their own power are there. Just as desert travelers approach the appearance of water with great expectations that cannot be met, so do we approach the appearance of delightful objects with the anticipation of pleasure but discover we have been deceived by false appearances.

When we look at our *reflection in a mirror,* though *it appears tangible and real,* we know that it is not our face. Nevertheless, we may react to it as if it were, generating much emotion regarding our appearances. In the same way, we believe there is a real me and agonize about the conditions of our lives: "Why can't I have what others have? Why are they better than me? Why are my needs and desires unfulfilled?" Yet when we investigate, we discover there is no inherently existent person there: there never has been and never will be. Exactly who, then, is the person we fret so much about? Yes, we exist, but not in the way we think we do. There is a dependently arisen person here who acts and experiences the results, but no matter where we look, an independent person who exists without depending on other factors can nowhere be found.

Morning fog in a valley *appears stable and enduring,* like it will endure all day, yet when conditions change, the fog lifts. Each moment the fog is arising, abiding, and disintegrating simultaneously. It cannot exist there forever even if we wanted it to.

All these examples illustrate false appearances: they appear to exist one way but in fact exist in another. Similarly, all phenomena appear to have their own inherent nature, although they do not. While such inherently existent things do not exist, dependently arisen things do. Since things function and causes produce their corresponding effects, we must pay attention to the actions we do, for they cause the experiences we will undergo.

105
This butcher enemy, the self, too is just the same;
Though ostensibly it appears to exist, it never has;
Though seemingly real, nowhere is it really;
Though appearing, it is beyond reification and denigration.

Consider the example of a tree: it looks like there's a real tree in the yard, but in fact there is a trunk, branches of various sizes, and leaves. There is the bottom of the tree and the top of the tree. None of these parts are a tree, and the collection of the parts also isn't a tree. A tree appears to us because we designate "tree" in dependence on these parts arranged in that particular formation. Only that merely designated tree is there, not a real tree that exists from its own side. However, when we think of our self-centered mind, our self-grasping ignorance, our low self-esteem, attachment, or resentment, they appear very real and solid to us. They certainly seem to exist with their own nature, independent of the mind that conceives and designates them.

However, none of these exist in the way they appear to our mind that is obscured by ignorance. Sometimes our low self-esteem seems so real: there is a real *me* who is inherently deficient, incapable, and unlovable. But look again: what we call "I" or "me" is simply a collection of different factors—a body and mind. If we search to see if I exist as something findable within the body and mind or as a totally separate entity from the body and mind, we cannot find a person. Yet, when we don't analyze, a person appears. Although that person appears to our conventional reliable cognizer, that appearance is mistaken. The person does not exist objectively as it appears to.

Furthermore, can we isolate something that is low self-esteem? Is there a truly existent thought that is low self-esteem, or is there just a series of moments of mind that have the similar quality of criticizing ourselves? Similarly, is our selfishness solid and real? Or is it merely designated in dependence on different moments of consciousness that have the similar function of placing our own interests before those of others?

Investigate the relationship between the I that has low self-esteem and the low self-esteem itself. *Am* I low self-esteem? Do I *have* low self-esteem? If I am low self-esteem, am I one and the same as the low self-esteem? That can't be so, because there are many aspects of me. Do I possess low self-esteem? If I do, I and my low self-esteem are two different things: I am the possessor of low self-esteem, and low self-esteem is my possession. In that case, who is the I who has the low self-esteem? Is it my body? Is it my mental consciousness? It feels like I and the low self-esteem are both objective, independent entities, yet when we look, we cannot find a distinct thing to identify as either of them.

Given how much our low self-esteem affects us, questioning its existence as an independent, identifiable entity can be unnerving. This afflictive mental state is very familiar and gives us a sense of identity that we hesitate to relinquish even though it is painful. "I'm the person with low self-esteem. Don't tell me I have buddha potential. Don't tell me I can do things well. Don't tell me I'm not awful; I know I am. That's my identity." Grasping at a truly existent image of low self-esteem keeps us trapped, when, in fact, there is no inherently existent person or inherently existent low self-esteem that can be found when searched for.

Discovering that we do not exist in the way we thought we did may sometimes trigger fear in us. If that occurs, see the fear itself as just an appearance. Fear is simply the self-grasping ignorance putting on its firework display to distract us. We don't need to follow the fear or believe in it. It arises dependent on causes; it is not permanent and does not exist under its own power.

In the same way, *this butcher enemy,* self-grasping, ostensibly appears to exist as having its own essence and existing under its own power. But it, too, cannot be found when we ask, "What really is the self-grasping?" or "To what does the word 'self-grasping' actually refer?" All we find is moments of consciousness that have a similar aspect. There is nothing findable we can isolate as being self-grasping.

Contemplating this gives us a different feeling about those aspects of ourselves that we don't like and the mental states that interfere with our attaining liberation and full awakening. We see that there is no solid enemy to hate or fight with inside ourselves. There are just series of similar moments of mind that we call "anger," "selfishness," "self-grasping," "low self-esteem," and so forth.

Though an inherently existent person, inherently existent self-esteem, inherently existent self-centeredness appear, they do not exist as they appear. All these things—like all phenomena everywhere—are beyond *reification and denigration* in that they are neither inherently existent nor totally nonexistent. They exist dependently, as appearances, nominally. They are like reflections of a face in a mirror. Just as there is no face in the mirror, yet the appearance of a face there enables us to comb our hair, there is no inherently existent person, yet a person exists as a mere appearance. This person creates karma and experiences the results. A person that exists by being merely designated by mind cycles in samsara and attains liberation.

Reification refers to the extreme of absolutism, eternalism, or permanence—thinking that all phenomena are truly existent. *Denigration* refers to the extreme of annihilation or nihilism, thinking that nothing whatsoever exists. That is, reification imputes a type of existence onto phenomena that they don't have, while denigration denies the level of existence they do have. The former doesn't negate enough; the latter negates too much. These two ways of thinking appear to be the opposite of each other, but they actually share an important premise—both hold that if something does not inherently exist, it does not exist at all, whereas if it exists, it must inherently exist. Both confuse emptiness with total nonexistence and conflate conventional existence with inherent existence.

Nagarjuna lived in the second century, when the great majority of philosophical systems asserted inherent existence. To help people overcome this wrong view, he wrote his *Treatise on the Middle Way*, where he presented multiple arguments that refute inherent existence. At the same time, he explained dependent arising, showing that phenomena exist. When Buddhism first spread to Tibet, some people misunderstood emptiness and fell to the extreme of nihilism, asserting that since phenomena did not exist inherently, nothing—including emptiness itself—existed at all. Delving into Nagarjuna's texts, Je Tsongkhapa showed that the reasoning of dependent arising disproved both reification and denigration. Even the word "dependent arising" refutes these two extremes. Because phenomena are "dependent," they are not independent or inherently existent—this negates the extreme of reification. Because they "arise," they exist—this disproves the extreme of denigration. In short, all phenomena lack inherent existence, yet exist conventionally, on the level of appearance, dependently, nominally.

Both the person who has fallen to the extreme of absolutism and the one who has fallen to the extreme of nihilism cannot see emptiness and dependent arising as complementary and compatible. However, when we have gained the right view, we can see that dependent arising, or nominal existence, and emptiness are two sides of the same coin. They exist together in a complementary fashion. At that time, we do not fall to either extreme view.

106

So how can there be a wheel of karma?
Although they are devoid of inherent existence,
Just as the moon's reflection appears in a glass of water,
Karma and its effects too manifest in diverse false guises.
So within this mere appearance, I will follow ethical norms.

If things are empty, how can karma function? Emptiness does not mean nonexistence. It means lacking independent existence and implies dependent existence. It is precisely because karma is empty and lacks inherent existence that it can bring effects. If our actions and their results were truly existent, they would be self-enclosed phenomena, independent of all other factors. In that case they could not arise due to causes and conditions and could not produce results. Being produced by causes and conditions means they depend on those causes and conditions; producing results means they change due to causes and conditions.

If things were truly existent, there would be no way a seed could grow into a tree, or an infant into an adult. We could not mix various ingredients together and make a cake. Nothing would be able to function, because every phenomenon would have its own independent essence, unrelated to everything else, unable to change. It is because things are empty that they can function. As Nagarjuna said, because phenomena are empty, everything is possible.

This is expressed by the analogy of *the moon's reflection appearing in a glass of water.* There is no moon in the glass of water, but the reflection of the moon appears due to causes and conditions. The reflection depends on the water, the light from the moon, and the position of the moon and the glass of water in relation to each other. While the glass of water is empty of a moon, the reflection of the moon exists as a deceptive appearance; it does not exist as it appears.

Likewise, *karma and its effects manifest in diverse false guises.* All the situations we find ourselves in are influenced by our previous karma. They arise in dependence upon the causes we created in the past and the particular constellation of conditions in the present. For example, the activity of hearing teachings is dependent—on the teacher's voice, on the lineage of masters, on the room, on us understanding language, and so forth. The situation is a dependent arising. There is not one part-less, isolated activity of listening to teachings; it consists of numerous moments that are in constant flux. Even though we cannot identify a single thing that is the event of listening to teachings, it is happening and will bring both immediate and long-term results. We know this, because if we spent this time watching television instead, the results would be different.

Although actions and their results exist conventionally, they cannot be found when we search for them with ultimate analysis. We cannot isolate one moment or one factor and say, "This is the action of kill-ing," or "This is the action of generosity." But when we don't search for a particular thing that the word "killing" or "generosity" refers to, we can talk about them and understand what each other means. They are appearances, existing due to the mind conceiving and designating them in dependence on a basis of designation.

Saying that things exist by being merely designated does not mean we can call something anything we want. Conventionally as a group, we have agreed to call certain arrangements of parts by a particular name and have given them specific definitions. We have agreed to call a yellow citrus fruit a "lemon." If I decided to call it "golf ball" instead, no one would know what I was talking about, and my saying "mix the juice of a golf ball with sugar, chill it, and drink it on a hot day" would be considered gibberish. The name "golf ball" does not fulfill the defi-nition or the function of a yellow citrus fruit.

In our normal perception, we consider happiness and suffering to be truly existent, when in fact they are also mere appearances that cannot be isolated and identified when analyzed. For example, we say, "I'm happy." What is that happiness? Does it exist on its own? Is it in my body? In my mind? Is it a primary consciousness? A mental factor? If it is a mental factor, can this mental factor exist independently of a pri-mary consciousness? Why did this happy feeling arise at this moment?

It must have a cause; thus it is changing moment by moment and is dependent on other factors.

Furthermore, happiness and suffering are designated and identified in relation to each other. Does one exists first, or are they defined in mutual relationship to each other? Do you call a particular feeling "happiness" one day and "suffering" the next, depending on whether you have felt a preponderance of happiness or suffering the previous day? A healthy person says, "Walking is painful," after he bumps his ankle against a pole, while a person recovering from a broken leg says, "I'm pretty comfortable when walking," even though he has a cast on and cannot go very far. The person with the broken leg may be experiencing more pain than the one who bumped his ankle, but in relation to what he experienced when he first broke his leg and his expectations of how he should feel now, he finds the present sensation somewhat comfortable.

Even though things do not truly exist and are unfindable when searched for with ultimate analysis, *within this mere appearance, we should follow ethical norms.* Following ethical norms is extremely important. Selflessness and emptiness are not excuses to act according to whatever impulse arises in our mind. Rather, because actions and their effects arise dependently and are empty of inherent existence, we should pay very close attention to what we think, say, and do. People who understand emptiness respect and adhere to the law of karma and its effects very closely.

People may say, "Since everything is empty, we can do whatever we want. There's no good and no bad." This reflects their misunderstanding of the meaning of emptiness. They have mistaken emptiness for total nonexistence, and by throwing ethical conduct to the wind, they create the causes to experience severe suffering. Those with a correct understanding of emptiness, see that emptiness, far from contradicting karma and its effects, is compatible with it. In fact, for the wise, emptiness indicates dependent arising, and dependent arising signals emptiness. Since observing ethical conduct is the most important type of dependent arising to understand, the wise greatly respect it.

107

When the fire at the end of the universe blazes in a dream,
I feel terrified by its heat, though it has no inherent reality.
Likewise, although hell realms and their likes have no inherent reality,
Out of trepidation for being smelted, burned, and so on, I will forsake
    {destructive actions}.

When we dream that the universe is ending with a raging fire consuming everything, we see the blaze and feel the heat, even though there is no real fire in the dream. The appearances of fire, heat, and me getting burned are there, but an actual fire, heat, and me are not present. While these appear real in the dream and we grasp them as real and react to them as real, they exist only on the level of deceptive appearances.

Similarly, in dependence on pixels on a screen, people appear on a computer screen. Are there actually people there? No. Do we respond as if they were real? Yes, we cringe when seeing refugees fleeing violence or villages struck by Ebola. We are enchanted seeing wild giraffes and lion cubs; we laugh at the antics in sitcoms. In fact, none of those are there in the screen; they are only appearances. However, these false appearances function to arouse emotions in us. Learning more about the situation of people or animals, we develop ideas about how they should be cared for, and that often motivates us to act and extend help.

While dreaming, the dream people and dream environment appear real. When watching a film, the people and their actions appear real. Likewise, when we listen to teachings, our teacher, ourselves, and the audience appear truly existent. Just as there is an appearance of fire in a nightmare and of people on a screen, but no real fire or people are actually there, there is an appearance of people at the teachings, but no truly existent people are there. Does that mean that there are no people at all? No, conventionally existent people that exist on the level of appearance attend the teachings of a dependently existing spiritual mentor.

Dreams and screens are analogies, but we should not take them too far. These analogies have the purpose of pointing out deceptive, false appearances to us. However, there is a difference between the fire in a dream and the people who are here listening to teachings with us. The dream fire cannot perform the function of burning anything, and the person on a screen cannot shake your hand. However, the people here in this room with us can shake our hands; they experience happiness and suffering. Our actions affect them. Nevertheless, they are deceptive in that they appear to be truly existent although they are not.

Although hell realms and their likes have no inherent reality, they do function as places of painful existence. If we are born there due to being reckless in our ethical conduct, we will experience suffering. Therefore, *out of trepidation for being smelted, burned, and so on, we will forsake {destructive actions}* and respect the functioning of karma and its effects.

As human beings, we see animals and know that the animal realm exists and beings are born in it. Do the hell, hungry ghosts, and celestial realms exist, or are they illusions like figures on a screen or in a dream? These environments and the sentient beings living in them are as "real" or "unreal" as our human realm. When beings whose minds are overwhelmed by grasping at inherent existence are born in these realms, everything appears completely real to them, and they grasp everything and everybody there to exist as inherently real as well. As in our human lives, the people and environment in the other realms, and ourselves as well, are empty of inherent existence. We suffer because we grasp ourselves, others, and environment as inherently existent, although they are not.

As in the previous verse, this verse emphasizes the importance of observing the functioning of karmic causality, even though the people and environment do not exist as they appear. Even though the hell realms do not truly exist, on a conventional level sentient beings can be born there due to destructive actions. Similarly, although human beings do not truly exist, sentient beings are born in the human realm by the force of virtuous ethical conduct.

108

When in feverish delirium, although there is no darkness at all,
One feels as if plunged and trapped inside a deep, dark cave.

So, too, although ignorance and so on lack inherent reality,
I will dispel ignorance by means of the three wisdoms.

In feverish delirium due to disturbance of the elements of our body, we feel as if we were *plunged and trapped inside a deep, dark cave.* Although the experience feels real, when we are aware that it is just a false appearance, we are not overcome by fear. Likewise, when we are in a bad mood, the people around appear to be particularly rude and critical, and when we feel depressed, the activities that we used to find interesting now appear useless and boring. These daily life examples show the power our mind has in creating our experiences. The situations and objects we encounter do not exist objectively "out there" as we believe them to. When we grasp these appearances to the mind as having an independent, inherent nature, they affect us strongly, and we think, "This person, from his own side, is a jerk," or "That person is really terrific." If these people existed objectively as they appear to us at that moment, everyone would see them in the same way. However, that is not the case. The person we adore appears dull to another person, and the person we think is obnoxious someone else loves dearly. Stopping the grasping at these false appearances as real will enable our minds to be peaceful and see others with equanimity.

All appearances in samsara—and even the ignorance that is samsara's root—do not exist inherently. Ignorance and cyclic existence depend on each other. They are causally related and mutually related; therefore, they do not exist with their own inherent nature. Ignorance exists by being merely designated in dependence on a series of moments of self-grasping, and cyclic existence exists by being merely designated in dependence on the six realms and the twelve links.

Precisely because ignorance and cyclic existence are empty of inherent existence, they can be eliminated. Ignorance grasps at inherent existence, which doesn't exist at all. This can be known by cultivating *the three wisdoms:* the wisdom of learning, the wisdom of reflection, and the wisdom of meditation. The wisdom of learning is gained through hearing, reading, and studying the teachings on emptiness. Based on that, the wisdom of reflection contemplates what we learned in order to develop a correct conceptual understanding of the meaning of emptiness. Following that, we cultivate the wisdom of meditation by focusing our mind on the meaning of emptiness until we can perceive it directly, without the medium of a conceptual appearance. This wisdom knows the lacks of inherent existence, which is directly contradictory to the inherent existence that ignorance erroneously perceives. As our mind becomes more and more familiar with this wisdom, it cuts away the layers of ignorance, until finally ignorance is completely eliminated. At that point, the afflictions based on ignorance no longer arise, and karma causing cyclic existence is no longer created. In this way cyclic existence comes to an end, and nirvana is attained.

109
When a musician plays a song of ecstasy,
If probed, there is no inherent reality to the sound.
Yet melodious tunes arise through the aggregation of unexamined facts
And soothe the anguish lying in people's hearts.

When a musician plays a song of ecstasy, where and what is that song? Is it in the musical instrument? In the musician? Is it the sound waves in space or the sound waves when they touch our ears? Is the song one note? A collection of notes? *If probed, there is no inherent reality to the sound,* yet the song still exists—the *melodious tunes arise through the aggregation of unexamined facts.* The individual sounds arise due to causes and conditions, and when they arise in a certain order, they form a song. Even though neither the sounds nor the song are findable under analysis, they still function to *soothe the anguish that lies in people's hearts.*

On the other hand, if the musician, the notes, and the song existed inherently as they falsely appear to, how could they function to bring joy to others? Someone could be a musician without depending on playing a musical instrument; the song could exist without the musician playing the instrument, and the instrument could play music without there being a musician or a song. Such are the logic conundrums of asserting that things exist from their own side or under their own power.

110

Likewise when karma and its effects are thoroughly analyzed,
Though they do not exist as inherently one or many,
Vividly appearing, they cause the rising and cessation of phenomena.
Seemingly real, one experiences joy and pain of every kind.
So within this mere appearance, I will follow ethical norms.

Similar to the example of the song, when we apply ultimate analysis
to karma and its effects—looking at how they exist and what their
ultimate nature is—we discover that they are empty of inherent existence. When we try to identify exactly what an action is and its effects
are, we cannot find things that exist independent of each other or of
everything else. Instead, we find only their emptiness. This emptiness
does not contradict the conventional existence of karma and its effects;
in fact, it supports and complements it by showing that while they lack
inherent existence, they arise dependent on other factors, such as their
own causes and conditions.

If an action were inherently existent, it would have to be either
inherently one or inherently many. There are no other options: it can't
be both one and many. Let's take the example of speaking harshly to
somebody out of anger. Is that action of speaking harshly one inherent
thing or many inherent things? There are factors contributing to the
action—the perception of the other person's face, the sound of his or her
voice, our thought ("He can't speak to me like that!"). Then there is the
motivation to put the person in his place, the brief contemplation of
how to word our response so it has the most hurtful effect, our mouth
opening, the words coming out, the completion of the angry stream of
words, and the other person hearing it. Investigating in this way, we see
that the action of harsh speech is not one thing with exact, well-defined
borders. Rather, there is a sequence of different events.

If it is not one thing, then is it many things? If it were many things,
then how come we say it is one action of harsh speech? In addition, if
the action of harsh speech were many actions, then which of those many
actions would it be?

When we analyze an action or karma, we see it is neither an inherently singular action nor an inherently multiple action. Thus it is empty of inherent existence. However, it does exist dependently, by being merely designated in dependence on the collection of various events. In the same way, the results of our actions—for example, the feelings of joy and pain we experience—are neither inherently one nor inherently many. Although we cannot isolate inherently existent causes or inherently existent effects, the law of cause and effect still functions. We know from our own experience that certain actions bring particular results. Therefore, it is important to observe the functioning of the law of karma and its results.

The Tibetan phrase here translated as *one or many* can also be translated as "one or different." This involves an analysis of the relationship between the designated object—for example, an action—and its basis of designation (its many parts). Is the designated object inherently the same as the basis of designation, or is it totally unrelated and separate? The same analysis can be applied to the result—the joy or pain experienced as a result of that action. Are those feelings identical with their basis of designation, or are they totally different from them?

Let's consider the generous action of making a donation to a charity. If that action existed inherently, it should be findable either within its basis of designation—the parts of the action, such as its motivation, the object given, the recipient, the action of giving, and the completion of that action of giving—or totally separate from those. Again, there are no other options: in terms of inherent existence, two things must be either identical or totally separate. When we investigate closely, we see that the action of making a donation cannot be identified with just one element of the scenario—giving is not identical to the motivation or to the gift or to the recipient, the action, and so forth. Giving is not identical to any of the parts of the action: holding the object, extending our hand, or releasing the object. Nor can the act of giving be identified separate from those. When we analyze and see that things are neither inherently one and the same, nor inherently separate from their basis of designation, we can safely conclude that they do not inherently exist.

When we apply the same analysis to the effect—the happiness experienced as the karmic result of generosity—we cannot find happiness in any of the individual mind moments of pleasurable feeling. Nor is happiness found separate from those mind moments. It is empty of existing by its own nature.

We can also analyze the relationship between the causal action and the resultant happiness. Does happiness exist in the action at the time the action is occurring? If it did, cause and effect would exist simultaneously, which is impossible. Does happiness arise from an inherently other phenomenon totally unrelated to that action that caused it? No, it cannot be identified there, because then any kind of action could produce happiness, and that certainly isn't the case. Is happiness inherently identifiable within both its cause and as something separate from its cause? No, that doesn't make sense. Does happiness arise without a cause? Certainly not, results are not random occurrences. Seeing that the result, happiness, cannot be found inherently in any of these ways, we conclude that is does not exist inherently. Nevertheless, we feel happiness and pain; these results do exist.

We do not plant crops in the spring, thinking nothing is going to happen; we plant crops because we know that seeds produce plants. We plant corn to get corn; we plant daisies to get daisies. In the same way, we want to create the causes for future lives. To "grow" happiness in future lives, we engage in virtuous actions now. If we want the results of liberation and awakening, we have to "plant" the causes of merit and wisdom now. We do not think, "Everything is random, so it doesn't matter what seeds I put in the ground." Similarly, we want to be careful what kind of karmic seeds we "plant" in our mindstream.

Karma and its effects, causes, and conditions are intricately involved: *the rising and cessation of phenomena*. We are born and die. Relationships come together, change, split apart, and new ones begin. These things *vividly appear* to arise and perish, but none of them exists as a self-enclosed, objective event. We experience happy, painful, and neutral feelings, but these experiences do not arise under their own power. Dependent, they arise due to causes. They are mere apparitions in the sense that when we investigate them with ultimate analysis, we cannot find them, yet when we do not investigate, they appear and function.

III

When drops of water fill a bucket,
It is not the first drop that fills it,
Nor the last drop, or each drop individually.
Through the gathering of dependent factors, the vase is filled.

II2

Likewise when someone experiences joy and suffering, the fruits
{of karma},
This is not due to the first instant of their cause,
Nor is it due to the last instant of the cause.
Joy and pain are felt through the coming together of dependent factors.
So within this mere appearance, I will observe ethical norms.

The example of the drops of water filling the bucket illustrates the dependent nature of causes and their effects. Neither the cause nor the effect can be isolated as a self-enclosed entity, yet both exist and function. One drop of water—be it the first drop, the last drop, or one in the middle—does not fill a bucket. Yet the bucket is filled depending on many drops, all of which must be present. If one is missing, the bucket will not be completely full.

Similarly, the result of an action—the experience of pleasure or pain—is not due solely to the first moment of the cause, the last moment, or any moment in between. Rather, all the moments of causal energy and all the various factors contributing to an action must come together in their own unique arrangement in order to produce that specific feeling of joy or misery. When we think of the complexity of the countless causes and conditions that assemble for each moment of our experience, it is mind boggling.

Our first introduction to the idea of karma and its effects is usually done in a simple manner. Our parents tell us, "In the sandbox, if you throw sand in someone's face, he'll throw sand in your face, so don't do to others what you don't want to experience yourself." Later the explanation expands to include future lives: "If you speak rudely to that person, someone will speak rudely to you in a future life." We then come to understand that karma and its effects is not a tit-for-tat affair always involving the same people. Our uttering of harsh words plants the seed in our mindstream to hear harsh words sometime in a future life. However, the person who criticizes us will not necessarily be the person we criticized; it may very well be someone else. Many other causes and conditions must come together for that karmic seed to ripen into that result.

The functioning of karma and its effects is not rigid. Conditionality allows room for change. For that reason, the environment we choose to put ourselves in and the actions we choose to do now are important for they will influence which karmas will ripen. If a person caused serious physical harm to someone in a previous life, there is a karmic seed on his mindstream that could ripen in his getting in a traffic accident. If he drinks and drives, he is creating the cooperative conditions for that karma to easily ripen. On the other hand, if he does purification practice, he can forestall the ripening of the karma or lessen the severity of the result. Perhaps that karma will ripen in his tripping instead.

Our being on the receiving end of harsh words is but one result of that action. As explained earlier, if the action of our speaking harshly is complete with preparation, action, and completion, it will also ripen in our being reborn in a certain realm, the habitual tendency to speak harshly, and the environment we live in. The functioning of karma and its effects is complex and many elements are involved, so much so that only an omniscient buddha is able to know the specific causes and conditions leading to a specific result or constellation of results in an individual's life.

This verse emphasizes once again that even though joy and suffering are empty of inherent existence, they exist dependently. Causes are created and results are experienced all within the sphere of emptiness. Since our experiences arise due to causes that we ourselves have created, we need to pay attention to our actions, realizing that they have an ethical dimension. It is within our ability to create the causes for the kind of lives we want to have in the future, for our liberation from cyclic existence, and for our full awakening. In the sutras, the Buddha explained what the causes for each of these are, and the great Indian masters fleshed out the details. The great Tibetan masters systematized these teachings and further commented on them. It is up to us to study and practice the instructions of this liberating path that we are so fortunate to have encountered.

When we do so, we learn that creating the causes for good rebirths involves taking refuge in the Three Jewels and then ceasing the ten nonvirtuous paths of action and engaging in the ten virtuous ones. The causes for liberation are the three higher trainings in ethical conduct, concentration, and wisdom. The causes for full awakening are generating bodhicitta, engaging in the six perfections—generosity, ethical conduct, fortitude, joyous effort, meditative stability, and wisdom—and eventually the tantric path.

113

Ah! So utterly delightful when left unanalyzed,
This world of appearance is devoid of any essence;
Yet it seems as if it really does exist.
Profound indeed is this truth, so hard for the weak to see.

When left unanalyzed, conventional things are delightful to use and experience. We can talk about agents who act, the actions they do, and the objects acted upon. There are a pitcher, a batter, and a baseball. There are friends and good conversations, projects to do and people to work with to accomplish them. All these daily life objects function, and we communicate about them.

However, when analyzed, *this world of appearance is devoid of any essence.* When we walk into the room, the apple on the table seems real, existing in and of itself. But when we investigate the apple with ultimate analysis to find out what it really is and how it really exists, we see that it lacks its own identifiable essence. If the apple had a findable essence, the more we examined it, the more obvious that essence would become. However, the opposite happens. When we ask, "Is the apple the peel? The core? The flesh? The top side? The bottom side?" we cannot identify anything that is an apple. There are only parts, none of which is an apple. Yet, when left unanalyzed, we say, "Here's an apple for you to eat," and the other person knows what we're talking about and eats the apple and enjoys it.

The apple exists dependent on many parts and causes, all of which are "non-apples." How strange that when many "non-apples" are put together in a certain arrangement, suddenly an apple appears by being merely designated! The apple appears but is empty. It is empty of its own essence, yet it appears. *Profound indeed is this truth, so hard for the weak to see.*

The same applies to our bodies, emotions, thoughts, and opinions. All these things that appear so real, that we believe we have to defend from harm, are similar in appearing when left unanalyzed and being unfindable when searched for with ultimate analysis. I and mine are similar: they seem so real and important, yet they vanish when we try to identify exactly what they are. Understanding this deeply gives us a newfound spaciousness in our minds.

114
Now as I place my mind on this truth in total equipoise,
What remains certain even of this mere appearance?
What exists and what does not exist?
What thesis is there anywhere of "is" or "is not"?

The mind placed *on this truth in total equipoise* is a special state of meditation that is the union of serenity (*shamatha*) and insight (*vipasyana*) that is focused on the emptiness of true existence. This is a nondual meditative state, free from the appearance of subject and object—of the mind as the perceiving subject cognizing a separate object, in this case emptiness. This nondual meditative state has no appearance of inherent existence or of conventional objects. In addition, there are no conceptual appearances at that time because the meditative equipoise directly perceiving emptiness is a totally nonconceptual consciousness.

Until that time, all phenomena have appeared to us as truly existent. When meditators are in this meditative concentration that directly perceives the lack of true existence, the only thing appearing to that mind is emptiness. Perceiving only emptiness, which itself lacks inherent existence, the mind and its object are merged like water poured into water, indistinguishable. This extremely peaceful, penetrative state of meditative wisdom counteracts the ignorance that is the root of cyclic existence.

Although this state of nondual meditation does not perceive conventional objects, that doesn't mean they no longer exist. Rather conventionalities are not in the purview of this nondual wisdom. For example, our auditory consciousness cannot perceive colors, yet this does not negate the existence of colors because colors are not the object of an auditory consciousness. They are the object of a visual consciousness. Similarly, conventionalities are not the object of ultimate analysis or of direct perceivers of emptiness. These ultimate consciousnesses do not negate the existence of conventional things; it negates only their inherent existence. The lines in the Heart Sutra, "There is no eye, no ear, no nose, no tongue, no body, and no mind," and so forth refer to meditative equipoise on the path of seeing when we have our first direct, nonconceptual perception of emptiness. To that mind, none of these other things appear. However, when these meditators arise from their meditative equipoise on emptiness, conventionalities again appear.

Before meditators have realized emptiness directly, they believe that everything—people, phenomena, samsara, nirvana—exist inherently. Upon perceiving emptiness directly, they realize that this is not true and that it has never been true. That is, perceiving emptiness does not make phenomena empty; they have always lacked inherent existence and only now is their ultimate nature known. However, when these meditators—who are now known as aryas—emerge from meditative equipoise, the appearance of subject and an object returns, as do the appearance of true existence and the appearance of conventionalities. Although in the postmeditation time, aryas see things that appear inherently existent, they do not assent to this appearance by grasping them as inherently existent. Thus it is exceedingly difficult for attachment, anger, arrogance, jealousy, and all the other afflictions to arise in their minds.

What exists and what does not exist? The emptiness of inherent existence exists and is known by a reliable cognizer apprehending ultimate truths. Conventional truths, which exist falsely in that they appear truly existent although they are not, exist and are apprehended by conventional, reliable cognizers. Inherent existence, however, does not exist.

What thesis is there anywhere of "is" or "is not"? refers to Nagarjuna stating that he did not have a thesis. Many people misunderstood that statement to mean that Madhyamakas do not believe in anything and make no positive statements at all, they only negate. This is not correct. Rather, Nagarjuna does not make any truly existent theses; all theses he makes exist only conventionally.

115

There is no object, no subject, nor ultimate nature {of things}.
Free of all ethical norms and conceptual elaborations,
If I abide naturally with this uncontrived awareness
In the ever-present, innate state, I will become a great being.

To review, while nothing exists inherently, phenomena do exist conventionally; they vividly appear when not searched for by ultimate analysis. *There is no {inherently existent} object or subject,* and even emptiness, the *ultimate nature,* lacks inherent existence. All these *conceptual elaborations* of true existence never existed and do not appear to the mind of meditative equipoise on emptiness, which perceives ultimate reality. *Ethical norms,* which depend on words and conceptuality, also do not appear to the meditative equipoise on emptiness. However, they exist conventionally and are established by conventional, reliable cognizers. Although *ethical norms* do not exist inherently, they exist dependently. As discussed before, constructive and destructive actions are so designated in dependence on the pleasant or painful effects they respectively bring about.

Misunderstanding the meaning of emptiness, some people think that since ethical norms do not exist inherently, once emptiness is realized we need not follow them. These people proceed to do whatever they like, reveling in unconventional behavior. Mistakenly thinking they are free, they "freely" create the causes for unfortunate rebirths.

Their actions create chaos now and bring suffering results in the future as well. To prevent this, Dharmarakshita, in several of the previous stanzas, spoke of the importance of keeping precepts and holding to ethical norms. While virtuous and nonvirtuous actions are empty on the ultimate level, they function conventionally, and causes indisputably bring results.

If . . . with this uncontrived awareness that does not fabricate inherent existence, *I abide naturally . . . in the ever-present, innate state,* without clinging, grasping, and conceptuality, we will *become a great being,* a *mahasattva,* somebody who crosses over to the other side and is free of cyclic existence and the two obscurations.

116

Thus by practicing conventional bodhicitta
And ultimate bodhicitta {as well},
May I accomplish the two collections without obstacles
And realize perfect fulfillment of the two aims.

In this verse, Dharmarakshita gives us his final advice and encouragement to study, reflect, meditate on, and actualize the path to full awakening. By practicing the *conventional bodhicitta* (the aspiration to become a buddha in order to benefit sentient beings most effectively) and *ultimate bodhicitta* (the wisdom directly realizing emptiness), we will complete the *two collections* of merit and wisdom. The resultant state of buddhahood is the *perfect fulfillment of the two aims*: the aim of self and the aim of others.

The aim or purpose of self refers to the truth body (dharmakaya) of a fully enlightened being, the omniscient mind that is completely free from all obscurations and directly perceives all phenomena, both conventional and ultimate. The aim of others is the form body, the manifestations of a buddha that directly benefit sentient beings. With form bodies, a buddha is able to guide sentient beings to temporal and ultimate happiness, especially by teaching them the Dharma. In this way form bodies fulfill the aim of others.

Thus Buddhist practice involves working for our own and others' goals and happiness. Our ordinary view believes our own happiness and that of others as separate—if others have something good, I will not have it. We believe that since objects of enjoyment are finite, if someone else obtains a wonderful possession or situation, that means we will not have it. Our ordinary mind also thinks that if we work for others' welfare, we'll have to sacrifice our own happiness and thus will abide in a state of misery—that working for our own benefit and working for others' benefit are incompatible and contradictory. This view is very narrow, and adhering to it traps us in a prison of our own making. In fact, there is not a limited amount of goodness and joy, such that if others have it, we do not. Rather, the more goodness and wisdom there are, the more there will be. The more we cherish others and work for their welfare, the happier we will be. The buddhas work for the benefit of others, and their happiness and bliss is so much greater than the happiness of ordinary beings who seek their own welfare.

14 Colophon and Conclusion

This text entitled *The Wheel of Weapons Striking at the Vital Points of the Enemy* was composed by the great Dharmarakshita—yogi of scriptural knowledge, reasoning and realizations—in accordance with the instructions of the sublime teachers. He composed this in a jungle where terrifying animals of prey roamed free and undertook his practice in the terrifying jungle of our degenerate age.

He gave this teaching to Atisha, who, in order to transform many sentient beings so difficult to tame, undertook this practice throughout all places where sentient beings lie, whether in cardinal or intermediate directions. As Atisha experienced the realizations of this practice, he uttered the following lines:

When I renounced my kingdom and practiced austerity,
I accumulated merit and met with my supreme teacher.
He revealed to me this sublime Dharma nectar and
    initiated me into it.
Having mastered the antidotes, today I commit the
    words to my heart.

By casting wide my intelligence free of prejudice
To a detailed study of diverse doctrinal systems,
I have witnessed immeasurable wonders,
But I have found this teaching most helpful in our
    degenerate age.

From among his inconceivable number of disciples in India and Tibet, Atisha bestowed this teaching to the most qualified vessel, Upasaka [Dromtonpa], who was prophesized by many meditation deities, such as the Bhagvati Tara. This teaching was given to help tame the hardened people of Tibet, a land outside the bounds of civilization. The father conqueror [Atisha] and his child [Dromtonpa] themselves acted as the scholar and translator of the text.

Atisha [gave this teaching] to Dromtonpa, [who then transmitted it to] Potowa, and thence, in a lineal order, to Sharapa, Chekawa, Chilbupa, Lha Chenpo, Lha Drowai Gonpo, Ojopa, Khenpo Marton, Khenpo Sherap Dorje, Buddharatna, Kirtishila, Gyalwa Sangpo, Nup Cholungpa Sonam Rinchen, and he to myself, Shonu Gyalchok Konchok Bang.

This text belongs to the cycle of Dharmarakshita's thought training [teachings].

Even though they are busy seeking pleasure and avoiding pain, people so often feel their lives are purposeless. Without being able to identify the source of the malaise, they unconsciously seek something bigger than their own egos and so join this movement or that, dive into one field of study or another, or simply try to stay afloat while forces outside of their control buffet them around. How fortunate we are to have encountered the Buddha's teachings that show us the way to make our lives meaningful for ourselves and others.

Reading the colophon, we become aware of the numberless beings who have given us our present opportunity, beginning with the Buddha, who, with great compassion, turned the Dharma wheel. Many Indian sages then held these teachings and taught them to others, until they came to Dharmarakshita. He, in turn, gave them to Atisha, who brought them to Tibet, and there began the Kadampa lineage that specialized in these thought-training teachings. These teachings were again passed down for centuries until they arrived at the recent generation of masters and now to us.

May we always have a sense of gratitude for the Buddha and all these sages who learned, practiced, realized, and taught the thought-training teachings, and may we pay it forward by practicing them well and sharing them with others.

May all the merit we created by our study and practice ripen in the long lives and good health of our Dharma teachers. May they compassionately teach and guide us until samsara ends. May the Dharma exist in pure forms forever, and may practitioners everywhere be harmonious and mutually support each other. May each sentient being attain the full awakening of a buddha.

Recommended Reading

Byrom, Thomas. *The Dhammapada*. Boston: Shambhala, 1993.

Chodron, Thubten. *Buddhism for Beginners*. Ithaca, N.Y.: Snow Lion, 2001.

———. *Don't Believe Everything You Think*. Ithaca, N.Y.: Snow Lion, 2012.

———. *Guided Meditations on the Stages of the Path*. Ithaca, N.Y: Snow Lion, 2007.

———. *Open Heart, Clear Mind*. Ithaca, N.Y.: Snow Lion, 1990.

———. *Taming the Mind*. Ithaca, N.Y.: Snow Lion, 2004.

———. *Working with Anger*. Ithaca, N.Y.: Snow Lion, 2001.

Dharmarakshita. *The Wheel of Sharp Weapons*. Dharamsala, India: Library of Tibetan Works and Archives, 2007.

Dilgo Khyentse Rinpoche. *Enlightened Courage: An Explanation of the Seven-Point Mind Training*. Ithaca, N.Y.: Snow Lion, 2006.

———. *The Heart of Compassion: The Thirty-Seven Verses of the Practice of a Bodhisattva*. Boston: Shambhala, 2007.

First Dalai Lama, Gyalwa Gendum Druppa. *Training the Mind in the Great Way*. Translated by Glenn H. Mullin. Ithaca, N.Y.: Snow Lion, 1997.

Gyaltsen, Geshe Tsultim. *Compassion: The Key to Great Awakening: Thought Training and the Bodhisattva Practices*. Boston: Wisdom Publications, 1997.

Gyatso, Lobsang. *Bodhicitta: Cultivating the Compassionate Mind of Enlightenment*. Ithaca, N.Y.: Snow Lion, 1997.

H. H. Tenzin Gyatso, the Fourteenth Dalai Lama. *Awakening the Mind, Lightening the Heart*. San Francisco: HarperSanFrancisco, 1995.

———. *Healing Anger: The Power of Patience from a Buddhist Perspective*. Ithaca, N.Y.: Snow Lion, l997.

———. *Kindness, Clarity, and Insight*. Rev. ed. Ithaca, N.Y.: Snow Lion, 2006.

———. *The Path to Bliss*. Ithaca, N.Y.: Snow Lion, 2003.

———. *The Path to Enlightenment*. Ithaca, N.Y.: Snow Lion, 1994.

———. *The Way to Freedom*. San Francisco: HarperSanFrancisco, 1994.

Hopkins, Jeffrey. *Cultivating Compassion*. New York: Broadway, 2002.

———. *A Truthful Heart: Buddhist Practices for Connecting with Others*. Ithaca, N.Y.: Snow Lion, 2008.

Jinpa, Thubten. *The Book of Kadam*. Boston: Wisdom Publications, 2008.

———. *Essential Mind Training*. Boston: Wisdom Publications, 2011.

———, trans. *Mind Training: The Great Collection*. Boston: Wisdom Publications, 2006.

———, trans. *Wisdom of the Kadam Masters*. Boston: Wisdom Publications, 2013.

Khandro Rinpoche. *This Precious Life: Tibetan Buddhist Teachings on the Path to Enlightenment*. Boston: Shambhala, 2005.

Khenchen Thrangu Rinpoche. *The Heart of the Dharma: Mind Training for Beginners*. New York: KTD Publications, 2010.

Loden, Geshe Acharya Thubten. *Path to Enlightenment in Tibetan Buddhism*. Melbourne: Tushita Publications, 1993.

Patrul Rinpoche. *The Words of My Perfect Teacher*. Rev. ed. Translated by the Padmakara Translation Group. Boston: Shambhala, 1998.

Rabten, Geshe, and Geshe Ngawang Dhargyey. *Advice from a Spiritual Friend*. Rev. ed. Boston: Wisdom Publications, 2001.

Rinchen, Geshe Sonam. *Atisha's Lamp for the Path to Enlightenment*. Ithaca, N.Y.: Snow Lion, 1997.

———. *The Six Perfections*. Ithaca, N.Y.: Snow Lion, 1998.

———. *The Thirty-Seven Practices of Bodhisattvas*. Ithaca, N.Y.: Snow Lion, 1997.

Sopa, Geshe Lhundub. *Peacock in the Poison Grove: Two Buddhist Texts on Training the Mind*. Boston: Wisdom Publications, 1996.

———. *Steps on the Path to Enlightenment: A Commentary on Tsongkhapa's Lamrim Chenmo*. 5 vols. Boston: Wisdom Publications, 2004.

Tegchok, Geshe Jampa. *The Kindness of Others: A Commentary on the Seven-Point Mind Training*. Weston, Mass.: Lama Yeshe Wisdom Archives, 2006.

———. *Transforming Adversity into Joy and Courage: An Explanation of the Thirty-Seven Practices of Bodhisattvas*. Ithaca, N.Y.: Snow Lion, 2005.

Thubten Zopa Rinpoche, Lama. *The Door to Satisfaction: The Heart Advice of a Tibetan Buddhist Master*. Boston: Wisdom Publications, 1994.

———. *Transforming Problems into Happiness*. Boston: Wisdom Publications, 2001.

Trichen, Chogye. *Parting from the Four Attachments*. Boston: Shambhala, 2003.

Tsering, Geshe Tashi. *The Awakening Mind: The Foundation of Buddhist Thought*. Boston: Wisdom Publications, 2008.

Tsong-kha-pa. *The Great Treatise on the Stages of the Path to Enlightenment*. 3 vols. Ithaca, N.Y.: Snow Lion, 2000–04.

Tsulga, Geshe. *How to Practice the Buddhadharma*. Boston: Wisdom Publications, 2002.

Yangsi Rinpoche. *Practicing the Path: A Commentary on the Lamrim Chenmo*. Boston: Wisdom Publications, 2005.

Also by Thubten Chodron

Buddhism for Beginners (Snow Lion Publications)

Buddhism: One Teacher, Many Traditions, with the Dalai Lama (Wisdom Publications)

Cultivating a Compassionate Heart: The Yoga Method of Chenrezig (Snow Lion Publications)

Don't Believe Everything You Think: Living with Wisdom and Compassion (Snow Lion Publications)

Guided Meditations on the Stages of the Path (Snow Lion Publications)

How to Free Your Mind: The Practice of Tara the Liberator (Snow Lion Publications)

Open Heart, Clear Mind: An Introduction to the Buddha's Teachings (Snow Lion Publications)

An Open-Hearted Life: Transformative Methods for Compassionate Living from a Clinical Psychologist and a Buddhist Nun, with Russell Kolts (Shambhala)

Taming the Mind (Snow Lion Publications)

Working with Anger (Snow Lion Publications)

BOOKS EDITED BY THUBTEN CHODRON

Blossoms of the Dharma: Living as a Buddhist Nun (North Atlantic Books)

Choosing Simplicity: A Commentary of the "Bhikshuni Pratimoksha," by Ven. Bhikshuni Master Wu Yin (Snow Lion Publications)

Insight into Emptiness, by Khensur Jampa Tegchok (Wisdom Publications)

Karmans for the Creation of Virtue: The Prescriptive Precepts in the Dharmaguptaka Vinaya, by Vinaya Master Bhikṣu Benyin (self-published by Sravasti Abbey)

Pearl of Wisdom, Books I and II: Buddhist Prayers and Practices (Sravasti Abbey)

Transforming Adversity into Joy and Courage: An Explanation of the Thirty-Seven Practices of Bodhisattvas, by Geshe Jampa Tegchok (Snow Lion Publications)

www.thubtenchodron.org

www.sravasti.org